GREAT OCCASIONS

GREAT OCCASIONS

READINGS FOR
THE CELEBRATION
OF BIRTH,
COMING-OF-AGE,
MARRIAGE,
AND DEATH

EDITED BY CARL SEABURG

Boston: Skinner House Books
Unitarian Universalist Association

Library of Congress catalog card number 68-24372

12 11 10 9 8 7 6 5
99 98 97 96 95 94 93 92 91

To the people

of the First Universalist Church

Norway, Maine

CONTENTS

CONTENTS

PREFACE

FROM THE DRAWINGS engraved on cave sides to flags flung upon the moon, we have been proclaiming to the universe, "We are here." No reply has yet come from the universe. Is the message getting through? Is there a cosmic ear to hear?

Our earliest efforts have been to speak to that assumed Great Cosmic Ear — by whatever name it was called. To beg it for rain for crops, to ask their fertility, to recover from sickness, to escape from danger, to win in battle — all the longings felt by human creatures during their little lives.

Those lives have centered around four great facts: that all people are born and die; that most of them reach maturity and marry. Around these central experiences of humanity have collected acts and words which proclaim that it is good to exist, to know the pleasures and duties of maturity, to live companioned, and to know life in its sorrow and joy.

These are crystallizing events — "distinguishable days." Peoples of every heritage have celebrated them. Despite theological trenches which have been dug to defend certain dogmatic interpretations of these events, the occasions themselves are "everyone's land." Liberals, conservatives, theists, atheists — let the names be what they will — all have joined in this *praise of creation*. In the human frame, these are the four corners of a person's life — significant junctions where ordinary human beings find themselves at an important transition point.

ix

GREAT OCCASIONS

No law compels these occasions to be marked by ceremonies. Civil society, in order to keep minimal track of its members, does require the recording of births, marriages, deaths, and registration for voting. It is our needs that have made these occasions ones of festivity and celebration. There are always some voices to be heard wanting to abandon such events. Yet if the function of religion is to help people understand and relate to what happens to them, it would seem as if these elemental transition points of human life ought to continue as occasions for celebration and thought.

It is to help church people more fully meet their opportunities in these areas that this collection has been compiled. Yet this is not a parochial anthology, and the general reader in search of thoughtful and moving meditations about the "great occasions" of life will discover in these pages much to reward browsing. The standards by which readings were chosen were that they should have a satisfactory literary quality, be intellectually and emotionally honest, and be suitable for such use, keeping in mind particularly that the piece was to be read aloud. The main requirement, however, was that it speak to the human condition today.

Certain assumptions underlie this work: that users of it would have access to their own denominational service manuals which would give information on the order and form of services in that communion; that those who use Biblical materials in their services would have an adequate knowledge of what was available to them. The need was felt to be for supplemental material; so, except in a few instances, readings from the Bible will not be found in this book. Besides the Bible itself, there are many books which give Biblical selections.

It is also assumed that the primary users of this book will freely adapt these readings to their own particular needs; that pronouns will be altered to fit the occasion of use, and individual names added where wanted. Not all selections are expected to be equally useful to everyone. Much will depend on the user's creative imagination. Some selections are deliberately "avant garde" — not to shock, but to stake out new areas of feeling and expression as people's sensitivities enlarge. It is hoped that some pieces, encountered here for the first time, will — through use — become "old favorites."

PREFACE

This compilation has deliberately drawn on the whole written-down expression of humanity. It ranges through time, through cultures. It is especially rich in contemporary readings, both poetical and prose, much of it previously uncollected. From those authors who have been much anthologized, some interesting rarities will be found. In some cases, standard selections will be found here in new form, since the older arrangements eliminated sentences which this editor thought worth including. In general, many of the "old chestnuts," pieces widely available in standard collections, are not here printed.

Some users may be surprised that no names are attached to certain pieces. They may even think some pieces credited to others are actually their own composition. All an anthologist can say is that in the case of such selections, a diligent search has been made for the original author. But so great has been the borrowing, the swapping, the lending, and then the subsequent altering and blending — here a word changed, there a phrase — that it is often impossible to learn who the original author was. Identifying information, where known, will be cheerfully received and proper credit given in future editions.

The book is in four sections, each preceded by a short commentary on the topic of that section. The material in each section is arranged by themes so that like items are grouped together and quickly available to the user. A subject index is also supplied for the section on death so that special material for particular memorial services can easily be found. The arrangement is planned to be the most useful to the reader, and a little experience in using the book will enable one to find the way quickly to the material wanted.

Some of these selections were slightly altered from their original version to better serve the purposes of this work. None of the pieces quoted in their entirety has been changed. Most of the pieces marked as "from" have not been changed other than having been taken from a longer original. But a few have been, and readers who need to see the selections in their original form should consult the indicated sources.

*   *   *

For the suggestion to undertake this work I am much indebted

xi

to Mr. Gobin Stair of Beacon Press. For suggestions of individual pieces, and for a generous outpouring of their own works and experiences, I am greatly obliged to my colleagues in the liberal ministry. Much of the work on this book was facilitated by the helpfulness of people connected with the Boston Athenaeum, the General Theological Library in Boston, Crane Library at Tufts University, and the library of Boston's Charles Street Meeting House. My thanks to them.

—*Carl Seaburg*

GREAT OCCASIONS

Within the flickering inconsequential acts of separate selves dwells a sense of the whole which claims and dignifies them. In its presence we put off mortality and live in the universal. The life of the community in which we live and have our being is the fit symbol of this relationship. The acts in which we express our perception of the ties which bind us to others are its only rites and ceremonies.

—JOHN DEWEY

In the shattering emotion of love, beyond the delusions of sensuality, men continue to find entrance to the still point of the turning world. Now, as always, the experience of death as man's destiny, if accepted with an open and unarmored heart, acquaints us with a dimension of existence which fosters a detachment from the immediate aims of practical life. Now, as always, the philosophical mind will react with awe to the mystery of being revealed in a grain of matter or a human face.

—JOSEF PIEPER

FOR THE OCCASION
OF BIRTH

FOR THE OCCASION
OF BIRTH

How OFTEN does a couple have a child? Two point eight times say the statistics. This is not often in the life of a family. Put it another way: how often is a child born? The statistics drop to a constant: one birth per child. We have not yet attained Auden's dream of a society of perfect freedom "where a foetus is able to refuse to be born." Nor have we found Naurois's beguiling land of Meipe: "Children in that country go to a shop and choose their parents."

So the children brought into our churches and temples and mosques after their birth, come coerced—as it were—into life, into a tribe, into a language group, into a faith. People who are complete strangers to them, and yet are called their parents, bring them to be presented, dedicated, christened, or baptized. The name of the act varies, the rites of the act differ, but the intentions are similar and universal.

It is quite common in these birth ceremonies to make use of one of the four ancient "elements"—water. As a symbol of cleansing, of purification, of washing away both the debris of birth and the sin of the past, it is one that would naturally occur in many diverse traditions. Some groups use oil to anoint the newborn. Others make use of lighted candles to symbolize the fresh life that has come into the world. A new gesture coming into use is the presenting of a budding rose to the child as a symbol of life and growth.

Frequently a name is given to the child on this occasion. Hopi

3

Indians with their seemingly instinctive respect for the individual give a number of names to their newborn, so that when the child is of age it can — like European royalty — choose the name which pleases it most as the one it shall thenceforth bear. Among some Eskimo tribes, an old woman stood around while the mother was in labor, calling out appropriate names. Their belief being that when the baby heard "its" name called it would emerge from the womb.

Over and above the theological meanings that various acts might have, there is the universal recognition of the awe and wonder of the new parents at the life they have jointly created out of their love for each other; there is a feeling of obligation to be worthy of the gift of this new life; and in the act of presenting the child before the parents' religious fellowship, there is a symbolic acceptance of the child into the larger society.

Water, candle, oil, or rose—what we are doing is affirming that it is good to live, and that the gift of life is a good gift. We are saying our pleasure in the sun that warms our body, the wind that invigorates us, the rain that refreshes us. We are saying our rapture in the excitements of sex, the ennoblements of love, the catharsis of creating, the joys in the simple gestures of our everyday living. And as we do, we take into our arms that which is loved, and "by the articulate breath," imprint a name upon the waiting future.

*   *   *

The 70 readings which follow center around five themes: joy and wonder, responsibility, integrity, commitment, and growth. Attention is called to Appendix A where an outline of a simple ceremony for adoption is given. Parents who are adopting children might wish such recognition by their religious fellowship.

An eye comes out of the wave

—THEODORE ROETHKE

Behold the child, the visitor. He has come from nowhere, for he was not before this, and it is nowhere that he goes, wherefore he is called a visitor, for the visitor is one who comes from the unknown to stay but awhile and then to the unknown passes on again.

The child has come forth out of the great womb of the earth. The child has come forth to stand with star dust in his hair, with the rush of planets in his blood, his heart beating out the seasons of eternity, with a shining in his eyes like the sunlight, with hands to shape with that same force that shaped him out of the raw stuff of the universe.

When one baby is born it is the symbol of all birth and life, and therefore all men must rejoice and smile, and all men must lose their hearts to a child.

—From *Man Is the Meaning*
KENNETH L. PATTON

5

GREAT OCCASIONS

The trumpet of morning blows in the clouds and through
The sky. It is the visible announced,
It is the more than visible, the more
Than sharp, illustrious scene. The trumpet cries
This is the successor of the invisible.

This is its substitute in stratagems
Of the spirit. This, in sight and memory,
Must take its place, as what is possible
Replaces what is not. The resounding cry
Is like ten thousand tumblers tumbling down

To share the day. The trumpet supposes that
A mind exists, aware of division, aware
Of its cry as clarion, its diction's way
As that of a personage in a multitude:
Man's mind grown venerable in the unreal.

—From *Credences of Summer*
WALLACE STEVENS

It is innocence that is full and experience that is empty.
It is innocence that wins and experience that loses.

It is innocence that is young and experience that is old.
It is innocence that grows and experience that wanes.

It is innocence that is born and experience that dies.
It is innocence that knows and experience that does not know.

It is the child who is full and the man who is empty,
Empty as an empty gourd and as an empty barrel:

That is what I do with that experience of yours.

Now then, children go to school.
And you men, go to the school of life.

BIRTH

Go and learn
How to unlearn.

—From *Innocence and Experience*
CHARLES PEGUY
(tr. ANN AND JULIAN GREEN)

I say that it touches a man that his blood is sea water and his tears are salt, that the seed of his loins is scarcely different from the same cells in a seaweed, and that of stuff like his bones is coral made. I say that physical and biological law lies down with him, and wakes when a child stirs in the womb, and that the sap in a tree, uprushing in the spring, and the smell of the loam, where the bacteria bestir themselves in darkness, and the path of the sun in the heaven, these are facts of first importance to his mental conclusions, and that a man who goes in no consciousness of them is a drifter and a dreamer, without a home or any contact with reality.

—From *An Almanac for Moderns*
DONALD CULROSS PEATTIE

And so the children come.
And so they have been coming.
Always in the same way they come—
Born of the seed of man and woman.
No angels herald their beginnings,
No prophets predict their future courses,

7

GREAT OCCASIONS

No wise men see a star to point their way
To find the babe that may save mankind.

Yet each night a child is born is a holy night.
Fathers and Mothers—
Sitting beside their children's cribs—
Feel glory in the wond'rous sight of a life beginning.
They ask: "When or how will this new life end?
Or will it ever end?"
Each night a child is born is a holy night.

—From *Each Night a Child Is Born*
SOPHIA LYON FAHS

What is this amazing vital force which flows through the cells which are the basic units of all living matter, each cell a chemical power plant of very complex structure to generate the energy to carry on the life process? It is the source of the marvelous ability of the living plant or animal to lay hold upon the special elements outside itself which it needs; to transmute them into the pattern of its own frame; to use them to transmit to another generation its own highly specialized form of existence.

We know very well that we never gather grapes from thorns or figs from thistles. The feathers of each variety of birds grow in definite patterns which enable us to identify the species; the scales of a particular kind of fish repeat the same arrangement and approximate number in every one of hundreds of millions of individuals. The feathers of each bird, the scales of each fish are numbered as truly as the hairs on our own heads. Yet although each plant or creature remains true to type, it is also a distinct individual not quite like any other even of the same species.

—From *The Religion of an Inquiring Mind*
HENRY WILDER FOOTE

BIRTH

from spiralling ecstatically this

proud nowhere of earth's most prodigious night
blossoms a newborn babe:around him,eyes
—gifted with every keener appetite
than mere unmiracle can quite appease—
humbly in their imagined bodies kneel
(over time space doom dream while floats the whole

perhapsless mystery of paradise)

mind without soul may blast some universe
to might have been,and stop ten thousand stars
but not one heartbeat of this child;nor shall
even prevail a million questionings
against the silence of his mother's smile

—whose only secret all creation sings

—from spiralling ecstatically this
E. E. CUMMINGS

We are your children. Out of the infinite we have come to you, and through you. We are the old, yet ever new, miracle of incarnation.

Give us a chance to grow, within the warmth of your unfailing love, into souls sensitive to beauty, hearts open to love and hungry for the imperishable values of life. Do not shrink and wither us with fear, but quicken with faith the springs of courage within us.

Enter with us, through the gates of wonder, into the wider perspectives of the morrow. Accept us, as we grow, into a fellowship of mutual respect and shared responsibilities, that we, in our turn, may be worthy fathers and mothers of the coming generation.

—From a selection by
W. WALDEMAR W. ARGOW

Begin
With singing
Sing
Darkness kindled back into beginning
When the caught tongue nodded blind,
A star was broken
Into the centuries of the child.

—From *Ceremony After a Fire Raid*
DYLAN THOMAS

I have an idea that there is a terrible force in everything that comes among us alive in the world, that is being hatched, born, that becomes young. And now: what a need of love at the same time! A thing strange and beautiful surpassing all dramatic conflicts, and novelistic plots; to be welcomed and loved by those who will have to give place; to be received into the house of life with pleasure and love. To be taken into the arms, to be led softly and carefully, to be supported—a conqueror! That divinely victorious trust; that thirst for life, that capacity of a child to enjoy itself, that happy pride that it can walk, talk, that it is growing into a big man! What a possession, what a victory, what a pleasant toy, what an achievement life must be!

—JOSEPH ČAPEK
(tr. M. WEATHERALL)

Each of us still at the outset of his or her individual life story is microscopic and one sole cell. By that cell's multiplication, and by its descendants' coherence, each of us attains his or her final form and size. Each at every stage of that astonishing "becoming" is never any less than a self-centered individual. The offspring has from outset its individuality. It is never at any time truly a part of the mother. The mother's body prepares a nest for it. The young creature, separate individuality as it is, finds the newly prepared nest ready for it, and occupies it. Ensconced there it thrusts thence suckers into the maternal tissue and draws from the circulation of the mother nutriment, and in effect breathes through its mother's circulation. The embryo is, however, never any part of the mother, never at any time at all a part of the maternal life. The new life is on its own though it lives as a parasite on the old, a benign parasite, doing the mother no harm and destined at term to set the hostess free. Then the old nest is shed with it, having served its purpose. The embryo even when its cells are but two or three is a self-centered society which is familial and a unity— an organized family of cells, with corporate individuality. This character of being an individual seems, as we look upon Nature, a feature peculiarly stressed in what is living.

—From *Man On His Nature*
CHARLES SHERRINGTON

GREAT OCCASIONS

I arrive where an unknown earth is under my feet.
I arrive where a new sky is above me.
I arrive at this land, a resting place for me.
O Spirit of the Earth!
The stranger humbly offers his heart as food for thee.

—POLYNESIAN SONG
(tr. ARTHUR S. THOMSON)

How have I labored?
How have I not labored
To bring her soul to birth,
To give these elements a name and a centre!
She is beautiful as the sunlight, and as fluid.
She has no name, and no place.
How have I labored to bring her soul into separation;
To give her a name and her being!

Surely you are bound and entwined,
You are mingled with the elements unborn;
I have loved a stream and a shadow.

I beseech you enter your life.
I beseech you learn to say "I"
When I question you:
For you are no part, but a whole;
No portion, but a being.

—*Ortus*
EZRA POUND

BIRTH

When I came to birth I found the universe awaiting me. Here it was with all its splendid and its awe-inspiring aspects, its beauty and its bounty, ready to give the new-born babe whatever he might be able to acquire with such measure of courage, strength, and wisdom as he could attain.

I had done nothing to prepare it for my advent and, when I emerged into conscious life from the unfathomed depths of mystery, I was under the necessity of taking it as I found it and of adjusting myself as rapidly as I was able to the terms which it imposed for my well-being.

The persons who took any notice of the arrival of another puny babe were few, but in my parents' house there was rejoicing and, for their sakes, kinsfolk and friends showed an affectionate interest in the little child. From the moment of my earliest cry I was surrounded with love which ministered to my needs, and with high ideals of life and faith to guide my growth in mind and spirit. These were my guardian angels.

—From *The Religion of an Inquiring Mind*
HENRY WILDER FOOTE

The urgent business of birth
Admits no verbal delays
Felicity is hardly the word
Of entrance to the savage world
To the flocking unlocking days
The myriad burdens
Of woe and wonder
So at your morning
To one of the harmless
One of the threshold people
Welcome—and warning

—*For Carolyn*
CARL SEABURG

GREAT OCCASIONS

For the gift of childhood, whose innocence and laughter keep the world young, we all rejoice and give thanks. May this sweet life, which we have accepted into our community of ideals and friendship, receive abundantly the blessings of health, love, knowledge, and wisdom, and in its turn give back richly to the common heritage that endures from generation to generation.

—ANONYMOUS

This mannikin who just now
Broke prison and stepped free
Into his own identity—
Hand, foot and brow
A finished work, a breathing miniature—
Was still, one night ago
A hope, a dread, a mere shape we
Had lived with, only sure
Something would grow
Out of its coiled nine-months nonentity.

.   .   .

How like a blank sheet
His lineaments appear;
But there's invisible writing here
Which the day's heat
Will show: legends older than language, glum
Histories of the tribe,
Directives from his near and dear—
Charms, curses, rules of thumb—

14

BIRTH

He will transcribe
Into his own blood to write upon an heir.

.   .   .

Welcome to earth, my child!

.   .   .

We time-worn folk renew
Ourselves at your enchanted spring,
As though mankind's begun
Again in you.

—From *The Newborn*
C. DAY LEWIS

Give back life for life

——H. D. THOREAU

Naked are we born, naked of body and mind and spirit, naked of knowing, dependent and helpless.

For parents is the awesome privilege to be the givers and shapers of the person of growing men and women.

Parents give to the baby the bright knowingness of its eyes.

Love they give with their eyes and lips.

From the smile of his father and mother the baby learns to smile in reply, and from their laughter comes his laughter.

To their speech he makes his sounds in answer, and by imitation words, and in the use of words his mind is formed.

From their walking he learns to follow; from their gestures he patterns the movements of his hands and the inflections of his voice.

Their goodness becomes his goodness and their evil his evil.

Their fear and doubt become his own, and also their wisdom, courage, openness, and the adventure of their beliefs.

Motherhood is the sacred and holy calling.

This is the highest of all dedications, to the creation of human nature, the husbanding of the growth of mind and love and character.

BIRTH

Fatherhood is man's first vocation and his worthiest pursuit, above all the power and business of the world.

What will it profit a man if he gain the influence and riches of things and fame, and loses his children and their companionship?

—*The Child and Its Parents*
KENNETH L. PATTON

Dear Friends: In asking from us today the dedication of this child, you offer the dedication of yourselves for his fullest development in every possible way. And in seeking for him the blessing of our free faith and of the universal church, you pledge to inculcate in him to the best of your ability, the love of truth and the dream of brotherhood and peace.

By your teaching and example you would help him to be reverent and strong, and equal to the tasks and temptations that will confront him.

He is the wonderful creation of your life together; and it is your desire to make life for him as wonderful as it can be. This ceremony is for you a symbol of your gratitude and your resolution.

—DANA MC LEAN GREELEY

We who now live are parts of a humanity that extends into the remote past, a humanity that has interacted with nature. The things in civilization we most prize are not of ourselves. They exist by grace of the doings and sufferings of the continuous human community in which we are a link. Ours is the responsibility of conserving, transmitting, rectifying, and expanding the heritage of values we have received that those who come after us may receive it more solid and secure, more widely accessible, and more generously shared than we have received it.

—From *A Common Faith*
JOHN DEWEY

Within the personal community of marriage, the orientation of both partners to the child is not another orientation than that of husband and wife to each other. Both desire the full personal good of the other. This personal good is the human perfection in disinterested service and loving responsibility. They make one another respectively a father and a mother and thus give each other the noblest task of love and care. And thus the mutual love of husband and wife and their creative love for the child are fused into one love.

—J. P. WALGRAVE
(tr. PETER SCHOONENBERG)

The coming of a child into the family circle widens its dimension far beyond the simple addition of another member.

It brings the miracle of a new personality struggling for its own fulfillment. Therefore, it is quite natural for us to be thrilled at the sight of new births.

However, as the years pass it is too easy for us to take our children for granted. Whatever their ages they deserve the tender love and firm guidance, which only we as parents, teachers, and friends can give.

Moreover, these children have a right to a faith in themselves, in the story of mankind, in their particular heritage, and in the vast universe-home which is theirs.

It is to symbolize these possibilities and responsibilities that we have come to this ceremony.

—From a selection by
DAVID H. MAC PHERSON

The parents of a child are but his enemies when they fail to educate him properly in his boyhood. An illiterate boy, like a heron amidst swans, cannot shine in the assembly of the learned. Learning imparts a heightened charm to a homely face. Knowledge is the best treasure that a man can secretly hoard up in life. Learning is the revered of the revered. Knowledge makes a man honest, virtuous, and endearing to the society. It is learning alone that enables a man to better the condition of his friends and relations. Knowledge is the holiest of the holies, the god of the gods, and commands the respect of crowned heads; shorn of it a man is but an animal. The fixtures and furniture of one's house may be stolen by thieves: but knowledge, the highest treasure, is above all stealing.

—From the *Garuda Purana*

GREAT OCCASIONS

The essential feature of life is a continued manifestation of energy, whether conscious or unconscious. Each newborn creature instinctively strives to acquire the strength and skill to find the food it needs, to avoid danger, and, later, to propagate and protect its young. I have stood above a sea gull's nest on a rocky ledge and watched a chick within its shell painfully pecking out a hole into open air, sinking back exhausted after each attempt. Had I broken away the edges of the shell to release it I should have deprived it of something of the growing strength it needed.

And when I returned a half-hour later and found it out of its shell it shrank from me and tried to hide from the danger I seemed to threaten, though I was the first human being it had ever seen and, so far as its experience went, might have been as normal a part of its surroundings as the lichen-covered ledge and the wind-blown spruce above. Similarly, for all of us, life from its beginning to its close always involves the putting forth of effort alternating with periods of rest.

—From *The Religion of an Inquiring Mind*
HENRY WILDER FOOTE

To the human infant, his mother *is* nature. She must *be* that original verification, which, later, will come from other and wider segments of reality. All the self-verifications, therefore, begin in that inner light of the mother-child-world, which Madonna images have conveyed as so exclusive and so secure; and, indeed, such light must continue to shine through the chaos of many crises, maturational and accidental.

—From *Insight and Responsibility*
ERIK H. ERIKSON

BIRTH

The weakness of the newborn is truly relative. While far removed from any measure of mastery over the physical world, newborn man is endowed with an appearance and with responses which appeal to the tending adults' tenderness and make them wish to attend to his needs; which arouse concern in those who are concerned with his well-being; and which, in making adults care, stimulate their active care-taking.

In life in general and in human life in particular, the vulnerability of being newly born and the meekness of innocent needfulness have a power all their own. Defenseless as babies are, they have mothers at their command, families to protect mothers, societies to support the structure of families, and traditions to give a cultural continuity to systems of tending and training. All of this is necessary for the human infant to evolve humanly, for his environment must provide that outer wholeness and continuity which, like a second womb, permits the child to develop his separate capacities and to unify them.

—From *Insight and Responsibility*
ERIK H. ERIKSON

All people start as children and all peoples begin in their nurseries. It is human to have a long childhood; it is civilized to have an ever longer childhood. Long childhood makes a technical and mental virtuoso out of man, but it also leaves a lifelong residue of emotional immaturity in him. While tribes and nations, in many intuitive ways, use child training to the end of gaining their particular form of mature human identity, their unique version of integrity, they are, and remain, beset by the irrational fears which stem from the very state of childhood which they exploited in their specific way.

—From *Childhood and Society*
ERIK H. ERIKSON

21

GREAT OCCASIONS

A child is a person in himself, but also the man who shall be. An uncreatured one whose life is bounded by the sensations he feels. the warmth and food he is given, and most important, by the love with which he is surrounded.

A child is man in potential, the flower whose unfolding takes place under the careful tutelage and shelter of love.

And upon each of us, parents, sponsors, teachers, rests the obligation for this love. Love freely, wisely, that the child may grow strong and straight into creative maturity. Love freely, love wisely, that the child may grow happily into manhood or womanhood. Love freely, love wisely, that the child may become. That the child may help himself fulfill himself. That the child may be all that lies within him. That the child may, in the life that lies ahead, be at peace with all that he is. Love with understanding, knowing that within each child are you and I and all humanity.

—From a selection by
RUDOLPH W. NEMSER

Perhaps the best function of parenthood is to teach the young creature to love with *safety,* so that it may be able to venture unafraid when later emotion comes; the thwarting of the instinct to love is the root of all sorrow and not sex only but divinity itself is insulted when it is repressed.

—From *The Journey's Echo*
FREYA STARK

BIRTH

Only recently is it becoming generally recognized that the role of the parent in relation to the upbringing of a child is perhaps the most important thing that happens in our culture. Also, it is being recognized that much has been learned about the process of development during the first five or six years of life. But very little of that knowledge is yet implemented. It should be obvious, then, that our responsibility now is to help our children learn things and learn in ways that were not available to us when we were children. If they are going to make the kind of world in which security can be found, they will have to develop free of many limitations that still bind us.

Yet many people who themselves have developed away from the "certainties"—religious and other—inculcated in them in their childhood, who no longer believe what they were taught when they were children, send their children back, by their own teaching or by that of others, to learn things in terms which they themselves have discarded.

This is unfair to children. Surely one's children should be given the advantages of one's own development. Surely they should not be tied hand and foot all over again as their parents were tied to the absolutes of the past generation. Millions of children in the world are now being tied to the certainties of ten and twenty and thirty generations ago by this mechanism wherein each generation refuses to let its children continue from the point it itself reached.

This is not to suggest that no one needs religion or that we should become antireligious and get rid of it. It is to suggest that children should not be tied to the system of beliefs to which their parents happen to adhere, beliefs often acquired through the accident of birth into a particular family at a particular time in a particular place. Surely the time has come when the human race should learn to take charge of its own destiny and no longer submit itself to the mercy of these accidents.

—From *Tomorrow's Children*
BROCK CHISHOLM

GREAT OCCASIONS

I am not yet born; O hear me.
Let not the bloodsucking bat or the rat or the stoat or the
   club-footed ghoul come near me.

I am not yet born, console me.
I fear that the human race may with tall walls wall me,
   with strong drugs dope me, with wise lies lure me,
      on black racks rack me, in blood-baths roll me.

I am not yet born; provide me
With water to dandle me, grass to grow for me, trees to talk
   to me, sky to sing to me, birds and a white light
      in the back of my mind to guide me.

I am not yet born; forgive me
For the sins that in me the world shall commit, my words
   when they speak me, my thoughts when they think me,
      my treason engendered by traitors beyond me,
         my life when they murder by means of my
         hands, my death when they live me.

I am not yet born; rehearse me
In the parts I must play and the cues I must take when
   old men lecture me, bureaucrats hector me, mountains
      frown at me, lovers laugh at me, the white
         waves call me to folly and the desert calls
            me to doom and the beggar refuses
               my gift and my children curse me.

I am not yet born; O hear me,
Let not the man who is beast or who thinks he is God
   come near me.

I am not yet born; O fill me
With strength against those who would freeze my
   humanity, would dragoon me into a lethal automaton,
      would make me a cog in a machine, a thing with
         one face, a thing, and against all those
            who would dissipate my entirety, would
               blow me like thistledown hither and
                  thither or hither and thither

24

BIRTH

like water held in the
hands would spill me.

Let them not make me a stone and let them not spill me.
Otherwise kill me.

—Prayer Before Birth
LOUIS MACNEICE

(*Note:* For use in dedication services it is suggested that the phrase "I am
not yet born" be changed to "I am just born," and that any inappropriate
stanzas be omitted.)

Let our children learn to be honest, both with themselves and
with all others. This is the basic human value. In its simplest terms,
it is the capacity to distinguish clearly between *what is* and *what is
not,* and thus to deal effectually with reality.

Let our children learn to love truth. No matter whence it comes,
so it be truth let them freely accept it, even when it goes against
them. If they do this, they will not be much hampered by prejudice,
for wherever truth can enter, prejudice cannot long remain. Moreover, by fidelity to truth the mind is nourished and becomes well
grown.

Let our children find courage and discover that they are stronger
than the things of which they are afraid. Courage in our dealings
with our own lives, courage in speaking out for the right, in
condemning injustice, in standing for good against evil, courage
to remain loyal to a deep conviction at whatever cost.

Let our children cultivate breadth of humanity: a cordial welcome not merely for the factional, the provincial, the sectarian
when they are good, but for whatever is beneficial to the human
race no matter whence it comes.

Let our children cultivate kindness, for it does not often come
without cultivation, and it is needed: the world is too harsh.

25

GREAT OCCASIONS

Let our children cultivate humility. Let our children learn that they are like other people, even the people they tend to despise; and that there is good and bad in all of us, and that each of us must make a hard struggle to bring the good out on top. Then, because of their own lost battles, they will acquire a gentle wisdom and walk softly where other people might get hurt.

—From a selection by
A. POWELL DAVIES

We take the future from ourselves

—RAYMOND J. BAUGHAN

And now may our hearts be open to all the children of the generations of man, that the circle of love and peace may grow forevermore.

—ANONYMOUS

Friends, by bringing your children to be dedicated into the fellowship of this church you are acknowledging the wonder of life; you are proclaiming the importance of an ethical perspective; you are sharing with this congregation some of the joy that is yours as parents.

As your children are here dedicated, the members of the congregation join you in a re-dedication to life's larger purposes.

—ROBERT ZOERHEIDE
(adapted by FRED A. CAPPUCCINO)

GREAT OCCASIONS

We give thanks for the gift of life, as we dedicate ourselves to the tenderness of understanding, the fairness of good care, and the intelligence of warm devotion.

May all of us honor the trust of children by giving to them, as they grow, the twin virtues of parenthood, which are to be found in the strength of good example and the love maturing in faith.

—ROBERT ZOERHEIDE

For the gift of childhood and its family setting in our lives, we lift up grateful hearts. Though we cannot save them from trial or danger, we would, by example and encouragement, help them to find courage, wisdom, and love in our midst. We would learn from them as they experience the days of their years with us, and we shall welcome the day when they shall stand among us challenging us and offering a new companionship.

—DONALD JOHNSTON

A baby is not like a picture that you hang on the wall and enjoy forever afterward. A baby is not even like a house which, once secured, must be kept up, or the roof will leak, the paint peel off, and the plumbing give out. A baby, more than anything else in the world, will grow and develop in accordance with what you do or do not do; in accordance with the devotion and the intelligence, the courage and the patience you bring to the task of caring for him.

With a newborn baby, the potential for good or ill is so great,

BIRTH

new parents sometimes feel virtually crushed by the weight of it. They know their own shortcomings. They know their ignorance. They know their frailties, their psychological problems, and all the other weaknesses to which human flesh is heir. They know that, resolve as they will to do their best, they will not always do it. They know they will be angry, thoughtless, intemperate, vindictive, and, more often than they suspect, ignorant of their own motives, unconsciously, even self-righteously, taking out on their children the frustrations from which they themselves suffer.

So we are possessed by a sense of obligation, of purpose, and of determination, that we shall be worthy of the gift that has been given into our hands.

—From a selection by
DUNCAN HOWLETT

Friends, in the light of ancient custom, by bringing this child to be received into the fellowship of the Church and dedicated to all that is good in life, you declare your desire to show him the ways that lead unto the life abundant.

On our part, we pledge this child the love and care of this Church. In following the ancient rite found in our own religious heritage, we rejoice in the promise your child bears. As the bud opens to glorious flowering, so may this child's life display a wealth of achievement only faintly suggested in this, the budding time of life.

We use the ancient symbol of water as a sign of our common heritage. Essential to existence, from primeval organism to modern man, water reminds us of our common bond with Mother Nature. As water quenches our thirst, so may it symbolize the water of life abundant for which Mankind has thirsted through the ages.

—ANONYMOUS

In presenting your children in this service of religion that they may be named and recognized by this church family, you are thereby taking a step as parents in the assumption of moral responsibility.

Let your child learn from your lips and your life how lovely is the path of virtue, how noble it is to become an apostle of truth, how holy it is to sacrifice oneself, if need be, for the good of others.

The great end of parental care, as Channing observed, "is not to stamp your minds upon the young but to stir up their own; not to make them see with your eyes but to look inquiringly and steadily with their own; not to form an outward regularity but to touch inward springs; not to burden memory but to quicken the power of thought, so that they may learn and approve for themselves what is everlastingly right and good."

—LON RAY CALL

Newborn, on the naked sand
Nakedly lay it.
Next to the earth mother,
That it may know her;
Having good thoughts of her, the food giver.

Newborn, we tenderly
In our arms take it,
Making good thoughts.
House-god, be entreated,
That it may grow from childhood to manhood,
Happy, contented;
Beautifully walking

BIRTH

The trail to old age.
Having good thoughts of the earth its mother,
That she may give it the fruits of her being.
Newborn, on the naked sand
Nakedly lay it.

—RIO GRANDE PUEBLOS
(tr. MARY AUSTIN)

As we contemplate the miracle of birth, as we renew in our hearts the sense of wonder and joy, may we be stirred to a fresh awareness of the sacredness of life and of the divine promise of childhood. May we so live that all our children will be able to acquire our best virtues and to leave behind our worst failings. May we pass on the light of courage and compassion, and the questing spirit; and may that light burn more brightly in these our children than it has in us.

—ROBERT MARSHALL

To thee, the creator, to thee, the Powerful,
I offer this fresh bud,
New fruit of the ancient tree.
Thou art the master, we thy children.
To thee, the Creator, to thee, the Powerful,
Khmvoum, Khmvoum,
I offer this new plant.

—PYGMY PRAYER
(tr. REX BENEDICT)

Friends, in bringing this child to be named, you declare your purpose in love to give freely of yourselves, and ultimately to perform the final act of love, which is to give freedom as you give love.

You here dedicate yourselves, as we dedicate ourselves, to give our holiest gifts—love and respect—to this new person. And we pray that we will be great-hearted enough to ask nothing in return. ————————————, we commit ourselves to the unfolding of your promise. May this flower remind those who love you of beauty, good, and truth, and of the infinite mystery of life.

—JAMES HUNT AND PAUL KILLINGER

Many of us, as parents, live with children from day to day. In a real sense this is an awesome fact. The clay of us is the clay of them, and the spirit of us, the holy, the sound, becomes the spirit of them as they look to us directly and subtly for shaping and guidance. The clay is all shaped but the holy is still being born. Out of our deep need for guidance and inspiration we pray for beauty and tenderness, for strength and integrity, for courage to face life strong and true, for joy to seize the delight of life and make it ever ring with laughter in the memories which shape the future.

—From a selection by
WILLIAM B. RICE

BIRTH

We pray for those who come after us, for our children, and the children of our friends, and for all the young lives that are marching up from the gates of birth, pure and eager, with the morning sunshine on their faces. We remember with a pang that these will live in the world we are making for them. We are wasting the resources of the earth in our headlong greed, and they will suffer want. We are building sunless houses and joyless cities for our profit, and they must dwell therein. We are making the burden heavy and the pace of work pitiless, and they will fall wan and sobbing by the wayside. We are poisoning the air of our land by our lies and our uncleanness, and they will breathe it.

We have cried out in agony when the sins of our fathers have been visited upon us. Save us from maiming the innocent ones who come after us by the ¹ded cruelty of our sins. Help us to break the ancient force of evil by a steadfast will and to endow our children with finer ideals and nobler thoughts. Grant us to leave the earth fairer than we found it; to build upon it cities of hope in which the cry of needless pain shall cease. May we be granted a vision of the far-off years as they may be if redeemed by us that we may take heart and do battle for our children.

—From *For Those Who Come After Us*
WALTER RAUSCHENBUSCH

From the beginning of time, men and women have brought their children to the houses of worship for dedication. In the presence of the congregation, the child is given his name and the parents declare their responsibility for him.

We come to a house of worship out of reverence for the mystery of life that we have seen in the miracle of reproduction and birth. We acknowledge the mystery of the power that is in us and works through us, and we are humble before that mystery.

We give the child a name in this ceremony. In this act we

declare that the child is an individual, a unique and separate person with a dignity and life of his own. He comes from us, but he is not ours. He is himself, an individual. In giving him a name we declare that we will respect him as himself, and give him the freedom to be himself.

We perform this ceremony publicly to declare that all of us, as parents and as representatives of society, are responsible for the care and development of all children. It is our task to give them a world of peace and justice in which to grow. It is our task to give them our ideals and our hopes. By presenting the child to the congregation, the parents acknowledge that the child is more than a private possession, but is a new being in whom we all have a responsibility, and whom we all welcome to the community.

We use a flower and water—time-honored symbols—in this ceremony. They remind us of the beauty and wonder and freshness of life. We dedicate ourselves to the task of nourishing the beauty and wonder and freshness of this child, and all children.

—JAMES HUNT AND PAUL KILLINGER

Obedient to the call of human will,
I now appear in form of flesh and bone;
Subject to loves that bless and hates that kill,
With griefs and joys and fears to match your own.
I cannot be your plaything, for the tides
That move your being surge the same in me.
Only a mortal sense of time divides
The fragile sapling from the sturdy tree.

I am your yesterdays; can you forget?
And your tomorrows; will you fail me, then?
Not all the shining goals your heart may set,

34

BIRTH

Nor pride of place, nor triumph of the pen
Can bring again to your repentant hand
The vanished child you failed to understand.

—The Child
SILENCE BUCK BELLOWS

Yourself! Yourself! Yourself, for ever and ever

—WALT WHITMAN

Nothing is strange to the child for whom everything is new.
Where all things are new nothing is novel.
The child does not yet know what belongs and what does not;
   therefore for him all things belong.
The ear of the child is open to all music.
His eyes are open to all arts.
His mind is open to all tongues.
His being is open to all manners.
In the child's country there are no foreigners.

—From *This World, My Home*
KENNETH L. PATTON

What is there yet in a son,
To make a father dote, rave, or run mad?
Being born it pouts, cries, breeds teeth.
What is there yet in a son? He must be fed

36

BIRTH

Be taught to go, and speak. Ay, or yet
Why might not a man love a calf as well?
Or melt in passion o'er a frisking kid,
As for a son? Methinks a young bacon,
Or a fine little smooth horse colt,
Should move a man as much as doth a son;
For one of these, in very little time,
Will grow to some good use; whereas a son,
The more he grows in stature, and in years,
The more unsquar'd, unbevell'd, he appears,
Reckons his parents among the rank of fools,
Strikes cares upon their heads with his mad riots;
Makes them look old, before they meet with age.
This is a son!

—From *The Spanish Tragedy*
THOMAS KYD

We have come here to welcome you in love, a new member of
the human community. Without a name you have come to us, but
henceforth your name shall be ——————————————.

By this name men will call you and to this name you will
respond. This is a new name for you, no matter how many other
persons have worn it. For whatever goodness or evil this name
comes to stand, that you will have given unto it by the life you
have lived. It is our hope that you will wear this name in honor
and in peace and in courage, and that men will come to look upon
your name and find it blessed.

—From *Man Is the Meaning*
KENNETH L. PATTON

GREAT OCCASIONS

Every child from its conception is a potential personality, though that personality may be nipped in the bud by some accident, deformity, or mental deficiency which from birth or later may limit its development. No one, not even parents well acquainted with their family history, can foresee with assurance the ways in which the potentialities of a normal infant may unfold, because of the multiple strands of its physical and psychical inheritance from its thousands of more remote ancestors.

The parents must protect the child's bodily welfare, train him to good habits, awaken and guide his sense of right and wrong, and nourish his mind with the cultural traditions of mankind. They may encourage him to acquire a wholesome self-reliance, or may unwisely warp his mind into conformity with their own prejudices, but they can never wholly determine for him the ways or the measure in which, as he advances into manhood, he will make use of what is given him, for his alone is the chief responsibility for the personality which he will develop in his intercourse with his fellow-men throughout the years of his life.

—From *The Religion of an Inquiring Mind*
HENRY WILDER FOOTE

I am an acme of things accomplish'd, and I am encloser of things
    to be.

My feet strike an apex of the apices of the stairs,
On every step bunches of ages, and larger bunches between the
    steps,
All below duly travel'd, and still I mount and mount.

Rise after rise bow the phantoms behind me,
Afar down I see the huge first Nothing, I know I was even there,
I waited unseen and always, and slept through the lethargic mist,
And took my time, and took no hurt from the fetid carbon.

38

BIRTH

Long I was hugg'd close—long and long.

Immense have been the preparations for me,
Faithful and friendly the arms that have help'd me.

Cycles ferried my cradle, rowing and rowing like cheerful boat-
   men,
For room to me stars kept aside in their own rings,
They sent influences to look after what was to hold me.

Before I was born out of my mother generations guided me,
My embryo has never been torpid, nothing could overlay it.

For it the nebula cohered to an orb,
The long slow strata piled to rest it on,
Vast vegetables gave it sustenance,
Monstrous sauroids transported it in their mouths and deposited
   it with care.

All forces have been steadily employ'd to complete and delight me,
Now on this spot I stand with my robust soul.

—From *Song of Myself*
WALT WHITMAN

Give your children your permission to grow up, to make their
own lives for themselves independent of you, and independent also of
your particular desires and ambitions. Give them a sense of truth;
make them aware of themselves as citizens of a dangerous universe, a universe in which there are many obstacles as well as ful-
fillments, and prepare them for human nature in all of its varieties
and forms and variabilities. Show them that they must anticipate in
their lifetime pitfalls and snares and fickleness on the part of human beings from whom they could expect faithfulness. Do not
make the mistake of giving your children a picture of the world
that is painted in unrealistic colors in which there are lights but

GREAT OCCASIONS

no shadows. Give your children a sense of proportion in the landscape of the world, a sense of the reality of life with its lights and
shadows, of human nature with its goodness and its evils.

—From a selection by
JOSHUA LOTH LIEBMAN

It is not to diffuse you that you were born of your mother and
  father, it is to identify you,
It is not that you should be undecided, but that you should be
  decided,
Something long preparing and formless is arrived and form'd
  in you,
You are henceforth secure, whatever comes or goes.

The threads that were spun are gather'd, the weft crosses the warp,
  the pattern is systematic.
The preparations have every one been justified,
The orchestra have sufficiently tuned their instruments, the baton
  has given the signal.

The guest that was coming, he waited long, he is now housed,
He is one of those who are beautiful and happy, he is one of those
  that to look upon and be with is enough.

You are not thrown to the winds, you gather certainly and safely
  around yourself,
Yourself! Yourself! yourself, for ever and ever!

—From *To Think of Time*
WALT WHITMAN

BIRTH

As an animal, man is nothing. It is meaningless to speak of a human child as if it were an animal in the process of domestication; or of his instincts as set patterns encroached upon or molded by the autocratic environment. Man's "inborn instincts" are drive fragments to be assembled, given meaning, and organized during a prolonged childhood by methods of child training and schooling which vary from culture to culture and are determined by tradition. In this lies his chance as an organism, as a member of a society, as an individual. In this also lies his limitation. For while the animal survives where his segment of nature remains predictable enough to fit his inborn patterns of instinctive response or where these responses contain the elements for necessary mutation, man survives only where traditional child training provides him with a conscience which will guide him without crushing him and which is firm and flexible enough to fit the vicissitudes of his historical era.

—From *Childhood and Society*
ERIK H. ERIKSON

Child, if betideth that thou shalt thrive and thee,
Thench thou wer ifostred up thy moder kne:
Ever hab mund in thy hert of thos thinges thre,
Whan thou commest, what thou art, and what shall com of thee.
Lollay, lollay, little child, child, lollay, lollay,
With sorrow thou com into this world, with sorrow shalt wend
    away.

(Child, if it happens that you thrive and prosper, think you were brought up upon your mother's knee: always remember in your heart those three things, Whence you have come, what you are, and what shall come of you.)

—ENGLISH, 14TH CENTURY
ANONYMOUS

41

GREAT OCCASIONS

Whether god-in-man or monster
lies a puzzle in your head
that will slowly work its answer,
nor be solved till you are dead.

Limpid in your infant skull
is eclectic, potent stuff,
that will fashion and be fashioned
neither little nor enough.

The currents now so neutral
soon will sway and will be swayed.
What is given is retaken;
may you suffer undismayed.

Yours is not the whole decision,
nor will it lie within your power
to be as innocent and happy
as you are this hour.

—To a Baby
KENNETH L. PATTON

The egg has a mind

—ROBINSON JEFFERS

Unto us our children are given as an encouragement of hope and strength.

What matter if our bodies stiffen and age, if our hearts falter and our hands tremble?

What matter if we become stubborn and stupid, unable to see the shapes of new visions, for we shall pass?

What tragedy it would be if mankind were never to be better than we, if the promise of the human venture were to be fastened and limited in us.

What tragedy it would be if men were to be limited to our feeble imaginings, to our perverse clinging to superstitions and darkness.

Rather let this be our song, that new life in a springtime freshet will cause sons and daughters, like the green grass of the fields, to come up and cover the scarred face of the earth.

For unto us are children born; unto us new chances given, generation upon generation.

—From *A Thanksgiving for Children*
KENNETH L. PATTON

43

GREAT OCCASIONS

We are mindful that within each child there exists an immense potential that emerges as the years pass—and we realize with some apprehension that the quality of our own lives will determine how well this potential is realized in full bloom and flower. On this day of great promise, we dedicate ourselves to the children here presented, and to all children.

—FRED A. CAPPUCCINO

Outrageous company to be born into,
    Lunatics of a royal age long dead.
Then reckon time by what you are cr do,
    Not by the epochs of the war they spread.
    Hark how they roar; but never turn your head.
Nothing will change them, let them not change you.

—From *To Lucia at Birth*
ROBERT GRAVES

Lo, to the battleground of life,
    Child, you have come, like a confident shout,
Out of a struggle—into strife;
    Out of a darkness—into doubt.

Girt with the fragile armor of youth,
    Child, you must ride into endless wars,

44

BIRTH

With the sword of protest, the buckler of truth,
  And a banner of love to sweep the stars.

About you the world's despair will surge;
  Into defeat you must plunge and grope.
Be to the faltering an urge,
  Be to the hopeless years a hope!

Be to the darkened world a flame;
  Be to its unconcern a blow—
For out of its pain and tumult you came,
  And into its tumult and pain you go.

—*Lo, to the Battleground of Life*
LOUIS UNTERMEYER

A baby's first responses can be seen as part of an actuality consisting of many details of mutual arousal and response. While the baby initially smiles at a mere configuration resembling the human face, the adult cannot help smiling back, filled with expectations of a "recognition" which he needs to secure from the new being as surely as it needs him. The fact is that the mutuality of adult and baby is the original source of hope, the basic ingredient of all effective as well as ethical human action.

A parent dealing with a child will be strengthened in *his* vitality, in *his* sense of identity, and in *his* readiness for ethical action by the very ministrations by means of which he secures to the child vitality, future identity, and eventual readiness for ethical action.

—From *Insight and Responsibility*
ERIK H. ERIKSON

45

GREAT OCCASIONS

O child of man,
Wombed in dark waters you retell
Millenniums, image the terrestrial span
From an unwitting cell
To the new soul within her intricate shell,
O child of man.

O child of man
Whose infant eyes and groping mind
Meet chaos and create the world again,
You for yourself must find
The toils we know, the truths we have divined—
Yes, child of man.

—From Requiem for the Living
C. DAY LEWIS

The surest thing there is is we are riders,
And though none too successful at it, guiders,
Through everything presented, land and tide
And now the very air, of what we ride.

What is this talked-of mystery of birth
But being mounted bareback on the earth?
We can just see the infant up astride,
His small fist buried in the bushy hide.

There is our wildest mount—a headless horse.
But though it runs unbridled off its course,
And all our blandishments would seem defied,
We have ideas yet that we haven't tried.

—Riders
ROBERT FROST

BIRTH

No one is born a new being. He bears in his psyche the imprint of past generations. He is a combination of ancestral units from which a new being must be fused, yet he also bears within him an essential germ, a potential of a unique individual value. The discovery of this unique essence and its development is the quest of consciousness.

—From *The Inner World of Childhood*
FRANCES G. WICKES

As a token I give you this rose that it may be a symbol of the beauty of life that we wish for you.

May you have joy in listening and joy in singing; joy in hearing and joy in seeing; joy in thinking and joy in learning. May your hours be forever bright in play and in work, and in friendship and in love.

—From a selection by
ROBERT EDWARD GREEN

The egg has a mind,
Doing what our able chemists will never do,
Building the body of a hatchling, choosing among the proteins:
These for the young wing-muscles, these for the great
Crystalline eyes, these for the flighty nerves and brain:

47

GREAT OCCASIONS

Choosing and forming: a limited but superhuman intelligence,
Prophetic of the future and aware of the past;
The hawk's egg will make a hawk, and the serpent's
A gliding serpent: but each with a little difference
From its ancestors—and slowly, if it works, the race
Forms a new race: that also is a part of the plan
Within the egg. I believe the first living cell
Had echoes of the future in it, and felt
Direction and the great animals, the deep green forest
And whale's-track sea; I believe this globed earth
Not all by chance and fortune brings forth her broods,
But feels and chooses. And the galaxy, the firewheel
On which we are pinned, the whirlwind of stars in
    which our sun is one dust grain, one electron,
    this giant atom of the universe
Is not blind force, but fulfills its life and intends
    its course.

—From *De Rerum Virtute*
ROBINSON JEFFERS

In our service of dedication, we give the child a flower. The flower
symbolizes the beauty of life. It also symbolizes the meaning of
your dedication. Whether a flower is beautiful or not; whether it
comes into full bloom or not; whether it fulfills itself as a flower
or not—depends upon the nurture it receives. No flower grows
alone, apart from the sunshine and the rain, apart from the soil in
which it lives. So, too, no child grows alone.

May the flower then be a reminder of the beauty of fulfillment,
and of the reward which comes from love and understanding, from
teaching and example.

_____ _____, I welcome you into the fel-
lowship of life, and dedicate you to the service of freedom and
righteousness and of love.

BIRTH

May the life of the child be rich in vision, full in accomplishment, and afire with the highest of ideals.

—RUDOLPH W. NEMSER

Wind and spirit, earth and being, rain and doing, lightning and awareness imperative, thunder and the word, seed and sower, all are one: and it is necessary only for man to ask for his seed to be chosen and to pray for the sower within to sow it through the deed and act of himself, and then the harvest for all will be golden and great.

—From *The Seed and the Sower*
LAURENS VAN DER POST

Now this is the day.
Our child,
Into the daylight
You will go out standing.
Preparing for your day.

Our child, it is your day,
This day.
May your road be fulfilled.
In your thoughts may we live,
May we be the ones whom your thoughts will embrace,
May you help us all to finish our roads.

—From a selection by
ZUÑI INDIANS

49

FOR THE OCCASION
OF COMING-OF-AGE

FOR THE OCCASION
OF COMING-OF-AGE

CEREMONIES to mark the attainment of adulthood, or coming-of-age, have been common in most societies throughout human history. Almost all primitive groups had some form of "rites of passage." Usually they involved a special period of preparation culminating in a painful, sometimes frightening, ordeal testing the courage of the participant. Circumcision was often one of these ordeals. After passing the test, the youth was accepted as a full member of the tribe, made privy to its secrets, and eligible to act in every particular as an adult.

For more than six hundred years, Jewish groups have marked the beginning of maturity by the ceremony of bar mitzvah. On the Sabbath nearest his thirteenth birthday, and after a period of study, the youngster is called up to read the Torah like an adult. The Rabbi will address him personally, and certain privileges of the society become his. Afterwards, the occasion is celebrated with a joyous family party and the presentation of gifts to the youth. While Orthodox congregations do not perform the ceremony for girls, Reform and Conservative groups do. Reform congregations also have confirmation services several years later when these young people become official members.

The Roman Catholic church holds confirmation services for its young members, although in Europe and Latin America those confirmed have usually been much under the age of seven. In this country, the custom has been to hold such services when the

53

participants were about eleven years old. But recent developments indicate a substantial feeling on the part of many clerics that the young people should be confirmed only after they have reached greater intellectual and psychological maturity, or about the time they graduate from high school.

This corresponds more with current Protestant practice. Generally between the ages of thirteen and sixteen, young people become communicants or members of their churches. Even liberal churches tend to follow this custom, preceded by membership classes for those joining. Youth Sunday services and "graduation" from Church School are part of these activities too.

Perhaps here is a possible basis for the development of a custom of bar mitzvah' rites, or coming-of-age ceremonies, within the tradition of these churches. Ecumenicity, after all, is a two-way street. Thought and discussion of the possibilities of such a service are needed by ministers and congregations. The format could include participation in various elements of the customary church service by the young people, extending to them the "right hand of fellowship," signing the membership book, and a church or family party afterwards. (If bylaws have to be amended so that they can in fact become voting members of the congregation, so be it.)

It is hard to date maturity, and our society reflects that confusion. Some elective offices cannot be held until the candidate is twenty-five, thirty, or even thirty-five. Certain professions require such a long period of training, notably medicine, that half a person's normal life expectancy has passed before they can begin their "life work." Yet the military services are anxious to recruit people at eighteen, and even seventeen, and consider them perfectly fit to kill people and blow up cities.

Our society has invented a strange concept called the "teenager" which keeps its most vigorous members in a weird in-between-land of superficialities, and then berates them for being "problems." Parents worry whether their youngsters are emotionally equipped to make decisions for themselves, but do they not see this as a reflection on their training and education of their children? How long can young people be told they have to learn from experience, but be denied the opportunity to acquire that experience? The abilities of young people are grossly underestimated by adults. A century ago they captained ships, led armies, founded families, settled the wilderness. Today, it's a major crisis if they cut their hair in an odd fashion. Why do we mistrust them so?

One way to help break down these barriers might be some form of coming-of-age ceremony that would help parents realize that their children are "children" no more, but adults. A widespread use of such services might eventually produce a better understanding in our society of the rights of people in this age group. Such services would also strengthen church life and be heartwarming occasions too. For in their spring — the loveliest season of the body with the spirit leaping and the mind reaching — they come to us and in joy we welcome them among us in the temple.

*　　　*　　　*

The 49 readings which follow center around three themes: selfhood and integrity, opportunity and growth, and fidelity and courage.

The lords and owners of their faces

—WILLIAM SHAKESPEARE

Act in repose;
Be at rest when you work;
Relish unflavored things.
Great or small,
Frequent or rare,
Requite anger with virtue.

Take hard jobs in hand
While they are easy;
And great affairs too
While they are small.
The troubles of the world
Cannot be solved except
Before they grow too hard.
The business of the world
Cannot be done except
While relatively small.
The Wise Man, then, throughout his life
Does nothing great and yet achieves
A greatness of his own.

Again, a promise lightly made
Inspires little confidence;

Or often trivial, sure that man
Will often come to grief.
Choosing hardship, then, the Wise Man
Never meets with hardship all his life.

—LAO TZU
(tr. R. B. BLAKNEY)

They that have pow'r to hurt and will do none,
That do not do the thing they most do show,
Who, moving others, are themselves as stone,
Unmoved, cold, and to temptation slow;
They rightly do inherit heaven's graces
And husband nature's riches from expense;
They are the lords and owners of their faces,
Others but stewards of their excellence.
The summer's flow'r is to the summer sweet,
Though to itself it only live and die;
But if that flow'r with base infection meet,
The basest weed outbraves his dignity:
    For sweetest things turn sourest by their deeds;
    Lilies that fester smell far worse than weeds.

—*Sonnet 94*
WILLIAM SHAKESPEARE

One who, being in a junior position, has not the confidence of his
superiors will never govern the people. There is a way to gain

the confidence of one's superiors. He who is not trusted by his friends will not gain the confidence of his superiors. And there is a way to gain the trust of one's friends. He who fails to give satisfaction in his duty to his kinsfolk will not be trusted by his friends. There is a way to give satisfaction to one's kinsfolk. He who, upon examining himself, discovers a lack of integrity will not give satisfaction to his kinsfolk. There is a way to ensure personal integrity. He who is unclear as to the nature of the good will not achieve personal integrity. Therefore, integrity is the Way of Heaven, and to be concerned about integrity is the way of man. No man of integrity fails to move others. But a man lacking integrity will never move others.

—MENCIUS
(tr. W. A. C. H. DOBSON)

Him I call indeed a Brahmin who without hurting any creatures, whether feeble or strong, does not kill nor cause slaughter.

Him I call indeed a Brahmin who is tolerant with the intolerant, mild with the violent, and free from greed among the greedy.

Him I call indeed a Brahmin from whom anger and hatred, pride and hypocrisy have dropped like a mustard seed from the point of a needle.

Him I call indeed a Brahmin who utters true speech, instructive and free from harshness, so that he offend no one.

Him I call indeed a Brahmin who takes nothing in the world that is not given him, be it long or short, small or large, good or bad.

—From *The Dhammapada*
BUDDHA
(tr. F. MAX MÜLLER)

COMING-OF-AGE

Let not young souls be smothered out before
They do quaint deeds and fully flaunt their pride.
It is the world's one crime its babes grow dull,
Its poor are ox-like, limp and leaden-eyed.
Not that they starve, but starve so dreamlessly;
Not that they sow, but that they seldom reap;
Not that they serve, but have no gods to serve;
Not that they die, but that they die like sheep.

—The Leaden-Eyed
VACHEL LINDSAY

In all he does, whether good or bad,
a wise man should consider the fact.
Deeds done too quickly ripen into thorns
that pierce the heart till death.

—From the Sanskrit
(tr. DANIEL INGALLS)

How can one tell what things are true?

We approach closest to reality in human terms when we set up
a picture that enables us to predict correctly the outcome of some
experiment or course of action. We do this by choosing those

illusions, from among a great number, which enable us to make verifiable predictions on as many separate but connected levels of existence as possible. There is no reason to suppose that we get any closer to reality when scientists take us down into the realms of the atom and molecule than we are when observing phenomena in the external world. The gain in studying atoms is the new set of illusions which enables us to examine truth from new angles. Reality may well exist on every level of manifestation, but it must be interpreted on each in terms of our illusions so as not to involve contradictions with the illusions we reach from other views.

—From *What Man May Be*
GEORGE R. HARRISON

Thou, O my son, art feared by war-makers.
Let there be no war, for a man of war can never
          be satiated.
Let my son be, instead, a man of wisdom and learning.
A keeper of traditions of his house.
Let there be no war.
Plant deeply the spirit of peace,
That your rule may be called the land of
          enforced peace.

—Polynesian song
(tr. STEPHEN SAVAGE)

COMING-OF-AGE

It is only through possessing a mind that Man has become the dominant portion of this planet and the agent responsible for its future evolution; and it will only be by the right use of that mind that he will be able to exercise that responsibility rightly. He could all too readily be a failure in the job; he will only succeed if he faces it consciously and if he uses all his mental resources— knowledge and reason, imagination and sensitivity, capacities for wonder and love, for comprehension and compassion, for spiritual aspiration and moral effort. And he must face it un- aided by outside help. In the evolutionary pattern of thought there is no longer either need or room for the supernatural.

—From *Essays of a Humanist*
JULIAN HUXLEY

Members and friends, I would remind you that we have a solemn obligation to build with these young people a world in which their horizons may continually expand and their spirits soar. May we participate as wisely as we are able in their religious growth. May we find the wisdom to guide them unto themselves, and the trust to free them to become themselves. Above all, may we offer a quality of fellowship in which they will feel the bonds of love and concern that bind us together with all mankind.

—MICHAEL G. YOUNG

Put from you childish thoughts and see that you keep guard upon the virtues of your manhood. Then shall your years all be fair, and your good fortune grow from more to more.

GREAT OCCASIONS

Guard reverently your demeanor, preserve the integrity of your virtue. Then will your years be without end, and good luck attend you forever and ever.

Your kinsmen are all here to perfect this virtuous act. May your years be agelong, and blessings attend you.

May you attain to eminence, holding fast to what is right, for right leads to happiness. May you receive and ever hold this gift.

> —From CHINESE CAPPING CEREMONY
> (tr. REX BENEDICT)

Ours is a free church, dedicated to the nourishing of the human spirit, and the hope of a human community. Here we would venture together to seek and to do the truth, knowing that venture to be bounded only by the limits of our own imagination. Here knowledge is trusted, and the unknown is not feared; for it is but the growing edge of life's creativity. Here we would wrap our being and doing in compassion, for the voice that speaks to us out of Life's mystery is a challenge to create and to care, and not to destroy.

We are those who would see life whole; accepting the partial character of that vision at any moment, yet pushing always beyond the momentary boundaries of that vision; seeking the fulfillment of our highest hopes and our deepest needs in this community where no man is a stranger.

Knowing this, certain young people, after due study and preparation, have freely indicated a desire to take their formal place in this community.

> —From a selection by
> MICHAEL G. YOUNG

COMING-OF-AGE

How can I say that I've known
just what you know and just where you are?

What I want to say is, let your body in,
let it tie you in,
in comfort.

What I want to say,
is that there is nothing in your body that lies.
All that is new is telling the truth.

I'm here, that somebody else,
an old tree in the background.
You,
stand still at your door,
sure of yourself, a white stone, a good stone—
as exceptional as laughter
you will strike fire,
that new thing!

—From *Little Girl, My String Bean*
ANNE SEXTON

Oh those who are my generation!
We're not the threshold, just a step.
We're but the preface to a preface,
a prologue to a newer prologue!
Oh you in years my equal,
                              my true friend!

My fate's
          contained in yours.
Then let us be extremely frank,
and speak the truth about ourselves.
Let us share our anxieties together,

discuss between us, tell others too,
what sort of men we can't be any longer,
what sort of men we now desire to be.
Fallen out of love with self-conceit,
we shall not regret the loss.

Character
        begins to form
at the first pinch of anxiety about ourselves.

—From *There's Something I Often Notice*
YEVGENY YEVTUSHENKO
(tr. GEORGE REAVEY)

The power of youth is a darkness
that obscures young men's sight.
It is not dispelled by the luster of gems
nor removed by the rays of the sun.

—From the Sanskrit
(tr. DANIEL INGALLS)

Believe nothing merely because you have been told it, or it has
been traditional, or because you yourselves have imagined it. Believe whatsoever you find to be conducive to the good, to benefit
the welfare of all things.

—BUDDHA

COMING-OF-AGE

The highest value we know is human life, nobly lived. What may exist elsewhere is beyond our ken, but earth knows nothing so precious as character that is wrought in the white light of sane ideals.

—From *Words of Aspiration*
ARTHUR WAKEFIELD SLATEN

Let us settle ourselves, and work and wedge our feet downward through the mud and slush of opinion, and prejudice, and tradition, and delusion and appearance, that alluvion which covers the globe, through Paris and London, through New York and Boston and Concord, through church and state, through poetry and philosophy and religion till we come to a hard bottom and rocks in place, which we can call reality, and say, This is, and no mistake; and then begin, having a *point d'appui,* below freshet and frost and fire, a place where you might found a wall or a state, or set a lamp-post safely, or perhaps a gauge, not a Nilometer but a Realometer, that future ages might know how deep a freshet of shams and appearances had gathered from time to time.

—From *Walden*
HENRY THOREAU

Love the earth and sun and the animals, despise riches, give alms to every one that asks, stand up for the stupid and crazy, devote your income and labor to others, hate tyrants, argue not concerning God, have patience and indulgence toward the people, take off your hat to nothing known or unknown, or to any man or number of men—go freely with powerful uneducated persons, and with the young, and with the mothers of families—re-examine all you have been told in school or church or in any book, and dismiss whatever insults your own soul; and your very flesh shall be a great poem, and have the richest fluency, not only in its words, but in the silent lines of its lips and face, and between the lashes of your eyes, and in every motion and joint of your body.

—From the 1855 Preface to *Leaves of Grass*
WALT WHITMAN

With the establishment of a good relationship to the world of skills and tools, and with the advent of sexual maturity, childhood proper comes to an end. Youth begins. But in puberty and adolescence all samenesses and continuities relied on earlier are questioned again, because of a rapidity of body growth which equals that of early childhood and because of the entirely new addition of physical genital maturity. The growing and developing youths, faced with this physiological revolution within them, are now primarily concerned with what they appear to be in the eyes of others as compared with what they feel they are, and with the question of how to connect the roles and skills cultivated earlier with the occupational prototypes of the day. In their search for a new sense of continuity and sameness, adolescents have to re-fight many of the battles of earlier years, even though to do so they must artificially appoint perfectly well-meaning people to play the roles of enemies; and they are ever ready to install lasting idols and ideals as guardians of final identity.

—From *Childhood and Society*
ERIK H. ERIKSON

COMING-OF-AGE

That our senses lie and our minds trick us is true,
    but in general
They are honest rustics; trust them a little:
The senses more than the mind, and your own mind
    more than another man's.
As to the mind's pilot, intuition—
Catch him clean and stark naked, he is first of
    truth-tellers; dream-clothed, or dirty
With fears and wishes, he is prince of liars.
The first fear is of death: trust no immortalist. The
    first desire
Is to be loved: trust no mother's son.
Finally I say let demagogues and world-redeemers
    babble their emptiness
To empty ears; twice duped is too much.
Walk on gaunt shores and avoid the people; rock and
    wave are good prophets;
Wise are the wings of the gull, pleasant her song.

—Advice to Pilgrims
ROBINSON JEFFERS

Appoint at once a commission,
build a huge block on the edge
of every city: New York, Canton,
London, Rio, Istanbul.
On each block engrave warning:

You who succeed us, who take over our continents,
wherever you come from: We have nothing against you,

but wish you more luck with the earth
than we had, who muffed it.
Be warned, however, by this stone:

Do not become nations,
do not become classes,
be equal and do not divide.
Do not build cities,
do not multiply greatly.
Keep the streams clean
and the earth young.
Do not be gluttons of things,
be spare, be lean, be free.
And last, best not even inquire
who built these scarred stones.

Thus only may you fare well.
Farewell.

—To Whom It May Concern: Greeting
FRANCIS C. COOK

The healthy individual will be one who is capable of collaboration with groups and institutions, but who will steadfastly refuse to be collectivized. He will never get lost in that no-man's land between individuality and collectivity. He will never become a faceless person. He will never cover up all his personal problems by joining a mass movement.

The healthy individual will be one who accepts certain securities even when they are granted by governments, but who at the same time refuses to abandon the decision-making responsibility.

The healthy individual will be one who is capable of dissent when what is proclaimed to be true does not seem true to him. You don't have to give in if you don't believe it.

He will not despise the criterion of success of his environment, but will not accept such criterion for his own career if he feels that he is making a downward compromise.

The healthy person will refuse to be used as a means or to use others as a means toward his end.

The healthy people will be those who persist in believing that the whole human enterprise is a perpetual experiment. There is no time of arrival. Always the fun will be in the experiment.

People who stay healthy will be those who realize that there is no escape from conflict. Frequently the things for which we strive are not consistent. We all want security, but most of us also want new experience. If you get too much security, you will get no new experience. If you get too much status, you will get less love. The higher you go, the colder it gets. Conflict is a given datum in life. Wherever there is life, there is conflict. Where there is no conflict, there is death.

—From *The Democratic Man*
EDUARD C. LINDEMANN

Now there is time and Time is young

—MAY SARTON

Be an opener of doors for such as come after thee, and do not try to make the universe a blind alley.

—*Journal,* June 15, 1844
RALPH WALDO EMERSON

Youth is a wave, rolling away in all directions,
Part of it to break against rocks, or die on the beaches,
Or in the great calms—
And yet, the wave itself must rush on, foaming, far
    out into the distance,
Into the darkness . . .
And the next wave,
And the next,
Forever rising, forever breaking . . .

—From *To a Young Friend*
ROBERT NATHAN

COMING-OF-AGE

A tree that it takes both arms to encircle grew from a tiny rootlet. A many storied pagoda is built by placing one brick upon another brick. A journey of three thousand miles is begun by a single step.

—LAO TZU
(tr. BHIKSHU WAI-TAO
and D. GODDARD)

We must grow with our universe! It is turning out to be much more marvelous than man has ever dreamed, more beautiful while more complex, fuller of that which we consider good than philosophers of earlier days could dare to expect. Man's new directions of thought are filled with meaning for the coming races of mankind, and will lead him into new fields of awareness, new challenges of attainment, and new realizations of human destiny.

There is still far more in heaven and earth than is dreamt of in all our philosophies, but man is climbing and nature loses nothing of its wonder as he climbs. Beyond the human state stretch apparently unlimited opportunities for further evolution. Man has seen the gods, the essences of perfection, and knows within his heart that by following his inner light, learning how to control himself and the ever-increasing reaches of his universe, he can become like them.

—From *What Man May Become*
GEORGE R. HARRISON

GREAT OCCASIONS

This is an important moment in your lives and in the life of this church. This decision is your own; and yet not your own, for in it you participate in the spirit that gives this community its vitality and its promise.

You come, each from your own yesterdays, retaining the integrity of who you are and who you are becoming, to share your own becoming with the free and hopeful tomorrows of this diverse and unique congregation. You will share in the possibilities and the responsibilities of membership in our church. Your voice will become a part of the drama of our life together, and we trust that as you are able you will take your place in the councils of our leadership.

Most important, you are taking upon yourselves the mantle of a free and open spirit, and of concern for that broad humanity in which all are brothers.

—MICHAEL G. YOUNG

We stand for a moment, like those who pause upon a mountain path, and gaze downward to the valley they have left below and upward to the heights above that allure to further effort. We have been brought to our present point by powers we know not of, but whether our feet shall ever stand upon those high and lonely levels depends upon ourselves.

We are like voyagers when the harbor dangers have been safely passed, the pilot dropped, and the ship heads out to sea. From now on, the voyage is our own: ours the task of making it a joy; ours to prepare to weather the unfeeling, destructive storm; ours to find in the pageantry of Nature and in comradeship with our fellows a sufficient inspiration.

—From *Words of Aspiration*
ARTHUR WAKEFIELD SLATEN

COMING-OF-AGE

Allow the ear to hear what it likes, the eye to see what it likes, the nose to smell what it likes, the mouth to say what it likes, the body to enjoy what it likes, and the mind to think what it likes.

—From a selection by
YANG CHU

And meet the road—erect

—EMILY DICKINSON

This great world, which some multiply further as being only a species under one genus, is the mirror in which we must look at ourselves to recognize ourselves from the proper angle. In short, I want it to be the book of my student. So many humors, sects, judgments, opinions, laws, and customs teach us to judge sanely of our own, and teach our judgment to recognize its own imperfection and natural weakness, which is no small lesson. So many state disturbances and changes of public fortune teach us not to make a great miracle out of our own. So many names, so many victories and conquests, buried in oblivion, make it ridiculous to hope to perpetuate our name by the capture of ten mounted archers and some chicken coop known only by its fall. The pride and arrogance of so many foreign displays of pomp, the puffed-up majesty of so many courts and dignities, strengthens our sight and makes it steady enough to sustain the brilliance of our own without blinking. So many millions of men buried before us encourage us not to be afraid of joining such good company in the other world. And likewise for other things.

—From *Essay No. 26*
MICHEL DE MONTAIGNE
(tr. DONALD M. FRAME)

COMING-OF-AGE

The choice is always ours. Then let me choose
The longest art, the hard Promethean way
Cherishingly to tend and feed and fan
That inward fire, whose small precarious flame,
Kindled or quenched creates
The noble or the ignoble men we are,
The worlds we live in and the very fates,
Our bright or muddy star.

—From *Orion*
ALDOUS HUXLEY

Fidelity is the ability to sustain loyalties freely pledged in spite of the inevitable contradictions of value systems. It is the cornerstone of identity and receives inspiration from confirming ideologies and affirming companions.

In youth, such truth verifies itself in a number of ways: a high sense of duty, accuracy and veracity in the rendering of reality; the sentiment of truthfulness, as in sincerity and conviction; the quality of genuineness, as in authenticity; the trait of loyalty, of "being true"; fairness to the rules of the game; and finally all that is implied in devotion—a freely given but binding vow, with the fateful implication of a curse befalling traitors.

—From *Insight and Responsibility*
ERIK H. ERIKSON

What we are usually invited to contemplate as "ripeness" in a man is the resigning of ourselves to an almost exclusive use of the reason. One acquires it by copying others and getting rid, one by one, of the thoughts and convictions which were dear in the days of one's youth. We believed once in the victory of truth; but we do not now. We believed in our fellow men; we do not now. We were zealous for justice; but we are not so now. We were capable of enthusiasm; but no longer. To get through the shoals and storms of life more easily we have lightened our craft, throwing overboard what we thought could be easily spared. But it was really our stock of food and drink of which we deprived ourselves; our craft is now easier to manage, but we ourselves are in a decline.

I listened in my youth, to conversations between grown-up people through which there breathed a tone of sorrowful regret which oppressed the heart. The speakers looked back at the idealism and capacity for enthusiasm of their youth as something precious to which they ought to have held fast, and yet at the same time they regarded it as almost a law of nature that no one should be able to do so. This woke in me a dread of having ever, even once, to look back on my own past with such a feeling; I resolved never to let myself become subject to this tragic domination of mere reason, and what I thus vowed in almost boyish defiance I have tried to carry out.

—From *Memories of Childhood and Youth*
ALBERT SCHWEITZER
(tr. C. T. CAMPION)

And if you cannot make your life as you want it,
at least try this
as much as you can: do not disgrace it
in the crowding contact with the world
in the many movements and all the talk.

Do not disgrace it by taking it,
dragging it around often and exposing it

to the daily folly
of relationships and associations,
till it becomes like an alien burdensome life.

—*As Much as You Can*
C. P. CAVAFY
(tr. RAE DALVAN)

To look out upon the astounding universe with eyes unblinking and a face unblanched; to ignore no truth and fear no fact; to be ready at all times to recast opinion in the crucible of new experience; to build high hopes upon a firm foundation; to forgive without demanding apology; to keep affection in spite of misunderstanding; to set our thought upon the things of value and spend our strength in the fulfilling of noble purposes; to reverence the reverences of others rather than what they revere; to be alert to Nature's pageantry of beauty, though we dwell amid the city's clamor; to get the most out of Life and give the most we can; to be sincere, faithful to responsibility, cherishing honor above indulgence and service above gain; to be guided in our conduct by the shining angel of Intelligence and not by the gaunt specter of Fear; to approach our last hour with the calm of a philosopher and the gentleness of a saint, and to leave the world enriched by a treasury of kindly deeds and a memory of love: this is our Aspiration, this is our Ideal.

—From *Words of Aspiration*
ARTHUR WAKEFIELD SLATEN

GREAT OCCASIONS

Thou shalt not profess that which thou dost not believe.

Thou shalt not heed the voice of man when it agrees not with the voice in thine own soul.

Thou shalt study and obey the laws of the Universe and they will be thy fellow-servants.

Thou shalt speak the truth as thou seest it, without fear, in the spirit of kindness to all thy fellow-creatures.

Let thy soul be open and thine eyes will reveal to thee beauty everywhere.

—From a selection by
RALPH WALDO EMERSON

And if we are obliged to pay
a savage price because this world
is beautiful—all right, I'll say,
I shall consent to pay the price.

But, life, are all the stringencies
of fate, the losses, sudden blows,
so great a price for me to pay
for all the beauty you contain?!

—From *The Third Memory*
YEVGENY YEVTUSHENKO
(tr. GEORGE REAVEY)

COMING-OF-AGE

Do not pity the young.
Look, if the day allows,
At the light upon their brows.
Salute them passing us by,
The quick, the strict, the strong
Who will never wait, or die.
Sooner than we can say,
The young will have their way;
And have us, too, and be told
That none who live to be old
Have time to pity the young.

—From *Do Not Pity the Young*
JOHN HOLMES

There's nothing right or good in fame,
there's nothing to exalt our spirits.
Don't pore and wear your eyesight dim
on what you write, to weigh its merits.

Give yourself wholly. That is art.
Not something born of noise and blaze.
When there's no meaning in the game,
what shame to hear the lies of praise.

Don't live upon pretenses, poised
over the void with veering fears.
To huge horizons yield your heart
and catch the voice of coming years.

Omit the pointless present, omit
long chapters which you estimate
irrelevant. But use your wit,
keep strictly to your life and fate.

.   .   .

GREAT OCCASIONS

Another man in time will follow
the devious imprints of your feet;
but you yourself won't pause to tell
your victories from your defeat.

Never one moment, one jot, betray
your creed or from your purpose bend.
But stay alive—the thing that matters—
alive until the very end.

—From a selection by
BORIS PASTERNAK
(tr. JACK LINDSAY)

I believe the truth lies in youth; I believe it is always right against us. I believe that, far from trying to teach it, it is in youth that we, the elders, must seek our lessons. And I am well aware that youth is capable of errors; I know that our role is to forewarn youth as best we can: but I believe that often, when trying to protect youth, we impede it. I believe that each new generation arrives bearing a message that it must deliver; our role is to help that delivery. I believe that what is called "experience" is often but an unavowed fatigue, resignation, blighted hope.

There are very few of my contemporaries who have remained faithful to their youth. They have almost all compromised. That is what they call "learning from life." They have denied the truth that was in them. The borrowed truths are the ones to which one clings most tenaciously, and all the more so since they remain foreign to our intimate self. It takes much more precaution to deliver one's own message, much more boldness and prudence, than to sign up with and add one's voice to an already existing party.

—From *The Journals*
ANDRÉ GIDE
(tr. JUSTIN O'BRIEN)

COMING-OF-AGE

Blessed are they who come
At need, in mercy's name
To walk beside the lame,
Articulate for the dumb.

Blessed who range ahead
Of man's laborious trek,
Survey marsh, desert, peak,
Signal a way to tread.

Blessed whose faith defies
The mighty, welds the weak;
Whose dreaming hopes awake
And ring like prophecies.

Blessed who shall release
At this eleventh hour
Us thralls of evil power
And lift us into peace.

—From *Requiem for the Living*
C. DAY LEWIS

The body of mankind
Lives by the work of those
Whose anguish is their mind,
To whom the cruel are foes:
Those who dare choose to die,
Those cells that hold thought high.

—From *They Who Choose To Die*
RAYMOND HOLDEN

GREAT OCCASIONS

Be equal to your talent, not your age.
At times let the gap between them be embarrassing.
Fear not
      to be young, precocious.
To be young and tardy—
              that is wrong!
What if ironic smiles do multiply;
more mature—
         fear not to make them laugh;
more mature,
        while you still have time to grow,
make haste,
      while there's somewhere you can hurry.

—From *Others May Judge You*
YEVGENY YEVTUSHENKO
(tr. GEORGE REAVEY)

We are the living, on this keel of earth,
Who hail the convoy stars across the night,
Or feed joy's bird, and stroke his folded wing,
Then fling him flying toward the stream of light.

We are the living; daylight in our eyes;
Earth under heel; and in the mouth a word;
Fire in the fingers; questions in the mind;
And round the throat a slowly tightening cord.

Now give heart's onward habit brave intent:
Hammer the golden day until it lies

COMING-OF-AGE

A glimmering plate to heap with memory;
Salute the arriving moment with your eyes.

We live, we are elected now by time,
Few out of many not yet come to birth,
And many dead, to use the daylight now,
To stand up under the sun upon the earth.

Then break the silence with a voice of praise;
Open the door that opens toward the sky;
Press mind and body hard against this world,
Before we fall asleep, before we die.

—From *Address to the Living*
JOHN HOLMES

Far from distrusting the temporal delights that come through the body, we should abandon ourselves to them with confidence. The way of the senses is the way of life. It is the people with their hands in the till and their eyes on heaven who ruin existence. There should be open-air temples in every town and village where philosophers could expound this soundest of doctrines. Why is half the population tormented with restraints, obedience to which in no way furthers the public good? Because the priests for generations have been confederate with the money-makers, and they both know very well that if natural happiness were allowed the generations would no longer accept their shrewd worldly maxims, no longer be so docile, so easy to be exploited. Without doubt half the ethical rules they din into our ears are designed to keep us at work. Our haughty minds are nothing but the senses in flower. When the senses wither and die the mind withers and dies with them.

—From *Earth Memories*
LLEWELYN POWYS

Do not be too timid and squeamish about your actions. All life is an experiment. The more experiments you make the better. What if they are a little coarse, and you may get your coat soiled or torn? What if you do fail, and get fairly rolled in the dirt once or twice? Up again; you shall never be so afraid of a tumble.

—*Journal,* November 11, 1842
RALPH WALDO EMERSON

Grown-up people reconcile themselves too willingly to preparing young ones for the time when they will regard as illusion what now is an inspiration to heart and mind. Deeper experience of life, however, advises their inexperience differently. It exhorts them to hold fast, their whole life through, to the thoughts which inspire them. It is through the idealism of youth that man catches sight of truth, and in that idealism he possesses a wealth which he must never exchange for anything else.

We must all be prepared to find that life tries to take from us our belief in the good and the true, and our enthusiasm for them, but we need not surrender them. That ideals, when they are brought into contact with reality, are usually crushed by facts does not mean that they are bound from the very beginning to capitulate to the facts, but merely that our ideals are not strong enough; and they are not strong enough because they are not pure and strong and stable enough in themselves.

—From *Memories of Childhood and Youth*
ALBERT SCHWEITZER
(tr. C. T. CAMPION)

COMING-OF-AGE

We are all of us the same—black skins, brown skins, yellow skins, and white skins; all of us no better than precocious apes snapping at shadows. We awake out of an infinite oblivion to find ourselves alive on a sturdy planet of miracle and mystery. The myths of antiquity trickily preserved in pot-hook ciphers hedge us in with erroneous conclusions. How can we be expected to envisage existence with a clear, disinterested intelligence?

We grow up obsessed with the legends of our particular locality. We are dominated by the persuasions of custom. Our kings on their gilded thrones, our dressed-up judges, convince our flighty minds as to the stability of society, and not once in a lifetime do we see behind such administrative expedients. The priest rises to bless us with pontifical fingers punctiliously arranged, and his large claim provokes no protest. We do not see him as a direct representative of sacerdotal Egypt, an obsolete witch doctor out of the remote past, invoking the aid of beings that never have existed except in the bewildered dreams of savages. Meanwhile, on every side the stir of life continues with its weasel wickedness, its May-fly triviality, and its inexplicable inclination towards what is gentle, altruistic, and good.

The cuckoo's hollow echo comes to us through our breakfast window, troubling with its promise both maid and yellow-hosed bachelor. Swift as a half-seen fairy, a mouse crosses the garden path, a diminutive questing beast, the quiver of a lobelia flower the only proof of its passing. The white campion in the hayfield gives out to the June night its sweet breath. With bellies full of the blood and flesh of fellow animals we stand up to practice self-interested pieties, the claws on our fingers carefully disguised with gloves.

—From *Earth Memories*
LLEWELYN POWYS

FOR THE OCCASION
OF MARRIAGE

FOR THE OCCASION
OF MARRIAGE

COUPLES are always surprised by how short a time it takes to get married. Yet as a thirteenth century Arabic poet noted, "the tale was brief, the words were few, the meaning was immense."

Poets, however, have seldom had too much to say about marriage. About physical love, past, present, and hoped-for, they are quite specific, yea verbose. Stepping into this poetical vacuum, Kahlil Gibran has made the territory virtually his own. Along with "O Promise Me" and "Because," his reading on marriage from *The Prophet* has become a staple item in many modern marriage services. Couples might well wonder if they were duly married without the verbal sanctification of the Lebanese prophet.

Perhaps the poetical lack of interest in matrimony stems from Protestantism's mixed feelings about such services. Roman Catholics, defining it as a sacrament, have always maintained that the church had an exclusive right to perform the service, only reluctantly accepting civil participation in the matter. In revolting against the authority of Rome, early Protestants also rejected much of the dogma on marriage. Luther advised ministers to leave the business to the lawyers and the magistrates. Calvin thought religion was no more involved in marriage than in "agriculture, architecture, shoemaking, and many other things."

Was this a subconscious reflection of the antisex attitude of

Christians? The church—in all its branches—has been the great conservative in sexual affairs. They have insisted on monogamy, proclaimed the marital union indissoluble, fought every easing of divorce and abortion laws, made adultery and fornication crimes and not misdemeanors, invented the idea of perversions, and continually worked against what Lippmann termed "all unprocreative indulgence."

Gradually Protestants have come to accept the idea that religion had something to do with marriage. Endless nit-picking was done on the meaning of Jesus' participation in the wedding at Cana. Solving these theological crossword puzzles to their satisfaction, Protestants today generally conclude that marriage is well-pleasing to God. Kirkegaard—who felt the only good Christian was a celibate Christian—caustically observed that the day would come when such Christians would discover God to be "a woman called Maggie matchmaker."

This peevish view reflects few current feelings. Celibacy seems to be going out of style. Marriage, as Christopher Lasch points out, even overdominates the life expectations of Americans. "All the institutions of American society, family, school, church, the economy itself which is geared to the production of 'homes' and all the things necessary to operate them—encourage this pervasive obsession with domesticity."

But this domesticity takes place in a society in which—depending on whose statistics you accept—from 20 to 33 percent of all marriages end in divorce. The problem of divorce itself is the obverse of the coin. Many legal and social reforms are needed before divorce can become a healthy, sensible procedure and not a problem.

Besides the wholesale infiltration of the marriage service by the Gospel according to Gibran, other changes in the ritual are becoming common. The ceremony of the wine cup, with roots in Judaism and Catholicism, has been used in a number of services at the choice of some couples. A form of such a service will be found on page 129. Another charming Jewish custom which some couples might like to try is that of having the bride and groom stand under a Hupah (a canopy stretched out on four poles) while they exchange vows. The canopy symbolizes their coming together in their future home. And why do not the members of the wedding cry out a "mazel tov"—good luck—when they toss their seeds of rice? (Those fertility symbols are now too often refined out of their sexual implications by the substitution of sterile confetti.)

While each service is different, the meanings are universal. In Duncan Howlett's words, marriage is a "public declaration of partnership between a man and a woman, which implies both permanence and the undertaking of mutual responsibilities." Floyd Ross cautiously says the "relationship of man with woman is a continuing laboratory where one can possibly come to a larger selfhood." Above all, it is the joy of being a creature susceptible to joy. It has in mind the anticipations of the joys of the body and — in the back of its mind — the joys of companionship, of sharing the intimacies of life, of completing the self in another self.

* * *

The 109 readings which follow center around the six themes of joy, fulfillment, discovery, adventure, contentment, and responsibility and faith. See Appendix B for a Ceremony of Divorce suggested by Rudolph W. Nemser.*

* A useful discussion of such rites can be found in "The Rite of Divorce and Other Rights" by Ronald Mazur, in the *Journal of the Liberal Ministry*, Winter, 1966, Vol. 6, No. 1, pp. 42–48.

Such music in a skin!

—THEODORE ROETHKE

Lift your arms to the stars
And give an immortal shout!
Not all the wells of darkness
Can put your beauty out.

You are armed with love, with love,
Not all the powers of fate
Avail to do you harm—
Nor all the hands of hate.

What of good and evil,
Hell, and Heaven above—
Trample them with love!
Ride over them with love!

—*Song II*
JOHN HALL WHEELOCK

MARRIAGE

Speak softly; sun going down
Out of sight. Come near me now.

Dear dying fall of wings as birds
Complain against the gathering dark . . .

Exaggerate the green blood in grass;
The music of leaves scraping space;

Multiply the stillness by one sound;
By one syllable of your name . . .

And all that is little is soon giant,
All that is rare grows in common beauty

To rest with my mouth on your mouth
As somewhere a star falls

And the earth takes it softly, in natural love . . .
Exactly as we take each other . . . and go to sleep.

—Fall of the Evening Star
KENNETH PATCHEN

Love is a sacred mystery.

To those who love, it remains forever wordless;
But to those who do not love, it may be but a heartless
    jest.

Love is a gracious host to his guests though to the
unbidden his house is a mirage and a mockery.

Love is a night where candles burn in space,
Love is a dream beyond our reaching;
Love is a noon where all shepherds are at peace and
    happy that their flocks are grazing;
Love is an eventide and a stillness, and a homecoming;
Love is a sleep and a dream.

93

GREAT OCCASIONS

When love becomes vast love becomes wordless.
And when memory is overladen it seeks the silent deep.

—From *Jesus*
KAHLIL GIBRAN

Spring bursts today,
For Love is risen and all the earth's at play.

Flash forth, thou Sun,
The rain is over and gone, its work is done.

Winter is past,
Sweet Spring is come at last, is come at last.

Bud, Fig and Vine,
Bud, Olive, fat with fruit and oil and wine.

Break forth this morn
In rose, thou but yesterday a Thorn.

Uplift thy head,
O pure white Lily through the Winter dead.

Beside your dams
Leap and rejoice, you merry-making Lambs.

All Herds and Flocks
Rejoice all, all Beasts of thickets and rocks.

Sing, Creatures, sing,
Fishes and Men and Birds and everything.

All notes of Doves
Fill all our world: this is the time of loves.

—From *An Easter Carol*
CHRISTINA ROSSETTI

MARRIAGE

He who binds to himself a joy
Doth the wingèd life destroy;
But he who kisses the joy as it flies
Lives in Eternity's sunrise.

—WILLIAM BLAKE

It is for the union of you and me
that there is light in the sky.
It is for the union of you and me
that the earth is decked in dusky green.

It is for the union of you and me
that night sits motionless with the world in her arms;
dawn appears opening the eastern door
with sweet murmurs in her voice.

The boat of hope sails along on the currents of
        eternity towards that union,
flowers of the ages are being gathered together
for its welcoming ritual.

It is for the union of you and me
that this heart of mine, in the garb of a bride,
has proceeded from birth to birth
        upon the surface of this ever-turning world
to choose the Beloved.

—RABINDRANATH TAGORE
(tr. INDU DUTT)

GREAT OCCASIONS

Rise, my love, my beautiful one, come away;
For, see, the winter is past, the rain is over and gone;
The flowers have appeared on the earth, the time of
        song has come;
And the call of the dove is heard in our land;
The fig tree is putting forth its figs
And the blossoming grapevines give forth fragrance.
Rise, my love, my beautiful one, come away.

O my dove in the clefts of the rocks, in the
        recesses of the cliffs,
Let me see your form, let me hear your voice;
For your voice is sweet, and your form is comely.
Rise, my love, my beautiful one, come away.

—SONG OF SONGS
(tr. T. J. MEEK)

Shine! shine! shine!
Pour down your warmth, great sun!
While we bask, we two together.

Two together!
Winds blow south, or winds blow north,
Day come white, or night come black,
Home, or rivers and mountains from home,
Singing all time, minding no time,
While we two keep together.

—From *Out of the Cradle Endlessly Rocking*
WALT WHITMAN

96

MARRIAGE

What bodies do together in the dark is beautiful
                       and lips
may move in wonder as a man does love with a woman
what is of her, his
      and it will be all fire and roads leading somewhere
not darkness, not rain on the tortured faces, nor shadows
falling, falling
      shadows that mean nothing, and no one to care
They won't be afraid
There will be birds flying through their upturned faces

                    —From *Poem*
                      KENNETH PATCHEN

Between us a new morning
Is being born from our flesh
Just the right way
To put everything into shape
We are moving just the right footsteps ahead
And the earth says hello to us
The day has all our rainbows
The fireplace is lit with our eyes
And the ocean celebrates our marriage

                  —From a selection by
                  PAUL ELUARD
                  (tr. WALTER LOWENFELS)

GREAT OCCASIONS

love is a place
& through this place of
love move
(with brightness of peace)
all places

yes is a world
& in this world of
yes live
(skilfully curled)
all worlds

—love is a place
E. E. CUMMINGS

Awed by the many meanings of this hour and overjoyed by its promises, we hope the spirit of trust, understanding, and love may be with —————— and —————— through all the years that lie ahead. Whatever trials and testings may come, may they trust each other wholly, for without such faith marriage is a mockery; may they understand each other, for without understanding there is neither acceptance nor forgiveness; and may they truly love each other, for without love marriage is only an empty shell from which the white bird has flown.

As they build together a new life and a new home, may that home be bright with the laughter of children and of many friends; may it be a haven from the tensions of our time and a wellspring of strength; and in all the world may it be the one place they most want to be, the place where they discover the ultimate human mystery—the secret of how two become one.

So may this shining hour be an open door through which —————— and —————— will go forth to build that dearest of all relationships, a happy, harmonious marriage. May the years deal gently with them; walking together may they find

98

far more in life than either would have found alone; and even more fully may they come to know this one supreme truth: that caring is sharing . . . that living is giving . . . that life is eternal . . . and that love is its crown.

—From a selection by
W. WALDEMAR W. ARGOW

We two—What the earth is, we are;
We lovers—how long we were fooled!
Now delicious, transmuted, swiftly we escape, as nature escapes,
We are nature—Long have we been absent, but now we return,
We become plants, weeds, foliage, roots, bark,
We are bedded in the ground—we are rocks,
We are oaks—we grow in the openings, side by side,
We browse—we are two among the wild herds, spontaneous as any,
We are two fishes swimming in the sea together,
We are what the locust-blossoms are—we drop scent around the
    lanes, mornings and evenings,
We are also the coarse smut of beasts, vegetables, minerals,
We are what the flowing wet of the Tennessee is—We are two
    peaks of the Blue Mountains, rising up in Virginia,
We are two predatory hawks—we soar above, and look down,
We are two resplendent suns—we it is that balance ourselves,
    orbic and stellar—We are as two comets,
We prowl, fanged and four-footed in the woods—we spring on
    prey,
We are two clouds, forenoons and afternoons, driving overhead,
We are seas mingling—we are two of those cheerful waves, rolling
    on and on over each other, and interwetting each other,
We are what the atmosphere is, transparent, receptive, pervious,
    impervious,
We are snow, rain, cold, darkness,—We are each product and
    influence of the globe,

GREAT OCCASIONS

We have circled and circled till we have arrived home again—
we two have,
We have voided all but freedom, and all but our own joy—

—From original draft *Enfans d'Adam* (7)
WALT WHITMAN

In the highest moment of love, thought itself dissolves away like hoar-frost in the sun. The mind becomes as nothing, the body as nothing, the whole of our being caught up, translated, until it is at one with the incomprehensible mystery that lies behind matter, at one with that incalculable dynamic that is nowhere and yet is every-where, and through whose agency the star clouds stream across the firmament, the daffodil lifts its head, the swallow chitters, and the ground-ivy delivers up its soul to the ditches. For let them say what they will, it is in the agony and ecstasy of corporeal love, it is under the ascendancy of this first-born of all the senses that mortals draw most near to the quivering secret of life.

—From *Earth Memories*
LLEWELYN POWYS

Let a joy keep you.
Reach out your hands
And take it when it runs by,
As the Apache dancer
Clutches his woman.
I have seen them

100

MARRIAGE

Live long and laugh loud,
Sent on singing, singing,
Smashed to the heart
Under the ribs
With a terrible love.
Joy always,
Joy everywhere—
Let joy kill you!
Keep away from the little deaths.

—Joy
CARL SANDBURG

An old willow with hollow branches
slowly swayed his few high bright tendrils
and sang:

Love is a young green willow
shimmering at the bare wood's edge.

—From *Epitaph*
WILLIAM CARLOS WILLIAMS

(The Woman sings)

Under the sun
The earth is dry.
By the fire
Alone I cry.

101

GREAT OCCASIONS

All day long
The earth cries
For the rain to come
All night my heart cries
For my hunter to come
And take me away.

(The Man replies)

Oh! listen to the wind,
You woman there;
The time is coming,
The rain is near.
Listen to your heart,
Your hunter is here.

—AFRICAN BUSHMAN SONG

Love's characters come face to face

—WALLACE STEVENS

I would not have this perfect love of ours
Grow from a single root, a single stem,
Bearing no goodly fruit, but only flowers
That idly hide life's iron diadem:
It should grow always like that Eastern tree
Whose limbs take root and spread for*h constantly;
That love for one, from which there doth not spring
Wide love for all, is but a worthless thing.
Not in another world, as poets prate,
Dwell we apart above the tide of things,
High floating o'er earth's clouds on faery wings;
But our pure love doth ever elevate
Into a holy bond of brotherhood
All earthly things, making them pure and good.

—Sonnet III
JAMES RUSSELL LOWELL

103

GREAT OCCASIONS

Believe in what is yours.
Believe in who you are.
Believe in the richness and the power
    of what lies in the depths you share.

—From a selection by
RUDOLPH W. NEMSER

Time wasteth years, and months, and hours,
    Time doth consume fame, honour, wit, and strength,
Time kills the greenest herbs and sweetest flowers,
    Time wears out youth and beauty's looks at length,
      Time doth convey to ground both foe and friend,
      And each thing else but love, which hath no end.

Time maketh every tree to die and rot,
    Time turneth oft our pleasures into pain,
Time causeth wars and wrongs to be forgot,
    Time clears the sky, which first hung full of rain,
      Time makes an end of all humane desire,
      But only this, which sets my heart on fire.

Time turneth into nought each princely state,
    Time brings a flood from new resolved snow,
Time calms the sea where tempest was of late,
    Time eats whate'er the moon can see below;
      And yet no time prevails in my behove,
      Nor any time can make me cease to love.

—THOMAS WATSON

MARRIAGE

If life has meaning to us at all, it possesses it because of love. It is that which enshrines and ennobles our human experience. It is the basis for the peace of family and the peace of the peoples of the earth. The greatest gift bestowed upon humans is the gift not of demanding but of giving love between man and woman.

—From *Be Patient and Loving*
MARTIN M. WEITZ

But of deep love is the desire to give
More than the living touch of warmth and fire,
More than the shy comfort of the little flesh and hands;
It is the need to give
Down to the last dark kernel of the heart,
Down to the final gift of mind;
It is a need to give you that release which comes
Only of understanding, and to know
Trust without whimpering doubt and fear.

—From *September*
JOSEPHINE JOHNSON

To love means to decide independently to live with an equal partner, and to subordinate oneself to the formation of a new subject, a "we." This depends neither upon thinking nor upon feeling, but upon the resolution of two subjects to accept life's most difficult task, the creation of a double subject, a "we," with complete disregard for egocentricity, all prejudices, training formulas, and drives. He who has enough courage so to love finds in living with

105

his partner the strongest positive experience imaginable—the appearance of super-personal purposes. He exchanges that part of his egocentricity which he renounces for a part of the great clarification which awaits all of us. And life reveals to him part of its meaning.

—From *Let's Be Normal*
FRITZ KUNKEL

Mutual love is the only basis of a human relationship; and bargains and claims and promises are attempts to substitute something else; and they introduce falsity into the relationship. No human being can have rights in another, and no human being can grant to another rights in himself or herself.

If you love a person you love him or her in their stark reality, and refuse to shut your eyes to their defects and errors. For to do that is to shut your eyes to their needs. I...e cannot abide deceit, or pretense or unreality. It rests only in the reality of the loved one, demands that the loved one should be himself, so that it may love him for himself.

The sexual relationship is one of the possible expressions of love, as it is one of the possible cooperations in love—more intimate, more fundamental, more fraught with consequences inner and outer, but essentially one of the expressions of love, not fundamentally different in principle from any others, as regards its use. It is neither something high and holy, something to venerate and be proud of, nor is it something low and contemptible, to be ashamed of. It is a simple ordinary organic function to be used like all the others, for the expression of personality in the service of love. In such a unity sex ceases to be an appetite—a want to be satisfied—and becomes a means of communion, simple and natural.

—From *Reason and Emotion*
JOHN MACMURRAY

106

MARRIAGE

My true love hath my heart, and I have his,
   By just exchange one for another given:
I hold his dear, and mine he cannot miss,
   There never was a better bargain driven:
    My true love hath my heart, and I have his.

His heart in me keeps him and me in one,
   My heart in him his thought and senses guides:
He loves my heart, for once it was his own,
   I cherish his, because in me it bides:
    My true love hath my heart, and I have his.

—Love's Tranquility
PHILIP SIDNEY

I believe that men as human beings must have in common certain values and that these begin with the belief that love is essential to life: functioning as sex, it is necessary not only for procreation of life but for the full health of the human organism; functioning as sympathy, compassion, devotion, willingness to suffer if others can be benefited by it, it gives man his dignity and his grace as a human being.

I believe that love is an expanding feeling that reaches out toward others and helps them find more abundant life; and that this expansion, this reaching out to people is necessary for man's health.

I believe love gives man his capacity for acceptance of life's experiences, for understanding (which brain alone can never give), his tolerance, his generosity, his strength. This is love as I see it: an act of the human spirit reaching out in tenderness and concern toward all people.

—From Killers of the Dream
LILLIAN SMITH

Because they wish to dedicate themselves unto each other, and because they seek that greater joy that comes when two become joined in body, mind, and spirit, ——————— and ——————— come seeking the greater fulfillment of their lives in marriage.

—ROBERT BOTLEY

We are gathered here to join ——————— and ——————— in marriage. It is fitting and appropriate that you, the families and friends of ——————— and ——————— be here to witness and to participate in their wedding, for the ideals, the understanding, and the mutual respect which they bring to their marriage have their roots in the love, friendship, and guidance you have given them. Marriage makes us aware of the changes wrought by time, but the new relationship will continue to draw much of its beauty and meaning from the intimate associations of the past.

—WILLIAM R. FORTNER

The breaking of a wave cannot explain the whole sea

—VLADIMIR NABOKOV

It is one of life's richest surprises when the accidental meeting of two life paths leads them to proceed together along the common path of man and wife, and it is one of life's finest experiences when a casual relationship grows into a permanent bond of love. This meeting and this growth bring us together today.

—ANONYMOUS

Open your heart, as if you could,
Let me come into it, like fire,
And let me know it as dry wood,
Pretend your being is desire:

Then turn to sandstone, as you can,
And let me flow like water through
Your pores toward air, where I began,
As if your earth were all of you.

—*Double Love Song*
THOMAS WHITBREAD

Love, now a universal birth,
From heart to heart is stealing,
From earth to man, from man to earth—
It is the hour of feeling.

One moment now may give us more
Than years of toiling reason;
Our minds shall drink at every pore
The spirit of the season.

No joyless forms shall regulate
Our living calendar;
We from today, my love, will date
The opening of the years.

Some silent laws our hearts will make,
Which they shall long obey;
We for the years to come may take
Our temper from today.

—From *To My Sister*
WILLIAM WORDSWORTH

A good relationship has a pattern like a dance and is built on some of the same rules. The partners do not need to hold on tightly, because they move confidently in the same pattern, intricate but gay and swift and free, like a country dance of Mozart's. To touch heavily would be to arrest the pattern and freeze the movement, to check the endlessly changing beauty of its unfolding. There is no place here for the possessive clutch, the clinging arm, the heavy hand; only the barest touch in passing. Now arm in arm, now face to face, now back to back—it does not matter which. Because they know they are partners moving to the same rhythm, creating a pattern together, and being invisibly nourished by it. The joy of such a pattern is not only the joy of creation or the joy of participation, it is also the joy of living in the moment. Lightness of touch and living in the moment are intertwined.

—From *Gift from the Sea*
ANNE MORROW LINDBERGH

Love does not consist in gazing at each other but in looking outward together in the same direction. There is no comradeship except through union in the same high effort.

—From *Wind, Sand, and Stars*
ANTOINE DE SAINT-EXUPÉRY
(tr. LEWIS GALANTIÈRE)

The more you love, the more love you are given to love with.

—LUCIEN PRICE

A togetherness between two people is an impossibility, and where it seems, nevertheless, to exist, it is a narrowing, a reciprocal agreement which robs either one party or both of his fullest freedom and development. But, once the realization is accepted that even between the *closest* human beings infinite distances continue to exist, a wonderful living side by side can grow up, if they succeed in loving the distance between them which makes it possible for each to see the other whole and against a wide sky!

—From *Letters*
RAINER MARIA RILKE
(tr. J. B. GREENE and M. D. H. NORTON)

When you love someone you do not love them all the time, in exactly the same way, from moment to moment. It is an impossibility. It is even a lie to pretend to. And yet this is exactly what most of us demand. We have so little faith in the ebb and flow of life, of love, of relationships. We leap at the flow of the tide and resist in terror its ebb. We are afraid it will never return. We insist on permanency, on duration, on continuity; when the only continuity possible, in life as in love, is in growth, in fluidity—in freedom, in the sense that the dancers are free, barely touching as they pass, but partners in the same pattern.

The only real security is not in owning or possessing, not in demanding or expecting, not in hoping, even. Security in a relationship lies neither in looking back to what it was in nostalgia, nor forward to what it might be in dread or anticipation, but living in the present relationship and accepting it as it is now. For relationships too, must be like islands, one must accept them for what they are here and now, within their limits—islands, surrounded and interrupted by the sea, and continually visited and abandoned by the tides. One must accept the security of the winged life, of the ebb and flow, of intermittency.

—From *Gift from the Sea*
ANNE MORROW LINDBERGH

112

MARRIAGE

It takes years to marry completely two hearts, even of the most loving and well-assorted. A happy wedlock is a long falling in love. Young persons think love belongs only to the brown-haired and crimson-cheeked. So it does for its beginning. But the golden marriage is a part of love which the Bridal day knows nothing of.

A perfect and complete marriage, where wedlock is everything you could ask and the ideal of marriage becomes actual, is not common, perhaps as rare as perfect personal beauty. Men and women are married fractionally, now a small fraction, then a large fraction. Very few are married totally, and they only after some forty or fifty years of gradual approach and experiment.

Such a large and sweet fruit is a complete marriage that it needs a long summer to ripen in, and then a long winter to mellow and season it. But a real, happy marriage of love and judgment between a noble man and woman is one of the things so very handsome that if the sun were, as the Greek poets fabled, a God, he might stop the world and hold it still now and then in order to look all day long on some example thereof, and feast his eyes on such a spectacle.

—From a selection by
THEODORE PARKER

When a man and woman are successfully in love, their whole activity is energized and victorious. They walk better, their digestion improves, they think more clearly, their secret worries drop away, the world is fresh and interesting, and they can do more than they dreamed that they could do. In love of this kind sexual intimacy is not the dead end of desire as it is in romantic or promiscuous love, but periodic affirmation of the inward delight of desire

113

pervading an active life. Love of this sort can grow: it is not, like youth itself, a moment that comes and is gone and remains only a memory of something which cannot be recovered. It can grow because it has something to grow upon and to grow with; it is not contracted and stale because it has for its object, not the mere relief of physical tension, but all the objects with which the two lovers are concerned. They desire their worlds in each other, and therefore their love is as interesting as their worlds and their worlds are as interesting as their love.

—From *Preface to Morals*
WALTER LIPPMANN

love's function is to fabricate unknownness

(known being wishless;but love,all of wishing)
though life's lived wrongsideout,sameness chokes oneness
truth is confused with fact,fish boast of fishing

and men are caught by worms(love may not care
if time totters,light droops,all measures bend
nor marvel if a thought should weigh a star
—dreads dying least;and less,that death should end)

how lucky lovers are(whose selves abide
under whatever shall discovered be)
whose ignorant each breathing dares to hide
more than most fabulous wisdom fears to see

(who laugh and cry)who dream,create and kill
while the whole moves;and every part stands still:

—love's function is to fabricate unknownness
E. E. CUMMINGS

114

MARRIAGE

Not from pride, but from humility
As mortals, with human weaknesses
And strengths
You stand alone today
And promise faith.
Your faith you find as you live,
Each moment consecrated to
A search for Truth
And for that Good
Whose presence you have deeply felt.

NOW:
From this time, until
The time you must rejoin the
Earth from which you came,
Love the love in you that underlies
Your actions.
And with each other,
Share your wonder at the beauty
That you find
As Man and Wife.

—JAMES LAWSON

The hand offered by each of you is an extension of self, just as is
your mutual love. Cherish the touch, for you touch not only your
own, but another life. Be ever sensitive to its pulse. Seek always
to understand and to respect its rhythm.

——————————, do you take ——————————, in all her gentleness
and sensitivity for her warm heart and her understanding of you
and your philosophy, for her search for truth and goodness and
her recognition of falseness and evil, and for her courage to em-

115

bark along new and untried paths as conscience and necessity demand?

Yes, I take her not only for these, but also in laughter and tears, in health and illness, in success and failure, in conflict and tranquility, in doubt and trust as my wife and equal. Let this ring be a symbol of my vow.

——————— do you take ——————— for his discernment of truth in face of discouragement, his pursuit of a simple life amid worldly distractions, his strength to follow the course his judgment dictates, and his deep love of his fellow man?

Yes, I take him not only for these, but also in laughter and tears, etc.

—ANONYMOUS

We are each a secret to the other. To know one another cannot mean to know everything about each other; it means to feel mutual affection and confidence, and to believe in one another. We must not try to force our way into the personality of another. To analyze others is a rude commencement, for there is a modesty of the soul which we must recognize just as we do that of the body. No one has a right to say to another: "Because we belong to each other as we do, I have a right to know all your thoughts." Not even a mother may treat her child in that way. All demands of this sort are foolish and unwholesome. In this matter giving is the only valuable process; it is only giving that stimulates. Impart as much as you can of your spiritual being to those who are on the road with you, and accept as something precious what comes back to you from them.

—From *Memories of Childhood and Youth*
ALBERT SCHWEITZER
(tr. C. T. CAMPION)

116

MARRIAGE

Ah, this star we live on is burning full in danger.
All we know is this: across existence
and across its lapse passes something unknown.
We name it love. And, love, we pray to you.
—It takes only a second to walk around a man.
Whoever wishes to circle the soul of a lover
needs longer than his pilgrimage of years.

> —From *To the Unborn Children*
> HANS CAROSSA
> (tr. MURIEL RUKEYSER
> and ELIZABETH MAYER)

A heart alone is not a heart
Until it is one with all hearts
And your body is every star
In a sky full of stars
In the orbit of a movement
From your eyes to all eyes
Gleaming with a patina of loveliness
Whose light is the weight of the earth.

> —From a selection by
> PAUL ELUARD
> (tr. WALTER LOWENFELS)

GREAT OCCASIONS

When the giving of Love is entire,
And what Love cries to is bygone in the stress
      of its crying,
Then a man verifies
What passion testifies:
Prayer is Unbelief
Once one knows.

—AL-HALLAJ
(tr. ERIC SCHROEDER)

I thought of love as a crooked knife,
As a soft and passionate lord;
Born when the kings' beards dipped in wine
And the gold cups clashed on the board.
But my love came like a blast of cold,
A straight, clean, sword.

I thought of love as a secret thing,
For an hour of incensed ease,
When breast and breast together cling,
Under sweet-scented trees.
My love is all good-comradeship,
More great than these.

I thought of love as a toy for a day,
Soon to be overpassed;
Light and frail as a hollow shell,
That into the brook is cast.
My love holds while the earth endures,
And the suns stand fast.

I thought of love as mixed with earth,
One with the bloom of the sods.
My love is air and wine and fire,

MARRIAGE

Breaker of metes and rods,
A slender javelin tipped with light,
Hurled at the gods.

—From *Lucullus Dines*
STEPHEN VINCENT BENÉT

No love, to love of man and wife;
No hope, to hope of constant heart;
No joy, to joy in wedded life;
No faith, to faith in either part:
    Flesh is of flesh, and bone of bone
    When deeds and words and thoughts are one.

No hate, to hate of man and wife;
No fear, to fear of double heart;
No death, to discontented life;
No grief, to grief when friends depart:
    They tear the flesh and break the bone
    That are in word or thought alone.

Thy friend an other friend may be,
But other self is not the same:
Thy wife the self-same is with thee,
In body, mind, in goods and name:
    No thine, no mine, may other call,
    Now all is one, and one is all.

—RICHARD EDES

GREAT OCCASIONS

Love is
    a rain of diamonds
    in the mind

    the soul's fruit
    sliced in two

    a dark spring
    loosed at the lips of light

    under-earth waters
    unlocked from their lurking
    to sparkle in a crevice
    parted by the sun

    a temple
    not of stone but cloud

    beyond the heart's roar
    and all violence

    outside the anvil-stunned domain
    unfrenzied space

    between the grains of change
    blue permanence

    one short step
    to the good ground

    the bite into bread again

—Love Is
MAY SWENSON

I love you. It is my deepest desire that we spend our days and years together. Our love shall unite us in a genuine union of hearts and lives, in which I shall cherish and care for you; and not merely materially, for I shall honor you for what you intrinsically are, for the richness and promise of your personality.

I love you. I love you unconditionally, hoping for your love freely given in return. My love is not a demanding love, nor does it find room for resentments and hostilities. I will seek ever to understand you, to admire you for what you are, to recognize your potentialities, and to help you to attain them. I have faith in you and in our future together, a future in which we may ever become persons more completely loving.

I love you. I love you now because I cannot help it, but I know there is more to love than I now feel. I promise to make the continuing effort to purge all feelings of boredom, guilt, or being threatened, and to learn to love more maturely. I will share with you my hopes, my dreams, my aspirations, and strive to make myself a sensitive receiver for your hopes, your dreams, your aspirations. And all this shall not be a grim and solemn task, but we shall be gay and laugh together through it all.

I love you. I say this freely, without any sense of being trapped or being under a compulsion which I resent. The togetherness for which I hope is one in which the strength in each of us will complement the weakness of the other. My love is the beginning of a great project, a new creation. Already the two of us constitute a family, united by an invisible bond, and providing a soil in which love can flourish, increase, and mature. To this bond, as well as to you, I pledge my devotion.

I love you. I shall become part of your clan, and you shall become a part of mine. Your responsibilities shall be my responsibilities. If there be children, they shall draw us closer together. In the community in which we live we will seek the companionship and fellowship of those who will enhance our love rather than endanger it. As the years bring their relentless changes, we will enrich the later years with memories of the earlier days. If together we live out the full span of our years, we will be able to look back over them rejoicing that our love has indeed bestowed upon us the blessings of a union which has led us out of the realm of law and convention into the realm of the spirit.

—From a selection by
ELMO A. ROBINSON

We are those two natural and nonchalant persons

—WALT WHITMAN

When all the world is young, lad,
And all the trees are green;
And every goose a swan, lad,
And every lass a queen;
Then hey for boot and horse, lad,
And round the world away;
Young blood must have its course, lad,
And every dog his day.

When all the world is old, lad,
And all the trees are brown;
And all the sport is stale, lad,
And all the wheels run down;
Creep home, and take your place there,
The spent and maimed among;
And grant you find one face there,
You loved when all was young.

—CHARLES KINGSLEY

122

MARRIAGE

Now in the time of your youth
You enter a phase of
The cycle of life
Ordained
Before you were born.
Let the ceaseless flow of time
Find your love as strong
As on this day.
For love alone is eternal
Not subject to change;
Outside the cycle, yet
Causing
Sustaining
Available always,
The basis of good in our souls.

Ephemeral, flickering, passing in haste
The time of man is short.
All the richness of your labors
Is called wisdom
And the essence of wisdom is love.

—JAMES LAWSON

We have come together to make a marriage of our love and understanding. We shall share with each other in all gladness, strengthen
each other in all labor, minister to each other in all sorrow, and be
one with each other in the memories of life.

We shall make a home of the place where we dwell and there
we shall gather wisdom from the seasons of life. It shall be a place
for the gladness of children and for the joy of youth. In it shall
be a dream to make our land a large home for its elders.

We invite friendship to enrich our home and we welcome beauty and kindness that our hopes may be more than a sentimental longing and that peace may abide with us.

—ERNEST H. SOMMERFELD

Thou and I,
Sweet friend! can look from our tranquility
Like lamps into the world's tempestuous night,—
Two tranquil stars, while clouds are passing by
Which wrap them from the foundering seaman's sight,
That burn from year to year with unextinguished light.

—From *To Mary*
PERCY BYSSHE SHELLEY

Love is a great thing, yea, a great and thorough good; by itself it makes everything that is heavy light; and it bears evenly all that is uneven.

It carries a burden which is no burden; it will not be kept back by anything low and mean; it desires to be free from all worldly affections, and not to be entangled by any outward prosperity, or by any adversity subdued.

Love feels no burden, thinks nothing of trouble, attempts what is above its strength, pleads no excuse of impossibility.

It is therefore able to undertake all things, and it completes many things, and warrants them to take effect, where he who does not love would faint and lie down.

Though weary, it is not tired; though pressed, it is not straitened; though alarmed, it is not confounded; but as a living flame it forces its way upward, and securely passes through all.

Love is active and sincere; courageous, patient, faithful, prudent, and manly.

—From *Imitation of Christ*
THOMAS À KEMPIS

What greater thing is there for two human souls than to feel that they are joined for life, to strengthen each other in all labour, to rest on each other in all sorrow, to minister to each other in all pain, to be one with each other in silent unspeakable memories at the moment of the last parting?

—From *Adam Bede*
GEORGE ELIOT

Rising Sun! when you shall shine,
    Make this house happy,

Beautify it with your beams;
    Make this house happy,

God of Dawn! your white blessings spread;
    Make this house happy.

Guard the doorway from all evil;
    Make this house happy.

GREAT OCCASIONS

White Corn! Abide herein;
  Make this house happy.

Soft wealth! May this hut cover much;
  Make this house happy.

Heavy Rain! Your virtues send;
  Make this house happy.

Corn Pollen! Bestow content;
  Make this house happy.

May peace around this family dwell;
  Make this house happy.

—NAVAJO INDIAN CHANT

When two individuals meet, so do two private worlds. None of our private worlds is big enough for us to live a wholesome life in. We need the wider world of joy and wonder, of purpose and venture, of toil and tears. What are we, any of us, but strangers and sojourners forlornly wandering through the nighttime until we draw together and find the meaning of our lives in one another, dissolving our fears in each other's courage, making music together and lighting torches to guide us through the dark? We belong together. Love is what we need. To love and to be loved. Let our hearts be open; and what we would receive from others, let us give. For what is given still remains to bless the giver—when the gift is love.

—From a selection by
A. POWELL DAVIES

MARRIAGE

nothing false and possible is love
(who's imagined,therefore limitless)
love's to giving as to keeping's give;
as yes is to if, love is to yes

must's a schoolroom in the month of may:
life's the deathboard where all now turns when
(love's a universe beyond obey
or command,reality or un-)

proudly depths above why's first because
(faith's last doubt and humbly heights below)
kneeling,we—true lovers—pray that us
will ourselves continue to outgrow

all whose mosts if you have known and i've
only we our least begin to guess

> *—nothing false and possible is love*
> E. E. CUMMINGS

Men marry what they need. I marry you,
morning by morning, day by day, night by night,
and every marriage makes this marriage new.

In the broken name of heaven, in the light
that shatters granite, by the spitting shore,
in air that leaps and wobbles like a kite,

I marry you from time and a great door
is shut and stays shut against wind, sea, stone,
sunburst, and heavenfall. And home once more

inside our walls of skin and struts of bone,
man-woman, woman-man, and each the other,
I marry you by all dark and all dawn

and learn to let time spend. Why should I bother
the flies about me? Let them buzz and do.
Men marry their queen, their daughter, or their mother

by names they prove, but that thin buzz whines through:
when reason falls to reasons, cause is true.
Men marry what they need. I marry you.

—*Men Marry What They Need*
JOHN CIARDI

Let me not to the marriage of true minds
Admit impediments; love is not love
Which alters when it alteration finds
Or bends with the remover to remove.
O, no, it is an ever-fixèd mark
That looks on tempests and is never shaken;
It is the star to every wand'ring bark,
Whose worth's unknown, although his height be taken.
Love's not Time's fool, though rosy lips and cheeks
Within his bending sickle's compass come;
Love alters not with his brief hours and weeks,
But bears it out even to the edge of doom.
    If this be error, and upon me proved,
    I never writ, nor no man ever loved.

—*Sonnet 116*
WILLIAM SHAKESPEARE

In the quiet of this very special moment we pause to give thanks
for all the rich experiences of life that have brought ————

and —————— to this high point in their lives. We are especially grateful for the values which have flowed into them from those who have loved them and nurtured them and pointed them along life's way. We are grateful that within them is the dream of a great love and the resources to use that love in creating a home that shall endure. We are grateful for the values which they have found by their own strivings.

And now as they make their promises to each other, may they make them with the deepest insight into their meaning and with their fullest sincerity. May this be but the beginning of a relationship that will grow and mature with each passing year until the latter days become even more wonderful than the first.

—ROBERT BOTLEY

As we stand here at the altar of life, where life is touched by love, and love by life, we share with these who are taking their marriage vows, their newfound happiness. We see the door open for comradeship and mystery, for growth and fulfillment.

So we pray that each may bring his whole and best self to the other. May they bring intelligence as well as faith, to the task that is set before them. May they maintain enduring trust and respect, remembering that to understand all is ever to forgive all.

—JAMES ZACHARIAS

The years of our lives are a cup of wine poured out for us to drink. The grapes when they are pressed give forth their good juices for the wine.

GREAT OCCASIONS

Under the wine press of time our lives give forth their labor and honor and love.

Many days you will sit at the same table and eat and drink together.

Drink now, and may the cup of your lives be sweet and full to running over.

(Then the bride and groom shall drink.)

—*Ceremony of the Wine Cup*
KENNETH L. PATTON

This is Love's nobility,—
Not to scatter bread and gold,
Goods and raiment bought and sold;
But to hold fast his simple sense,
And speak the speech of innocence,
And with hand and body and blood,
To make his bosom-counsel good.
He that feeds men serveth few;
He serves all who dares be true.

—From *The Celestial Love*
RALPH WALDO EMERSON

Sweet are the thoughts that savour of content;
The quiet mind is richer than a crown;
Sweet are the nights in careless slumber spent;

MARRIAGE

The poor estate scorns fortune's angry frown:
Such sweet content, such minds, such sleep, such bliss,
Beggars enjoy, when princes oft do miss.

The homely house that harbours quiet rest;
   The cottage that affords no pride nor care;
The mean that 'grees with country music best;
   The sweet consort of mirth and music's fare;
Obscuréd life sets down a type of bliss:
A mind content both crown and kingdom is.

—Farewell to Folly
ROBERT GREENE

Love is the great Asker

—D. H. LAWRENCE

You are about to enter into a union which is most sacred and most serious, requiring of those who enter into it a complete and unreserved giving of self. It will bind you together for life in a relationship so close and so intimate that it will profoundly affect your whole future.

That future, with its hopes and disappointments, its successes and its failures, its pleasures and its pains, its joys and its sorrows, is hidden from your eyes.

Love can make it easy, and perfect love can make it a joy. May, then, this love with which you join your hands and hearts today never fail, but grow deeper and stronger as the years go on.

—From *Exhortation Before Marriage*
Collectio Rituum

Now I wish too that you make in your marriage no fetters for your spirits. Rather may the courage which love alone can give, guide your lives together into a fuller strength and into a greater freedom. Love is a concern with the true happiness of the other.

132

MARRIAGE

Love is a respect for the preciousness and worth of a person. Love gives and love receives. Love cannot live in itself, it must be nurtured with a mutual and ultimate sharing, a giving and a taking. Love is the noblest passion a man or woman can feel for it surpasses all lesser desires. Love is precious because it is an ethical commitment to another, which honors the duties of the promises here made, not only from a sense of obligation, but from the depths of the most divine sentiment a man or a woman can enjoy.

—BRANDOCH LOVELY

We have been called together as witnesses to the happiness which this couple has found together and to the pledge which they will now make, each to the other, for the mutual service of their common life.

We rejoice with them that out of all the world they have found each other, and that they will henceforth find the deeper meaning and richness of human life in sharing it with each other.

Taught by our own joys, by our own sorrows, even by our own failures, we remind them that in marriage as in all life, whosoever insists upon saving his lesser goods and his little self shall miss what is greater, but whosoever forgets himself in devotion to his beloved and in consecration to their common enterprise, is surest to find a full and happy life.

—ANONYMOUS

We have gathered to hear this couple give their vows of marriage. Those who enter into this relationship will cherish for each other a mutual esteem and love; they will bear each other's weaknesses and comfort each other in sickness and sorrow. They will, in honor and industry, provide for each other and for their household. In the trials of life they will sustain and encourage one another. For marriage is a mutual adventure, complex and rewarding; and the stimulation of intimacy is a gracious acknowledgment of human needs.

Understanding and patience are beacons to the satisfaction and enrichment which marriage can provide. Share the responsibilities of care and devotion and the home you establish will have laughter and warmth.

—KARL HULTBERG

It used to be thought that marriage was part of the permanent structure of the universe, like the cycle of the seasons or the rising of the sun. Marriage is nothing of the kind. There is no such thing as a single pattern of normal marriage. Furthermore, marriage is not dependable, and, in spite of the storybooks, it is not like the nesting of birds.

Marriage is a very recent development—particularly monogamous marriage—a matter of an uneasy few thousand years at best against previous millions—and therefore extremely unstable. It does not work automatically at all. And it is not instinctive. Mating is instinctive but marriage is not. And the difference is measured by the entire scope of civilization. It is not instinctive to be civilized—it has to be learned—and just as it is difficult to be civilized, so it is difficult to be married.

Nothing matrimonial is absolutely certain. Different kinds of people make different sorts of marriages. For a good beginning, physical attraction and compatibility are about equally necessary.

134

MARRIAGE

A marriage without physical attraction is almost hopeless from the beginning. A marriage with *only* physical attraction becomes hopeless after a short time. Only upon the dual basis of attraction and interests and temperaments that can be harmonized is a marriage gradually built up.

A marriage must be built exactly like anything else. Young people who know this need not be afraid. A marriage will work if you mean it to work.

—From a selection by
A. POWELL DAVIES
and MURIEL DAVIES

Here in the space between us and the world
lies human meaning.

Into the vast uncertainty we call.

The echoes make our music,
sharp equations which can hold the stars,
and marvelous mythologies we trust.

This may be all we need
to lift our love against indifference and pain.

Here in the space between us and each other
lies all the future
of the fragment of the universe
which is our own.

—From *Sound of Silence*
RAYMOND J. BAUGHAN

GREAT OCCASIONS

true lovers in each happening of their hearts
live longer than all which and every who;
despite what fear denies,what hope asserts,
what falsest both disprove by proving true

(all doubts,all certainties,as villains strive
and heroes through the mere mind's poor pretend
—grim comics of duration:only love
immortally occurs beyond the mind)

such a forever is love's any now
and her each here is such an everywhere,
even more true would truest lovers grow
if out of midnight dropped more suns than are

(yes;and if time should ask into his was
all shall,their eyes would never miss a yes)

—true lovers in each happening of their hearts
E. E. CUMMINGS

New musics! One the music that we hear,
this is the music which the masters make
out of their minds, profound solemn & clear.

Marriage is the second music, and therefore
we hear what we can bear, faithful & mild.

Therefore the streaming torches in the grove
through dark or bright, swiftly & now more near
cherish a festival of anxious love.

—From *Canto Amor*
JOHN BERRYMAN

MARRIAGE

——————— and ———————, in presenting yourselves here today, you are performing an act of faith in each other—a faith which should grow and mature and endure. If you would have your love set on such faith, not just at this moment, but in all the days ahead, then ever cherish the hopes and dreams you now hold. Resolve that love not be blotted out by the commonplace, nor blurred by the mundane in life. Faults will appear where now there is satisfaction; talents will fade in bleaching experience; wonder will flatten in the rituals of daily living—but devotion, joy, and love can remain, as you build them together. Stand fast in hope and confidence, believing in yourselves and believing in each other. In this spirit you can create a marriage which will radiate to one another and give new hope and strength to all who watch your quest with interest.

—PETER RAIBLE

The secret of love and marriage is that of religion itself; it is the emergence of the larger self; it is the finding of one's life by losing it. Such is the privilege of husband and wife—to be each himself, herself, and yet another; to face the world strong with the strength of two, wise with the wisdom of two, and brave with the courage of two. And the high and fine art of married life is in this mutual enrichment, mental and spiritual, this give and take between two personalities.

—ANONYMOUS

To ——————— and ——————— who gather to pledge their love and join their lives: May theirs always be a shared adventure, rich with moments of serenity, as well as excitement; vital with problems that test, as well as successes that lift; marked by a sense of personal freedom, as well as mutual responsibility.

May they find in each other companionship as well as love; understanding as well as compassion; challenge as well as agreement.

May the home they establish be an island where the pressures of a cluttered world can be sorted out and brought into focus; where accumulated tensions can be released and understood; where personal needs do not tower over concern for others and where the immediate does not blur more distant goals; where the warmth of humor and love puts both crisis and dullness into perspective.

And above all, may they find an ever richer meaning and joy in the high adventure of lifelong loving and learning together.

This is our wish for ——————— and ———————.

—ANONYMOUS
(arranged ERNEST D. PIPES, JR.)

In every passing era, new challenges are revealed to those who strive for a larger determination of their destinies. This is as true of marriage as it is for any other part of life's adventure.

A husband and father can no longer expect his position to be one of unquestioned authority. Nor can a woman expect the full measure of those words—wife and mother—to be hers as her due.

Each worthwhile goal must be earned by the degree of insight and unbounded love which we bring to it. So may you continue to grow in separateness and togetherness that your marriage may truly illuminate the challenges of your years.

—DAVID H. MACPHERSON

138

MARRIAGE

I ——————— take you ——————— to be the wife of my days, to be the mother of my children, to be the companion of my house; we shall keep together what share of trouble and sorrow our lives may lay upon us, and we shall hold together our store of goodness and plenty and love.

I ——————— take you ——————— to be the husband of my days, to be the father of my children, to be the companion of my house; we shall keep together what share of trouble and sorrow our lives may lay upon us, and we shall hold together our store of goodness and plenty and love.

—From *Man Is the Meaning*
KENNETH L. PATTON

Today we are privileged to share with ——————— and ———————
a moment of supreme joy in the new life they now begin together.
It is not our hour for exultation, but theirs. Yet would we speak
our hopes for them.

In the years ahead may their wisdom be steadily increased, that they may always apply tenderness and strength to the trials which will surely befall them.

May they never allow changing customs and fashions to dull the sense of loyal love and utter devotion now theirs.

When new lives are added to the fellowship which is their home, may they give thanks for the blessing of a child and bring it to the fullness of its promise by the same light of love which now glows in them.

139

And may they look beyond the limits of their own existence to the larger family of man, realizing its just claim upon them. For no marriage ought to be celebrated, nor none fulfilled lest a portion of its end be directed toward the ennoblement of all mankind.

—ANONYMOUS

Give all to love;
Obey thy heart;
Friends, kindred, days,
Estate, good-fame,
Plans, credit and the Muse,—
Nothing refuse.

'T is a brave master;
Let it have scope:
Follow it utterly,
Hope beyond hope.
It was never for the mean;
It requireth courage stout.
Souls above doubt,
Valor unbending,
It will reward,—
They shall return
More than they were,
And ever ascending.

—From *Give All to Love*
RALPH WALDO EMERSON

MARRIAGE

Most of us have far too many illusions about life, and a vast number of those illusions are concentrated in marriage. We think it should be all joy and gladness, all wonder and delight, and we are disappointed when it turns out not to be. We forget that life is not like that, and since marriage is for life, marriage cannot be that way either. Marriage is whatever life is, except that it thrusts the landscape of life into much sharper relief. The terrain is the same but the heights are far higher and the valleys much deeper. The plains are much broader, the woodland and fields much greener and more lovely. But the deserts are broader, too, and the heat more intense, the thorns are thicker, the briars sharper, the storms of wind and weather blow much harder. If the sunlight is brighter and the landscape more lovely, the nights are darker and colder and more lonely.

If you would keep your emotions safe from harm, if you would banish from yourself all danger of fear and anxiety, if you would protect yourself from a desolating sorrow, keep your emotions on the surface. Do not let the love that stirs within you deepen into the commitments of marriage. Keep your sexual relationships at the casual level. Do not let children come into your home. For if you do you will never be safe again. If you do you will expose yourself to the possibility of anguish your soul may not be able to bear. But know this, too: you will also expose yourself to a depth of feeling, a richness of emotion, to joy and happiness which will reduce the life you previously knew to the dimensions of the flickering shadows on your television screen. Marriage, when it is right, is like a secret society. Cynics on the outside will scoff. But the initiates within will know that I speak the truth.

—From a selection by
DUNCAN HOWLETT

No speed of wind or water rushing by
But you have speed far greater. You can climb

GREAT OCCASIONS

Back up a stream of radiance to the sky,
And back through history up the stream of time.
And you were given this swiftness, not for haste,
Nor chiefly that you may go where you will,
But in the rush of everything to waste,
That you may have the power of standing still—
Off any still or moving thing you say.
Two such as you with such a master speed
Cannot be parted nor be swept away
From one another once you are agreed
That life is only life forevermore
Together wing to wing and oar to oar.

—The Master Speed
ROBERT FROST

Out of all the hosts of earth, these two have come, have looked in each other's faces, and have seen their uniqueness and their oneness. Here they have pledged each to the other, to make their future common. Out of the depth of their love they will make their home and in it rear their children. Out of their wisdom they will face the varied experiences of life and draw from each event of the day that which will make them stronger for the next day's adventure. Out of their faith in the love with which they make this venture, may they find growing a courage sufficient to meet all the perilous chance and change which must touch us all.

May all their living be so bright and shining that no darkness about, no sorrow or separation, ever dim the light by which they walk on life's road. Throughout all the days of their years may they remember this day with tenderness and joy, remember it as the day when the glory and the beauty of our precious mortality began to open before them.

—WILLIAM B. RICE

MARRIAGE

Death is a mystery we see and meet, but love is a mystery in which we live and breathe and have our being. It is an eternal truth which surrounds us to be touched and treasured and known of man. It is an abiding element which has no bounds of time, no limits to its generous outpouring, no fears to make it weak.

It is our great adventure of faith, our lifelong giving and receiving of the unending blessings of life.

—From a selection by
WILLIAM B. RICE

Yesterday I stood at the temple door interrogating the passers-by about the mystery and merit of Love.

And before me passed an old man with an emaciated and melancholy face, who sighed and said: "Love is a natural weakness bestowed upon us by the first man."

But a virile youth retorted: "Love joins our present with the past and the future."

Then a woman with a tragic face sighed and said: "Love is a deadly poison injected by black vipers, that crawl from the caves of hell. The poison seems fresh as dew and the thirsty soul eagerly drinks it; but after the first intoxication the drinker sickens and dies a slow death."

Then a beautiful, rosy-cheeked damsel smilingly said: "Love is a wine served by the brides of Dawn which strengthens strong souls and enables them to ascend to the stars."

After her a black-robed, bearded man, frowning, said: "Love is the blind ignorance with which youth begins and ends."

Another, smilingly, declared: "Love is a divine knowledge that enables men to see as much as the gods."

Then said a blind man, feeling his way with a cane: "Love is a blinding mist that keeps the soul from discerning the secret of existence, so that the heart sees only trembling phantoms of desire among the hills, and hears only echoes of cries from voiceless valleys."

A young man, playing on his viol, sang: "Love is a magic ray emitted from the burning core of the soul and illuminating the surrounding earth. It enables us to perceive Life as a beautiful dream between one awakening and another."

And a feeble ancient, dragging his feet like two rags, said, in quavering tones: "Love is the rest of the body in the quiet of the grave, the tranquility of the soul in the depth of Eternity."

And a five-year-old child, after him, said laughing: "Love is my father and mother, and no one knows Love save my father and mother."

And so, all who passed spoke of Love as the image of their hopes and frustrations, leaving it a mystery as before.

Then I heard a voice within the temple: "Life is divided into two halves, one frozen, the other aflame; the burning half is Love."

Thereupon I entered the temple, kneeling, rejoicing, and praying:

> Make me, O Lord, nourishment
> for the blazing flame . . .
> Make me, O God, food for the
> sacred fire . . . Amen.

—KAHLIL GIBRAN
(tr. ANTHONY FERRIS)

MARRIAGE

We have come here to join this man and woman in marriage. Society has encouraged and protected the institution of marriage through the sanctions of its laws, but the relationship of marriage is more fundamental than any law. For marriage is the willing acceptance by man and woman that they shall live with each other both in good fortune—and it will be good—and in bad fortune—and such there will be for every marriage. Marriage is the acceptance by man and woman that they shall be prepared to bring forth children and to nourish and rear them physically and spiritually. Each of us was brought into the world without any decision of his own; each of us was stamped with the condition of mortality from the moment of his conception. And so of the three most significant events in our lives, birth, marriage, and death, it is only in marriage that we have the full power of personal decision.

In marriage the greatest courage will be required. We shall be put to the test of continuing to accept husband or wife with all defects revealed; but beyond this we shall be faced with the anguish of having to accept our own weaknesses. In the eyes of our husband or wife we shall see our most deeply hidden defects reflected. And this is the most difficult of all that is required of us: to accept that we are not as we should like to think we are, and that we are not as we should like the world to think we are.

But marriage also offers us the condition for the supreme fulfillment of human life: for our acceptance of our spouse with all his strengths and weaknesses, our works of love for our companion in marriage and for our children, and above all our acceptance of ourselves as we are, all these open us to receive the very ground of our being; all these bring us the glory of existence.

—ROBERT SENGHAS

145

Love has the longest history

—GEORGE BARKER

All lesser reasons for loving die away
Before this one: that you had power to make
Demand on me which I had power to meet;
That you could make demand so deep that I
Could meet it only by an act of birth,
Watching creation like a looker-on,
Myself the thing created out of dust.
Well may I own the power that does this thing.
With shaken breath I fear to look on the face
Of this great-statured self that bowed in the dark.
Decision now out of my hand is torn
And passes to this other at its birth,
And what shall happen I no longer know.

—Come to Birth
ABBIE HUSTON EVANS

MARRIAGE

Two there are who look so deep
Into each other's night, they see
Yet further than their meeting bodies
And earliest most brilliant star,
To where is nothing but a vow
That is their truth. Those instruments
Of world made flesh, they bore to prove
Before all change, their changeless word.

—From *Earth-Treading Stars That
Made Dark Heaven Light*
STEPHEN SPENDER

These are two individual souls, who nonetheless embody certain universal and enduring truths: that we need each other, that we can achieve unity only through tenderness, and that the protection of one human being by another is a solemn responsibility.

—KENNETH CLARK

This marriage is an event in the lifetime of a love. Neither I nor all society can join these two lovers today. Only they could do what they have chosen. They have joined themselves, each to the other. As they have found union with one another, they proclaim that union today and pledge its future. We by our participation in this celebration do but recognize and honor their intention to dwell together as husband and wife.

—From a selection by
RUDOLPH W. NEMSER

May your ring be always the symbol of the unbroken circle of love. Love freely given has no beginning and no end. Love freely given has no giver and no receiver. You are each the giver and each the receiver. May your ring always call to mind the freedom and the power of this love.

—RUDOLPH W. NEMSER

——————— and ———————, This is the second occasion upon which each of you takes the vow of matrimony. The informality of this service ought not in any way lessen the significance of this act, for it is a most solemn pledge which you are about to undertake. No other human ties are more tender, no vows more sacred than these which you now assume. This is no light compact which you enter today. Rather you are to partake of a relationship so close that its success literally shall depend upon how well you can merge your two loves into one.

You are both mature people. You both have established individual patterns of living. Yet you have found not only a need for companionship, but the satisfaction of that need in each other's company. It is this love, based upon a responsible understanding, that will aid you in creating out of two separate lives the family and the happiness you may share together.

—ROBERT EDWARD GREEN

MARRIAGE

The law of reality in the relationship of persons is this: "the integrity of persons is inviolable." You shall not use a person for your own ends, or indeed for any ends, individual or social. To use another person is to violate his personality by making an object of him; and in violating the integrity of another you violate your own.

—From *Reason and Emotion*
JOHN MAC MURRAY

Take Time while Time doth last,
Mark how Fair fadeth fast,
Beware if Envy reign,
Take heed of proud Disdain.
Hold fast now in thy youth,
Regard thy vowed Truth,
Lest when thou waxeth old
Friends fail and Love grow cold.

—*Song Set by John Farmer*
ANONYMOUS (c. 1600)

I love you. I will always try to be patient and kind, rather than envious or boastful. I will not put on airs, nor behave myself unseemly, nor keep insisting upon my rights. I will not be provoked to anger, nor harbor resentment by taking account of fancied evils. I will rejoice, not over unrighteousness, but only with the truth. I will try to bear all things and to endure any fate which may come to us, and in spite of change, to believe in you and to hope for our happiness together. I shall never fail you. This is what I mean when I say, "I love you."

—PAUL OF TARSUS
(arr. ELMO A. ROBINSON)

We pray for concord and creativity as well as for love and laughter in their life together; and when there is pain, may there be peace that passes not away. We pray for joy that they will share with other people, and for their home; may it be a temple for that which is beautiful and good and true. As they share the richer experiences of life, so may their hearts and minds and souls be knit ever more closely together. And yet may their bonds of sympathy strengthen their separate personalities. We pray for courage for them when the road is rough, and for humility for them when fortune favors them. May they carry the past gratefully with them in all the years of their sojourn, and with an equal measure of hope ever face the future unafraid.

—*A Wedding Prayer*
DANA MCLEAN GREELEY

The circle is the symbol of the sun and the earth and the universe. It is a symbol of holiness and of perfection and of peace. In this ring it is the symbol of unity, in which your two lives are now joined in one unbroken circle, in which, wherever you go, you will always return unto one another to your togetherness.

MARRIAGE

(*The one giving the ring shall say:*) I give you this ring to wear upon your hand as a symbol of our unity.

—*Ring Ceremony*
KENNETH L. PATTON

The metal in these rings
Has little real value
Except in its use today.
These words are gone
As I say them
But as I say them,
Your lives are changed forever.
You are man and woman,
Born to trouble and to joy;
And this is your greatest triumph—
That the greatest of gifts
Are yours for the risk
Of asking.

We are to witness now
The sealing of this promise with these rings
Sign and token before the world
Of the world you will create—
      single, whole, and quiet—
Within the world outside.
Together you are one; as one you are a world.

—JAMES LAWSON

Love is possible only if two persons communicate with each other from the center of their existence, hence if each one of them experiences himself from the center of his existence. Only in this "central experience" is human reality, only here is aliveness, only here is the basis for love. Love, experienced thus, is a constant challenge; it is not a resting place, but a moving, growing, working together; even whether there is harmony or conflict, joy or sadness, is secondary to the fundamental fact that two people experience themselves from the essence of their existence, that they are one with each other by being one with themselves, rather than by fleeing from themselves. There is only one proof for the presence of love: the depth of the relationship, and the aliveness and strength in each person concerned; this is the fruit by which love is recognized.

—From *The Art of Loving*
ERICH FROMM

Man, for all his ingenuity, has not yet designed a vow impossible to break. He has developed law and conscience, even pride, as keepers of his sacred pledges, and in his cunning he has found devices to mitigate each one. So it is not to man's institutions that we look this day of uniting. It is not this church, nor this state, which truly sanctifies, but the deepest well of human need, the need to live united and complete before the broken and imperfect world.

—ANONYMOUS

MARRIAGE

be of love(a little)
More careful
Than of everything
guard her perhaps only

A trifle less
(merely beyond how very)
closely than
Nothing,remember love by frequent

anguish(imagine
Her least never with most
memory)give entirely each
Forever its freedom

(Dare until a flower,
understanding sizelessly sunlight
Open what thousandth why and
discover laughing)

—*be of love(a little)*
E. E. CUMMINGS

For maintaining a happy marriage over a long period, the most important requirement is that you *like* each other. Love can sometimes be stormy, and in a stormy way you can feel your need of each other. But the storm can subside, and so can the need. If you do not *like* each other, your marriage will then be in a bad way.

—From a selection by
A. POWELL DAVIES
and MURIEL DAVIES

153

GREAT OCCASIONS

Love . . . consists in this, that two solitudes protect and touch and greet each other.

—From *Letters to a Young Poet*
RAINER MARIA RILKE
(tr. M. D. HERTER NORTON)

It was a wise man who said that it is important not only to pick the right mate but to *be* the right mate. And contrary to many popular love stories, it is not during the first year of bliss that most dangers crop up. Marriages do not, like dropped chinaware, smash as a result of that first quarrel which the newly married hope is unthinkable. Marriage is a rooted thing, a growing and flowering thing that must be tended faithfully.

Lacking that mutual effort, we are apt to find some day that our marriage, so hopefully planted, has been withering imperceptibly. Gradually we realize that for some time the petals have lost their luster, that the perfume is gone. Daily watering with the little gracious affectionate acts we all welcome, with mutual concern for the other's contentment, with self-watchfulness here and self-forgetfulness there, brings forth ever new blossoms.

—From *The Basic Axiom of Marital Felicity*
DONALD CULROSS PEATTIE

We are here as witnesses
To a promise and a gift:
The promise, faith; the gift, love.

154

MARRIAGE

You have lived to see good and evil; and to know
That these are bounded
By time
And come and go.

But in the ceaseless succession of
Good and evil,
Alone of man's Works,
Not subject to time or to change.
These remain:
Faith, your power,
And love, your strength.
Through all of this,
Enjoy
What you can
Endure
What you must
With love and charity always.

Here is your primal promise
This is the gift you bring.

—JAMES LAWSON

Throughout the memory of man, the founding of a new home has been noted as an act of a high and holy order. It has been celebrated with a service of marriage—in sacred groves, in humble meetinghouses, under vaulted arches, in temples with ancient rites, and in bombed-out cellars with hurried words.

Yet neither state, church, nor family relations can by the sole weight of tradition, ceremony, or expectation create a genuine joining of man and woman. Such a wedlock comes only through the ripening of love freely given.

155

GREAT OCCASIONS

[To the couple] It is in your power, therefore, and your power alone to bless this service—by the sincerity of your purpose, the strength of your common devotion, and the enduring character of your dedication.

—From a selection by
DAVID H. MACPHERSON

We have come here together that this man and this woman might bear witness before you and to the world of the oneness that has grown up between them; that they might affirm this oneness and this dedication here, as they have affirmed it to each other. As they now exist as one in their own eyes, so may they exist in your eyes. The mysterious union of two persons in marriage has already occurred in them in the giving and receiving of their love. In witness to this mystery, they do pledge their love and the sharing of their lives.

—MICHAEL YOUNG

May these two souls
Find a communion of ideal being and perfect grace.
May their love reach the level of every day's
Most quiet need. By sun and candlelight,
May they love freely as men strive for right.
May they love purely as men turn from praise.
May they find strength to meet the adversities;
Tolerance for the prejudices, Reverence

MARRIAGE

For the Beauties, Respect for the Truths,
And Faith for the Uncertainties
Which will come their way.

—CHARLES WHITE MC GEHEE
Adapted from
ELIZABETH BARRETT BROWNING

I. Thou shalt guard thine ability for lifelong learning and thereby expand the range of what thou canst know and feel and control.

II. Thou shalt retain the glow of romance by keeping before thee thine own ideal self, and by faithfully rediscovering and nourishing the ideal self of thy loved one, arranging the daily drama so that these ideal selves may more easily emerge from the wings and occupy center stage.

III. Thou shalt so live, free from deception, concealment, and pretense, that others may appreciatively understand thee.

IV. Thou shalt cast aside indifference and hostility, and thereby widen and deepen thine appreciative understanding of others.

V. Thou shalt cultivate concern for another's needs and interests, and thereby develop thy capacity to become a loving person.

VI. Thou shalt not by deed or word threaten thy beloved, guarding thyself against such conduct by seeing thine actions as others see them and hearing thy words as others hear them.

VII. Thou shalt not regard thy beloved object as a threat to thee, inquiring of thyself, if so tempted, what remnant of childhood is preventing thee from acting like a mature person.

VIII. Thou shalt search within for the criminal, and thus avoid accusing another of being the cause of thine own querulous resentment.

IX. Thou shalt not become irresponsible, or permit thy beloved to become irresponsible, for thou shalt be faithful in all thine obligations and respect such faithful conduct in others.

X. Thou shalt keep open the channels of communication, often by a word, but sometimes by a look, a handclasp, a kiss; sometimes by sharing a common task in unspoken communication. Thou shalt not let the barriers of silence hide thine ideal self, nor when thou speakest shalt thou create new barriers by thy words.

—HENRY NELSON WIEMAN
(arr. ELMO A. ROBINSON)

FOR THE OCCASION
OF DEATH

FOR THE OCCASION
OF DEATH

WHAT CAN BE SAID of death—except that nothing can be said. After ten thousand years of death we do not talk about it, we weep. But of our dead—of them we have much to say.

It would be mean and contemptible to cast them into the ground or the fire without a backward glance, as if they were only some leaf falling off an autumn tree. The Harvard anthropologist asked the primitive African Bushman why he stayed near his dead. The naked Bushman answered quietly, "He is our person, whom we love." Civilization has no better reply.

The excrescences that surround death in civilized society—the indignities of hospitals, the commercialism of morticians, the vulgarities of cemeteries—will change as we educate ourselves *and society*. But the simple human needs that death makes us conscious of, remain.

A constant one percent of the population in America die each year. They are spared our words. But their survivors need them. This is — as Hillary said — because the survivor is always a "debtor." And therefore guilty. Guilty of still being alive. Guilty of being glad of being alive. Guilty of suddenly recognizing how they should have behaved toward the deceased. Guilty of knowing they will not reform toward the living. Guilty and sorry too that in spite of the crutch of memory they know that they are unavoidably going to begin to forget the person who has died. Certainly a matter for

161

lamentation and regret. Bitter indeed it is that life simply has no time for the not-alive. Those we do remember, we change into ideas we can manipulate to serve us. And this is part of our grief too.

Studies have shown that the Protestant clergy believe their major task at funerals is to attend to the living. Few now believe, at least do not assert, that their words will mean the difference between the dead body's going to heaven or to hell, or to some halfway station in between. Roman Catholics say they believe this, but many of them do not—see the studies of Robert Fulton, Herman Feifel, S. D. Strut, and others—and more of them will not. Jewish belief and practice have largely taken on the protective coloration of the American environment, with some small distinctions made among Orthodox, Conservative, and Reform groups.

But funerals, or memorial services, fill a social need as well as an individual one. They provide, as Mandelbaum has pointed out, for a dignified disposal of the body, aid the bereaved to reorient themselves, and while publicly acknowledging and commemorating the dead person, reassert the viability of the group. For every close death makes us stop and ask ourselves Frank O'Hara's question: "Are we just muddy instants?"

Based on his studies of the Hiroshima survivors, Robert Lifton spoke of the continuous encounter we all face with death in this atomic age, and put the social significance of funerals thus: "For the sake of the dead and of our own sense of worth, we must give our experience significance by enabling it to serve wider moral purposes."

The funeral or memorial service then must be far more than what Samuel Beckett calls an occasion of "wordshed." It is rather a chance to restate the relationships between ourselves and what we value, and between an individual and the others. In essence, we say that it is good to have lived, that death fits into life and helps it make what little sense it does, and that all remains well with Life and the universe. It is not the place for an empty eulogy of the departed. Many of today's clergy are showing great skill in their ability to blend honest personal comments into an artistic whole. For one such example see Appendix C.

The studies of Feifel show that half the populace think of death as "the end," "time to go," "you're through." Less than a

162

quarter think of it as preparation for another life. The remainder either don't know or don't think about it or (15 percent) think of it as "rest and peace." These are the people to whom memorial services are addressed.

With 35 percent of the population nonchurch affiliated, with old theological ideas going to the wall — who actually believes in Heaven and Hell as real existent locatable places? — with a vigorous assault being waged by memorial societies on the traditional funeral, the alert cleric will consider carefully their special qualifications to serve the larger community with the kind of assistance which can be most helpful to them.

*　　*　　*

The 451 readings which follow center around the twelve themes of helplessness, desolation, grief, loss, resignation, acceptance, courage, hope, memory, commemoration, love, and affirmation. The attention of the reader is called to the special index provided for this section of the book.

The long custom of surrender

—ALICE JAMES

Be not disquieted either by kindness or by insult—
    empty joy or sorrow.
Do not count on good or evil—you will only waste
    your time . . .
And why seek advice from the Authorities or the Sages?
Who knows but that we all live out our lives in the
    maze of a dream?

—From a selection by
WANG WEI
(tr. L. C. WALMSLEY
and CHANG YIN-NAN)

After your burial on Stone-tower Mountain,
The mourners in their chariots wind downward through
    dark pines and cypresses.
Your bones interred beneath the white clouds, your

DEATH

life forever ended;
Only the flowing stream lives on in the world of men.

—WANG WEI
(tr. L. C. WALMSLEY
and CHANG YIN-NAN)

. . . The song is done, the slow string and quick pipe have
    ceased.
At the height of joy, sorrow comes with the eastern moon rising.
And I, a poor old man, not knowing where to go,
Must harden my feet on the lone hills, toward sickness and despair.

—TU FU
(tr. WITTER BYNNER)

That she must change so soon her curving city;
Leave this travel scarcely started; never see
Stars again reposeful in that dear room
Where death strays not and little birds
Are never split by shot—is it like this,
Dying? Just the moment going over
            the edge of the body, nothing left there
That grass can not solve?

I'd wish to settle nothing here with chisel;
No cold angel with well-fed eyes
            shall rest above her . . .
She once said "The Snow Queen must be very beautiful."

GREAT OCCASIONS

She was so tiny . . . she won't know what the dead are
    supposed to do.

—Peter's Little Daughter Dies
KENNETH PATCHEN

No one has found a way to avoid death,
To pass around it;
Those old men who have met it,
Who have reached the place where death stands waiting,
Have not pointed out a way to circumvent it.
Death is difficult to face.

—OMAHA INDIANS

What passing-bells for these who die as cattle?
   Only the monstrous anger of the guns.
   Only the stuttering rifles' rapid rattle
Can patter out their hasty orisons.
No mockeries for them from prayers or bells,
   Nor any voice of mourning save the choirs,—
The shrill, demented choirs of wailing shells;
   And bugles calling for them from sad shires.

What candles may be held to speed them all?
   Not in the hands of boys, but in their eyes
Shall shine the holy glimmers of good-byes.
   The pallor of girls' brows shall be their pall;

166

DEATH

Their flowers the tenderness of silent minds,
And each slow dusk a drawing-down of blinds.

—Anthem for Doomed Youth
WILFRED OWEN

It is a God-damned lie to say that these
Saved, or knew, anything worth any man's pride.
They were professional murderers and they took
Their blood money and impious risks and died.
In spite of all their kind some elements of worth
With difficulty persist here and there on earth.

—Another Epitaph on an Army of Mercenaries
HUGH MAC DIARMID

I kept my answers small and kept them near;
Big questions bruised my mind but still I let
Small answers be a bulwark to my fear.

The huge abstractions I kept from the light;
Small things I handled and caressed and loved.
I let the stars assume the whole of night.

But the big answers clamoured to be moved
Into my life. Their great audacity
Shouted to be acknowledged and believed.

Even when all small answers build up to
Protection of my spirit, still I hear
Big answers striving for their overthrow

167

GREAT OCCASIONS

And all the great conclusions coming near.

—*Answers*
ELIZABETH JENNINGS

Beneath this vast serene of sky
Where worlds are but as mica dust,
From age to age the wind goes by;
Unnumbered summer burns the grass.
On granite rocks, at rest from strife,
The aeons lie in lichen rust.
Then what is man's so brittle life?—
The humming of the bees that pass!

—*Time*
JOHN GALSWORTHY

He died in December. He must descend
Somewhere, vague and cold, the spirit and seal,
The gift descend, and all that insight fail
Somewhere. Imagination one's one friend
Can't see through. Both of us at the end.
Nouns, verbs do not exist for what I feel.

—*Epilogue*
JOHN BERRYMAN

DEATH

Perhaps to speak at all is false; more true
Simply to sit at times alone and dumb
And with most pure intensity of thought
And concentrated inmost feeling, reach
Towards your shadow on the years' crumbling wall.

—From *An Elegy*
DAVID GASCOYNE

Here in the dark, O heart;
Alone with the enduring Earth, and Night,
And Silence, and the warm strange smell of clover;
Clear-visioned, though it break you; far apart
From the dead best, the dear and old delight;
Throw down your dreams of immortality,
O faithful, O foolish lover!
Here's peace for you, and surety; here the one
Wisdom—the truth!—"All day the good glad sun
Showers love and labour on you, wine and song;
The greenwood laughs, the wind blows, all day long
Till night." And night ends all things.

—From *Second Best*
RUPERT BROOKE

I always knew the death sleeping inside you
Would awake on a sleepless night,
And wake everyone but you,
That hands would close in on the clock

169

GREAT OCCASIONS

Unable to hide its face ticking on the edge of tears,
That I would look through a thousand mornings
For my rareblooded bird to flash from her niche.

—From *Proposed Elegy for Jane
Elizabeth Should She Die Young*
ROBERT BAGG

Clocks cannot tell our time of day
For what event to pray
Because we have no time, because
We have no time until
We know what time we fill,
Why time is other than time was.

Nor can our question satisfy
The answer in the statue's eye:
Only the living ask whose brow
May wear the roman laurel now;
The dead say only how.

What happens to the living when we die?
Death is not understood by death; nor you, nor I.

—*No Time*
W. H. AUDEN

I shall lose my earthly dwelling-place
and find myself once more mother-naked.
The stars, the fishes,
will climb again the courses of their inverted skies.

DEATH

All that is color, bird or name,
will become once more a scant fistful of night,
and over the spoil of cyphers and feathers
and love's body, compounded of fruit and of music,
we fall at last, like dream or shadow,
the unremembering dust.

—From a selection by
JORGE CARRERA ANDRADE
(tr. MUNA LEE)

The earth goes on the earth glittering in gold,
The earth goes to the earth sooner than it wold;
The earth builds on the earth castles and towers,
The earth says to the earth—All this is ours.

—INSCRIPTION IN MELROSE ABBEY

Ah, love, let us be true
To one another! for the world, which seems
To lie before us like a land of dreams,
So various, so beautiful, so new,
Hath really neither joy, nor love, nor light,
Nor certitude, nor peace, nor help for pain;
And we are here as on a darkling plain
Swept with confused alarms of struggle and flight,
Where ignorant armies clash by night.

—From *Dover Beach*
MATTHEW ARNOLD

171

GREAT OCCASIONS

We are lived by powers we pretend to understand:
They arrange our loves; it is they who direct at the end
The enemy bullet, the sickness, or even our hand.

It is their tomorrow hangs over the earth of the living
And all that we wish for our friends: but existence is
              believing

We know for whom we mourn and who is grieving.

                 —From *In Memory of Ernst Toller*
                 W. H. AUDEN

I am but a murmur of winds,
I am but a dark vision,
A dream in the night.

O children and ye old men,
Lament for the birth of a babe;
Lead on, lead on to the bourn.

Farewell, mysterious earth,
Farewell, O sea,
Farewell, farewell.

Now for ever shall my lips be still
And now for ever my hands be at rest.

I flatter no gods with prayer,
They are subject and mortal as we,
Crushed by inscrutable Fate.

Farewell, mysterious earth,

DEATH

Farewell, impregnable sea,
Farewell,
Farewell.

—From *Valediction*
RICHARD ALDINGTON

Agonies are one of my changes of garments

—WALT WHITMAN

Sorrow is my own yard
when the new grass
flames as it has flamed
often before but not
with the cold fire
that closes round me this year.
Thirtyfive years
I lived with my husband.
The plumtree is white today
with masses of flowers.
Masses of flowers
load the cherry branches
and color some bushes
yellow and some red
but the grief in my heart
is stronger than they
for though they were my joy
formerly, today I notice them
and turn away forgetting.
Today my son told me
that in the meadows
at the edge of the heavy woods
in the distance, he saw
trees of white flowers.

DEATH

I feel that I would like
to go there
and fall into those flowers
and sink into the marsh near them.

—*The Widow's Lament in Springtime*
WILLIAM CARLOS WILLIAMS

She went her unremembering way,
    She went, and left in me
The pang of all the partings gone,
    And partings yet to be.

She left me marveling why my soul
    Was sad that she was glad;
At all the sadness in the sweet,
    The sweetness in the sad.

The fairest things have fleetest end:
    Their scent survives their close,
But the rose's scent is bitterness
    To him that loved the rose!

Nothing begins, and nothing ends,
    That is not paid with moan;
For we are born in others' pain,
    And perish in our own.

—From *Daisy*
FRANCIS THOMPSON
    (arranged KENNETH L. PATTON)

GREAT OCCASIONS

When I have seen by Time's fell hand defaced
The rich proud cost of outworn buried age,
When sometimes lofty towers I see down-rased
And brass eternal slave to mortal rage;
When I have seen the hungry ocean gain
Advantage on the kingdom of the shore,
And the firm soil win of the wat'ry main,
Increasing store with loss and loss with store;
When I have seen such interchange of state,
Or state itself confounded to decay,
Ruin hath taught me this to ruminate,
That Time will come and take my love away.
 This thought is as a death, which cannot choose
 But weep to have that which it fears to lose.

—Sonnet 64
WILLIAM SHAKESPEARE

He was a man, take him for all in all; I shall not look upon his like again.

—From *Hamlet*
WILLIAM SHAKESPEARE

How shall we mourn you who are killed and wasted,
Sure that you would not die with your work unended.
As if the iron scythe in the grass stops for a flower?

—From *Five Groups of Verse*
CHARLES REZNIKOFF

176

DEATH

Underneath the growing grass,
    Underneath the living flowers,
    Deeper than the sound of showers:
    There we shall not count the hours
By the shadows as they pass.

Youth and health will be but vain,
    Beauty reckoned of no worth:
    There a very little girth
    Can hold round what once the earth
Seemed too narrow to contain.

—The Bourne
CHRISTINA ROSSETTI

How pitiful is her sleep.
Now her clear breath is still.
There is nothing falling tonight,
Bird or man,
As dear as she;
Nowhere that she should go
Without me. None but my calling.
Nothing but the cold cry of the snow.

How lonely does she seem.
I, who have no heaven,
Defenseless, without lands,
Must try a dream
Of the seven
Lost stars and how they put their hands

177

Upon her eyes that she might ever know
Nothing worse than the cold cry of snow.

—In Memory of Kathleen
KENNETH PATCHEN

If I could find one word
that would shudder the air
like that frightened sob,
that wordless prayer
of my newly-born,
who drew one breath,
and with unopened eyes
sank back into death;
If I could break the world's cold heart
with that cry,
then this grief would lift
and I could die.

—Mother-Loss
KENNETH L. PATTON

You have left me to linger in hopeless longing,
Your presence had ever made me feel no want,
You have left me to travel in sorrow.
Left me to travel in sorrow; Ah! the pain,
Left me to travel in sorrow; Ah! the pain, the pain,
    the pain.

178

DEATH

You have left me to linger in hopeless longing,
In your presence there was no sorrow,
You have gone and sorrow I shall feel, as I travel,
    Ah! the pain, the pain.

You have gone and sorrow I shall feel as I travel,
You have left me in hopeless longing.
In your presence there was no sorrow,
You have gone and sorrow I shall feel as I travel;
   Ah! the pain, the pain, the pain.

Content with your presence, I wanted nothing more,
You have left me to travel in sorrow; Ah! the pain,
    the pain, the pain.

—OSAGE INDIANS

Move him into the sun—
Gently its touch awoke him once,
At home, whispering of fields unsown.
Always it woke him, even in France,
Until this morning and this snow.
If anything might rouse him now
The kind old sun will know.

Think how it wakes the seeds,—
Woke, once, the clays of a cold star.
Are limbs, so dear-achieved, are sides,
Full-nerved—still warm—too hard to stir?
Was it for this the clay grew tall?
—O what made fatuous sunbeams toil
To break earth's sleep at all?

—*Futility*
WILFRED OWEN

GREAT OCCASIONS

A few brief moments in the garden of life, going where the primroses go, and then the night came, and we lost him, lost our boy in the midst of darkness. As he entered the darkness, the little subdued cry of "I must confess, I feel a little frightened"; and then the quiet resignation, and, last, the rambling, broken by clear periods, and then the rambling again, and lastly, the quiet, calm, disappearance.

—Under a Greenwood Tree
SEAN O'CASEY

A philosophy that does not work as the handmaiden of repression responds to the fact of death with the Great Refusal—the refusal of Orpheus the liberator. Death can become a token of freedom. The necessity of death does not refute the possibility of final liberation. Like the other necessities, it can be made rational— painless. Men can die without anxiety if they know that what they love is protected from misery and oblivion. After a fulfilled life, they may take it upon themselves to die—at a moment of their own choosing. But even the ultimate advent of freedom cannot redeem those who died in pain. It is the remembrance of them, and the accumulated guilt of mankind against its victims, that darken the prospect of a civilization without repression.

—From *Eros and Civilization*
HERBERT MARCUSE

DEATH

When a death has come about by particularly tragic circumstances we say with one voice, "How horrible!" And when that death is self-inflicted we say, "How could it be?"

There is no one single answer, nor can any words, no matter how well thought out, give immediate satisfaction. The fact is that in our normal relationships it is almost impossible to plumb the depths of another's fears and anxieties.

But this we can affirm with certainty; that the struggle by a person to know life and love, regardless of the apparent outcome, that struggle to become, is what finally counts.

For some, living involves no obvious self-conflict. While for others, there is deep inner stress. Now we must realize we shall always be indebted to those who have struggled, perhaps more so to those who in their aloneness could not see a chance of winning. For it is from these last that we shall learn in the days and years ahead to labor more earnestly to share our common stores of beauty, joy, and love.

—From a selection by
DAVID H. MAC PHERSON

At ten one morning
the youth forgot.

His heart was growing full
of broken wings and artificial flowers.

He noted in his mouth
but one small word was left.

When he removed his gloves, a fine
thin ash fell from his hands.

From the balcony he saw a tower.
He felt himself both balcony and tower.

181

GREAT OCCASIONS

Of course he saw how in its frame
the stopped clock observed him.

He saw his shadow stretched out still
upon the silken white divan.

And the boy, rigid, geometric,
broke the mirror with an axe.

When it broke, one huge stream of shadow
flooded his chimeric chamber.

—*Suicide*
FEDERICO GARCÍA LORCA
(tr. EDWIN HONIG)

I do not know
How to exist, how to love.
Whether I sit at night or lie down.
The night is long, the time sad;
Troubles there are, low is my strength.
Long drawn-out are my evenings,
Grievous are my mornings;
Then at night it is more unpleasant,
While I am awake more grievous.
It is not long drawn-out because of the evenings,
Not grievous because of the mornings,
Not an affliction merely because of other times;
It is long drawn-out because of my lovely one
Grievous because of my beloved,
An affliction because of my darling.

—From the *Kalevala*
(tr. FRANCIS MAGOUN, JR.)

182

DEATH

Men lied to them and so they went to die.
Some fell, unknowing that they were deceived,
And some escaped, and bitterly bereaved,
Beheld the truth they loved shrink to a lie.
And those there were that never had believed,
But from afar had read the gathering sky,
And darkly wrapt in that dread prophecy,
Died hoping that their truth might be retrieved.
It matters not. For life deals thus with Man;
To die alone deceived or with the mass,
Or disillusioned to complete his span.
Thermopylae or Golgotha, all one,
The young dead legions in the narrow pass,
The stark black cross against the setting sun.

> —*Thermopylae*
> ROBERT HILLYER

No worst, there is none. Pitched past pitch of grief,
More pangs will, schooled at forepangs, wilder wring.
Comforter, where, where is your comforting?
Mary, mother of us, where is your relief?
My cries heave, herds-long; huddle in a main, a chief
Woe, world-sorrow; on an age-old anvil wince and sing—
Then lull, then leave off. Fury had shrieked "No lin-
gering! Let me be fell: force I must be brief."

O the mind, mind has mountains; cliffs of fall
Frightful, sheer, no-man-fathomed. Hold them cheap
May who ne'er hung there. Nor does long our small

183

GREAT OCCASIONS

Durance deal with that steep or deep. Here! creep,
Wretch, under a comfort serves in a whirlwind: all
Life death does end each day dies with sleep.

—GERARD MANLEY HOPKINS

It is not death that is bitter—*that* for all men stands fated—
But when, before his parents, a boy's young life has fled.
No bride I had, no bridal-song. I died unmated,
In life beloved of many, dear now to the myriad dead.

—GREEK EPIGRAM
(tr. F. L. LUCAS)

If we had known all that we know
We never would have let him go.

We had the stronger argument
Had we but dreamed his dark intent.

Or if our words failed to dissuade him
Unarguing love might still have stayed him.

But what we know, we did not know.
We said good-bye and saw him go.

—From *If We Had Known*
ROBERT FRANCIS

DEATH

Is it right to take your life
Or better to let life take it?
Is it superiority of man
When things have come to such a pass
As this, the whole truth none else knowing,
To make a final affirmation
In a final, great negation?
Is it an intellectual grace
So to do, and, Oh far deeper,
Is it a spiritual unity
Known once and forever known
Between the doer and the Creator?

Or is it a cold, implacable knowledge
Of the lessening river in the blood,
A last defeat before a mask
Life always wears and never loses,
Inscrutable in its designs?
As who would say, I am the lost,
Forever, lost, I am nothing now,
Of nothing, neither bad nor good,
My action is my final statement,
I too will be inscrutable
And none shall know my final meaning,
Mysterious action of a man.

To walk into the river waters
Leaving wife, sons, time behind him,
The tidal river of the marshes
Sinuous and ancient, seaward
And landward ever moving,
As years move forward to our future
And backward to our past remembered,
Or caught in stillness at full tide
When time seems not, is not insistent,

185

GREAT OCCASIONS

And then the river seems a gauze
And we are perfect in its laces
Beyond action, within contemplation.

—From *The Parker River*
RICHARD EBERHART

They say that "Time assuages"—
Time never did assuage—
An actual suffering strengthens
As Sinews do, with age—

Time is a Test of Trouble—
But not a Remedy—
If such it prove, it prove too
There was no Malady—

—EMILY DICKINSON

Thine absence overflows the rose,—
    From every petal gleam
Such words as it were vain to close,
    Such tears as crowd the dream

So eyes that mind thee fair and gone,
    Bemused at waking, spend
On skies that gild thy remote dawn
    More hopes than here attend.

DEATH

The burden on the rose will fade
    Sped in the spectrum's kiss.
But here the thorn in sharpened shade
    Weathers all loneliness.

—Old Song
HART CRANE

Mourn not the dead that in the cool earth lie—
Dust unto dust—
The calm, sweet earth that mothers all who die
As all men must;

Mourn not your captive comrades who must dwell—
Too strong to strive—
Each in his steel-bound coffin of a cell,
Buried alive;

But rather mourn the apathetic throng—
The cowed and the meek—
Who see the world's great anguish and its wrong
And dare not speak!

—RALPH CHAPLIN

I told a lie once in verse. I said
I said I said I said "the heart will mend,
Body will break and mend, the foam replace

187

For even the unconsolable his taken friend."
This is a lie. I had not been here then.

—JOHN BERRYMAN

When I shall be divorced, some ten years hence,
From this poor present self which I am now;
When youth has done its tedious vain expense
Of passions that for ever ebb and flow;
Shall I not joy youth's heats are left behind,
And breathe more happy in an even clime?
Ah no! for then I shall begin to find
A thousand virtues in this hated time.
Then I shall wish its agitations back,
And all its thwarting currents of desire;
Then I shall praise the heat which then I lack,
And call this hurrying fever, generous fire,
And sigh that one thing only has been lent
To youth and age in common—discontent.

—*Youth's Agitations*
MATTHEW ARNOLD

Looking at death is dying

—EMILY DICKINSON

Lovely the rose; and yet—its beauty Time deflowers:
Lovely in spring the violet—but brief its hours:
White is the lily—but fast it falls and fades away:
White is the snow—but it melts from earth where it lay:
Lovely the loveliness of youth—yet lives but a day.

—From a selection by
THEOCRITUS OF SYRACUSE
(tr. F. L. LUCAS)

It can be said that only man grieves. Only man loses a part of himself and knows he loses a part of himself and feels the loss intensely. The more deeply man feels, the more deeply man is involved in life, the more he grieves. Furthermore, grief is an almost inevitable part of the life of any normal person. The only way to avoid grief is not to live. The very fact that we are alive and involved in the lives of other people means the virtual certainty of eventual grief. The minute we marry we invite the likelihood of grief. The minute we have children we invite the pos-

189

sibility of grief. Life means grief—in time. Love means grief—in time.

During the period of grief, the emotional ties to the lost person are broken, even as the physical ties have been broken and mentally recognized. The emotional ties must be broken so that new emotional ties may be created.

In the normal course of grief there will be a feeling of loneliness and unreality, an emptiness in the stomach, a feeling of insecurity, a strong temptation to withdraw from all activities. Questions will be asked that can not be answered like, "Why did God permit it?" There will be feelings of guilt. A tendency to lash out against anyone who presumably might have prevented the loss.

To facilitate grief's work, let there be tears. Tears, as has been pointed out, are a mechanism for reducing the tension caused by grief. Tears are not a distortion of nature nor evidence of weakness. They are a means by which the grieving person works his way up from the depths.

And let there be talk. Repeat over and over again all the details surrounding the grief-producing tragedy. This makes the loss more realistic and the expectation that the loved one will return is dissipated.

When tears and talk flow freely, grief's work is being done and in time the bereaved will come to realize what Jesus meant when he said, "Blessed are they who mourn for they shall be comforted."

—CHADBOURNE A. SPRING

Out of the day and night
A joy has taken flight;
   Fresh spring, and summer, and winter hoar,
Move my faint heart with grief, but with delight
    No more—Oh, never more!

—From *A Lament*
PERCY BYSSHE SHELLEY

190

DEATH

Harsh my heart is,
Scalded with grief:
My life a limp
Worm-eaten leaf.

White flower unfeeling,
You star the mould:
Evolvéd calmness,
My heart enfold.

—From *The Sorrows of Unicume*
HERBERT READ

Rifle goes up:
Does what a rifle does.

Star is very beautiful:
Doing what a star does.

Tell them, O Sleeper, that some
Were slain at the start of the slaughter

Tell them, O Sleeper, that sleet and rain
Are falling on those poor riderless heads

Tell them, O Sleeper, that pitiful hands float on the water . . .
Hands that shall reach icily into their warm beds.

—*The Soldier and the Star*
KENNETH PATCHEN

GREAT OCCASIONS

Thou art a moon
That will not rise again,
O son, O son of mine,
     O son!
The chill dawn breaks without thee,
O son, O son of mine,
     O son!

—Polynesian song
(tr. PETER H. BUCK)

She was this world's, that for fairest things disposes
   The saddest destiny.
Rose as she was, her span was but a rose's:
   A single morn had she.

—FRANÇOIS DE MALHERBE
(tr. F. L. LUCAS)

When the white mist of her name drifts in our talking,
And the white flower stalk of her body comes into our minds,
Then the throat is tight and the word of quick grief
Springs to the lip and the talking is tender
For the white flower driven to earth,
For the sun-reaching flower chilled.

—*For Elisabeth Morrow Morgan*
MARGARET I. LAMONT

192

DEATH

We bereaved are not alone. We belong to the largest company in all the world—the company of those who have known suffering. When it seems that our sorrow is too great to be borne, let us think of the great family of the heavy-hearted into which our grief has given us entrance, and inevitably, we will feel about us their arms, their sympathy, their understanding.

Believe, when you are most unhappy, that there is something for you to do in the world. So long as you can sweeten another's pain, life is not vain.

—From *We Bereaved*
HELEN KELLER

What ceremony can we fit
You into now? If you had come
Out of a warm and noisy room
To this, there'd be an opposite
For us to know you by. We could
Imagine you in lively mood

And then look at the other side,
The mood drawn out of you, the breath
Defeated by the power of death.
But we have never seen you stride
Ambitiously the world we know.
You could not come and yet you go.

But there is nothing now to mar
Your clear refusal of our world.
Not in our memories can we mould

GREAT OCCASIONS

You or distort your character.
Then all our consolation is
That grief can be as pure as this.

—For a Child Born Dead
ELIZABETH JENNINGS

It is very sad to lose your child just when he was beginning to bind himself to you, and I don't know that it is much consolation to reflect that the longer he had wound himself up in your heartstrings the worse the tear would have been, which seems to have been inevitable sooner or later. One does not weigh and measure these things while grief is fresh, and in my experience a deep plunge into the waters of sorrow is the hopefullest way of getting through them on one's daily road of life again. No one can help another very much in these crises of life; but love and sympathy count for something.

—THOMAS H. HUXLEY

Journeying over many seas & through many countries
I come dear brother to this pitiful leave-taking
the last gestures by your graveside
the futility of words over your quiet ashes.
Life cleft us from each other
pointlessly depriving brother of brother.
Accept then, in our parents' custom
these offerings, this leave-taking

194

echoing for ever, brother, through a brother's tears.
    —"Hail & Farewell."

—GAIUS VALERIUS CATULLUS
(tr. PETER WHIGHAM)

Here a pretty baby lies
Sung asleep with lullabies;
Pray be silent, and not stir
Th' easy earth that covers her.

—*Upon a Child*
ROBERT HERRICK

Had you been old I might be reconciled
   To see you gathered to the silent wild,
Were your days darkened, weary, shattered, told,
   Had life with disillusion been defiled,
And grief poured on your head its molten gold—
   Had you been old—

But you were young: your faith a fire unshaken,
   Your hair bright tossed with wind, your breath swift taken
With dear delight of earth, with arms outflung
   To joy. Just then, just then to be forsaken
Of breath! to leave the melody unsung,
   When you were young!

—From *Had You Been Old*
ELIZABETH HOLLISTER FROST

The gracious boy, who did adorn
The world whereinto he was born,
And by his countenance repay
The favor of the loving Day,—
Has disappeared from the Day's eye;
Far and wide she cannot find him;
My hopes pursue, they cannot bind him.
Returned this day, the South-wind searches,
And finds young pines and budding birches;
But finds not the budding man;
Nature, who lost, cannot remake him;
Fate let him fall, Fate can't retake him;
Nature, Fate, men, him seek in vain.

The eager fate which carried thee
Took the largest part of me:
For this losing is true dying;
This is lordly man's down-lying,
This his slow but sure reclining,
Star by star his world resigning.

—From *Threnody*
RALPH WALDO EMERSON

When sorrow comes, let us accept it simply, as a part of life. Let
the heart be open to pain; let it be stretched by it. All the evidence
we have says that this is the better way. An open heart never
grows bitter. Or if it does, it cannot remain so. In the desolate
hour, there is an outcry; a clenching of the hands upon emptiness; a burning pain of bereavement; a weary ache of loss. But

anguish, like ecstasy, is not forever. There comes a gentleness, a returning quietness, a restoring stillness. This, too, is a door to life. Here, also, is a deepening of meaning—and it can lead to dedication; a going forward to the triumph of the soul, the conquering of the wilderness. And in the process will come a deepening inward knowledge that in the final reckoning, all is well.

—From a selection by
A. POWELL DAVIES

Inevitably our anguish frames the question "Why?" if not on our lips, in our hearts. There is no answer that removes this question— no answer that can bridge the chasm of irreparable separation. Life will never be the same, and this is as it should be, for our loved ones are not expendable.

We can meet such loss only with our grief, that uncontrived mixture of courage, affirmation, and inconsolable desolation. Grief is enough; for, in our grief we live an answer, as in the depths love and selfishness conjoin until, if we allow it, love asserts its dominance, and we become more aware of the community of living of which life makes us a part.

—From a selection by
PAUL N. CARNES

Give way to grief,
And, unashamed,
Abandon stoic fortitude a while.

197

GREAT OCCASIONS

Set free, a while, the soul,
Better to bear its load.
Tears unshed are stones upon the heart
That choke the healing stream.
Unlock the flood-gates;
Loose the waters.
Give way, and cope with grief.

—Give Way to Grief
MELVILLE CANE

I wonder in what fields today
He chases dragonflies in play,
My little boy—who ran away.

—CHIYO
(tr. CURTIS H. PAGE)

For the eyes loved,
For the face lifted
In that still light,
Dark trees are groved,
The snow drifted,
And the mound white.

And the grave dug
And the words spoken
And the flowers shed—
And the eyes tearless

198

DEATH

But the heart broken
For the brave dead.

Though a soul thrill
To the stars' fire
And a mind sing
To a keen will
Of a high desire
And a great thing,—

Ah, who listens?
Who—who hearkens
Or answer makes,—
Though the moon glistens
And the night darkens
And the heart breaks?

—From *Perpetual Light*
WILLIAM ROSE BENÉT

Strew on her roses, roses,
  And never a spray of yew.
In quiet she reposes:
  Ah! would that I did too.

Her mirth the world required:
  She bath'd it in smiles of glee.
But her heart was tired, tired,
  And now they let her be.

Her life was turning, turning,
  In mazes of heat and sound.
But for peace her soul was yearning,
  And now peace laps her round.

Her cabin'd, ample Spirit,
  It flutter'd and fail'd for breath.

199

GREAT OCCASIONS

To-night it doth inherit
The vasty Halls of Death.

—Requiescat
MATTHEW ARNOLD

Music I heard with you was more than music,
And bread I broke with you was more than bread.
Now that I am without you, all is desolate,
All that was once so beautiful is dead.

Your hands once touched this table and this silver,
And I have seen your fingers hold this glass.
These things do not remember you, beloved:
And yet your touch upon them will not pass.

For it was in my heart you moved among them,
And blessed them with your hands and with your eyes.
And in my heart they will remember always:
They knew you once, O beautiful and wise!

—From *Discordants*
CONRAD AIKEN

Egypt and Greece good-bye, and good-bye Rome

—WILLIAM BUTLER YEATS

The rainbow comes and goes,
And lovely is the rose,
The moon doth with delight
Look round her when the heavens are bare,
Waters on a starry night
Are beautiful and fair;
The sunshine is a glorious birth;
But yet I know, where'er I go,
That there hath passed away a glory from the earth.

—From *Ode on Intimations of Immortality*
WILLIAM WORDSWORTH

This bird died flying,
And fell in flowers.
Oh, what a world
Went in him. Ours.

—*End*
MARK VAN DOREN

GREAT OCCASIONS

Why are the things that have no death
The ones with neither sight nor breath.
Eternity is thrust upon
A bit of earth, a senseless stone.
A grain of dust, a casual clod
Receives the greatest gift of God.
A pebble in the roadway lies—
       It never dies.

The grass our fathers cut away
Is growing on their graves today;
The tiniest brooks that scarcely flow
Eternally will come and go.
There is no kind of death to kill
The sands that lie so meek and still.
But man is great and strong and wise—
       And so he dies.

—*Irony*
LOUIS UNTERMEYER

Death is the lot of cities and of States;
Pomp, luxury, 'neath sand and grass do lie,
Yet man, it seems, is wroth that he must die.

—From *Gerusalemme Liberata*
TORQUATO TASSO

DEATH

Some have left
and others are about to leave;
so why should we be sorry
that we too must go?
And yet our hearts are sad
that on this mighty road
the friends we meet can set
no place to meet again.

—From the Sanskrit
(tr. DANIEL INGALLS)

Bit by bit, nevertheless, it comes over us that we shall never again hear the laughter of our friend, that this one garden is forever locked against us. And at that moment begins our true mourning, which, though it may not be rending, is yet a little bitter. For nothing, in truth, can replace that companion. Old friends cannot be created out of hand. Nothing can match the treasure of common memories, of trials endured together, of quarrels and reconciliations and generous emotions. It is idle, having planted an acorn in the morning, to expect that afternoon to sit in the shade of the oak.

—From *Wind, Sand, and Stars*
ANTOINE DE SAINT-EXUPÉRY
(tr. LEWIS GALANTIÈRE)

GREAT OCCASIONS

I cried over beautiful things, knowing no beautiful thing lasts,

The field of cornflower yellow is a scarf at the neck of the copper sunburned woman, the mother of the year, the taker of seeds.

The northwest wind comes and the yellow is torn full of holes, new beautiful things come in the first spit of snow on the northwest wind, and the old things go, not one lasts.

—*Autumn Movement*
CARL SANDBURG

No consolation for despair will do:
Death is absolute, demanding no
Display, no epitaph to shape our grief
Beyond the simple folding of the hands.
The process of despair will mark our way.
Love cannot hold its gain or justify
Its loss, and cannot keep tomorrow from
Today. My friends, your sorrow is the stone
Of his finality, what can I say:
That he was good beyond most men? That he
Endures in memory. A man is not
The sum or fortune of his gifts—
You want his life. Somewhere some still eat
Their bread in happiness, abundant breath;
And you must know your early joy depended
Necessarily upon this death.

—*To the Family of a Friend on His Death*
ROBERT PACK

DEATH

O shallow ground
That over ledges
Shoulders the gentle year,

Tender O shallow
Ground your grass is
Sisterly touching us:

Your trees are still:
They stand at our side in the
Night lantern.

Sister O shallow
Ground you inherit
Death as we do.

Your year also—
The young face,
The voice—vanishes.

Sister O shallow
Ground
      let the silence of
Green be between us
And the green sound.

—Words To Be Spoken
ARCHIBALD MACLEISH

I am not resigned to the shutting away of loving hearts
    in the hard ground.
So it is, and so it will be, for so it has been, time out
    of mind:

GREAT OCCASIONS

Into the darkness they go, the wise and the lovely. Crowned
With lilies and with laurel they go; but I am not resigned.

Lovers and thinkers, into the earth with you.
Be one with the dull, the indiscriminate dust.
A fragment of what you felt, of what you knew,
A formula, a phrase remains,—but the best is lost.

Down, down, down into the darkness of the grave
Gently they go, the beautiful, the tender, the kind;
Quietly they go, the intelligent, the witty, the brave.
I know. But I do not approve. And I am not resigned.

—*Dirge Without Music*
EDNA ST. VINCENT MILLAY

O Love! In what secret closets of forever
we lock your images from rust and fading.

How, sentenced, we conspire to baffle death
with all the careful windings of our vows.

And to what small avail we utter: Always!
against the noise of nothing's climbing wave.

O Love! For all our protest, when that wave
is reeled back by the sea in lapsing thunder,
we hear the one word: Hush.

—From *Elegy for an Engineer*
DILYS LAING

206

DEATH

Because I came, blossoms opened.
Abundance is abroad because I am.
At my ear, the nightingale
Spellbinds my heart.
I am father to all,
To everyone on the stars
And in the farthest reaches.
And because I left
There was night.

—PAUL KLEE

. . . remember us.
Give us a little nobility at last!
Make us worthy of the color of our wounds,
That high wild burning hue, brave as a trumpet's throat,
For now men fall in battle and that noble flower flowing
   from their bodies
Tells nothing except how beautiful they might have been.

—From *That Noble Flower*
ROBINSON JEFFERS

It is our minds that bring
Their death to everything.
It is our way of seeing

GREAT OCCASIONS

That draws their stature up
To stone, to buildings. Whole
Tragedies that they felt
As private, as their own.
We now possess and feel
The act they willed alone
As part of us. We dress
Death in our loneliness.

—From *The Humanists*
ELIZABETH JENNINGS

The woman I loved has stepped into silence:
Shut is the wood where the gods walked.
Still as the still leaves about me
I think of her who was both flame and frost to me.
Fallen is the house, and I the stone left standing—
Who will sing of her when I too am forgotten?

—*The Woman I Loved*
SCHARMEL IRIS

Then the time comes when we must leave all this.
What will this "all this" be? For some people it will be
Hoards of accumulated wealth, estates, libraries.
Divans on which to enjoy pleasure,
Or simply leisure;
For many others it will be toil and trouble;

DEATH

To leave family and friends, children who are growing up;
Tasks begun, a work to accomplish,
A dream on the point of fulfillment;
Books they wanted to read;
Perfumes they had never breathed;
Unsatisfied curiosities;
Unfortunates who counted on their help;
The peace, the serenity they were hoping to attain—
And then suddenly "les jeux sont faits; rien ne va plus."

—From *Fruits of the Earth*
ANDRÉ GIDE
(tr. DOROTHY BUSSY)

The sun went up the morning sky with all his light, but the landscape was dishonored by this loss. For this boy, in whose remembrance I have both slept and awakened so oft, decorated for me the morning star, the evening cloud.

A boy of early wisdom, of a grave and even majestic deportment, of a perfect gentleness.

Every tramper that ever tramped is abroad, but the little feet are still.

He gave up his little innocent breath like a bird.

Sorrow makes us all children again,—destroys all differences of intellect. The wisest knows nothing.

—*Journal, January 30, 1842*
RALPH WALDO EMERSON

GREAT OCCASIONS

Never more will the wind
cherish you again,
never more will the rain.

Never more
shall we find you bright
in the snow and wind.

The snow is melted,
the snow is gone,
and you are flown:

Like a bird out of our hand,
like a light out of our heart,
you are gone.

—H.D. (HILDA DOOLITTLE)

On Sunday in the sunlight
With brightness round her strown
And murmuring beauty of the sky
At last her very own,
She who had loved all children
And all high things and clean
Turned away to silentness
And bliss unseen.

Rending, blinding anguish,
Is all a man can know;
Yet still I kneel beside her
For she would have it so,
Kneel, and pray beside her
In light she left behind—
Light and love in silentness,
Sight to the blind.

DEATH

Oh living light burn through me!
Oh speak, as spoke to me
Her deep sweet eyes and faithful,
Voice on Calvary!
Oh light be near and shining,
Nearer than I guess,
And teach me that true language
Of silentness!

—From *Perpetual Light*
WILLIAM ROSE BENÉT

The drunken torrents are falling—
the blueness is dying now
and the corals are pale as the water
round the island of Palau.

The drunken torrents are broken,
grown alien, to you, to me,
our only possession the silence
of a bone washed clean by the sea.

The floods, the flames, the questions—
till the ashes tell you one day:
"Life is the building of bridges
over rivers that seep away."

—*Epilog*
GOTTFRIED BENN
(tr. MICHAEL HAMBURGER)

GREAT OCCASIONS

A song alone
   comes down—and of the skylark
      the last trace is gone.

—Ampū
(tr. HAROLD E. HENDERSON)

The goal of all life is death

—SIGMUND FREUD

Everything that man esteems
Endures a moment or a day.
Love's pleasure drives his love away,
The painter's brush consumes his dreams;
The herald's cry, the soldier's tread
Exhaust his glory and his might:
Whatever flames upon the night
Man's own resinous heart has fed.

—From *Two Songs from a Play*
WILLIAM BUTLER YEATS

Our mothers depart from us,
gently depart
                on tiptoe,
but we sleep soundly,
                        stuffed with food,
and fail to notice this dread hour.
Our mothers do not leave us suddenly,
                        no—
it only seems so "sudden."

213

GREAT OCCASIONS

Slowly they depart, and strangely,
with short steps down the stairs of years.
One year, remembering nervously,
we make a fuss to mark their birthday,
but this belated zeal
will save neither their souls

                 nor ours.
They withdraw ever further,

                       withdraw even further.

Roused from sleep,
               we stretch toward them,
but our hands suddenly beat the air—
a wall of glass has grown up there!
We were too late.

               The dread hour had struck.
Suppressing tears, we watch our mothers,
in columns quiet and austere,
departing from us . . .

                      —*Our Mothers Depart*
                        YEVGENY YEVTUSHENKO
                        (tr. GEORGE REAVEY)

A slumber did my spirit seal;
   I had no human fears:
She seemed a thing that could not feel
   The touch of earthly years.

No motion has she now, no force;
   She neither hears nor sees;
Rolled round in earth's diurnal course,
   With rocks, and stone, and trees.

                    —*A Slumber Did My Spirit Seal*
                     WILLIAM WORDSWORTH

DEATH

O blessed vision! happy child!
Thou art so exquisitely wild,
What hast thou to do with sorrow,
Or the injuries of tomorrow?

Thou art a dew-drop, which the morn brings forth,
Ill fitted to sustain unkindly shocks,
Or to be trailed along the soiling earth;
A gem that glitters while it lives,
And no forewarning gives;
But, at the touch of wrong, without a strife
Slips in a moment out of life.

—From *To H. C.*
WILLIAM WORDSWORTH

. . . time, that takes us all, will at the last
In taking us, take the whole world we are dreaming:
Sun, wind and sea, whisper of rain at night,
The young, hollow-cheeked moon, the clouds of evening
Drifting in a great solitude—all these
Shall time take away, surely, and the face
From which the eyes of love look out at us
In this brief world, this horror-haunted kingdom
Of beauty and of longing and of terror,
Of phantoms and illusion, of appearance
And disappearance—magic of leger-de-main,
Trick of the prestidigitator's wand—
The huge phantasmagoria we are dreaming:
This shall time take from us, and take forever,
When we are taken by that receding music.

—From *Night Thoughts in an Age*
JOHN HALL WHEELOCK

215

GREAT OCCASIONS

When·I shall die there'll be no sign in all this world,
    and nothing changed,
Only the hearts of some will quiver like flowers at
    morning in the dew.
Thousands are dead and thousands are dying, thousands are
    longing for death to come,
For in dying as in birth no one has ever been alone.
Death does not frighten me, death is not evil, death's
    but a harder fragment of life.

           —From a selection by
            JIŘÍ WOLKER
            (tr. DORA ROUND)

All the flowers of the spring
Meet to perfume our burying;
These have but their growing prime,
And man does flourish but his time:
Survey our progress from our birth—
We are set, we grow, we turn to earth.
Courts adieu, and all delights,
All bewitching appetites!
Sweetest breath and clearest eye
Like perfumes go out and die;
And consequently this is done
As shadows wait upon the sun.
Vain the ambition of kings
Who seek by trophies and dead things
To leave a living name behind,
And weave but nets to catch the wind.

           —*A Dirge*
           JOHN WEBSTER

DEATH

I wonder how you take your rest,
   Whose restless vigor tossed and burned;
And if you find earth's stoney breast
   Warmer than those from which you turned?
Are you content with this, the goal
   Of all your purposes and pains;
Knowing the iron in your soul
   Will not corrode, for all the rains?

An end to questions now; you are
   Their silent answer on this red
Terrain where every flickering star
   Is a last candle by your bed.
The day has gone, and you are part
   Of the clean winds that smooth your brow.
O vigilant mind, O tireless heart,
   Try sleeping now.

—From *I Wonder How You Take Your Rest*
LOUIS UNTERMEYER

To me death is a thing to be left alone. It comes when it is least expected and there are no ifs and buts about it. Once it has happened nothing could have stopped it. There's nothing more that I can say.

—From *Green Memories*
GEDDES MUMFORD

GREAT OCCASIONS

Do not go gentle into that good night,
Old age should burn and rave at close of day;
Rage, rage against the dying of the light.

Though wise men at their end know dark is right,
Because their words had forked no lightning they
Do not go gentle into that good night.

Good men, the last wave by, crying how bright
Their frail deeds might have danced in a green bay,
Rage, rage against the dying of the light.

Wild men who caught and sang the sun in flight,
And learn, too late, they grieved it on its way,
Do not go gentle into that good night.

Grave men, near death, who see with blinding sight
Blind eyes could blaze like meteors and be gay,
Rage, rage against the dying of the light.

And you, my father, there on the sad height,
Curse, bless, me now with your fierce tears, I pray.
Do not go gentle into that good night.
Rage, rage against the dying of the light.

—*Do Not Go Gentle into That Good Night*
DYLAN THOMAS

We are not sure of sorrow,
    And joy was never sure;
Today will die tomorrow,
    Time stoops to no man's lure;
And love, grown faint and fretful
With lips but half regretful
Sighs, and with eyes forgetful
    Weeps that no loves endure.

218

DEATH

From too much love of living,
    From hope and fear set free,
We thank with brief thanksgiving
    Whatever gods may be
That no life lives for ever;
That dead men rise up never;
That even the weariest river
    Winds somewhere safe to sea.

Then star nor sun shall waken,
    Nor any change of light:
Nor sound of waters shaken,
    Nor any sound or sight:
Nor wintry leaves nor vernal,
Nor days nor things diurnal;
Only the sleep eternal
    In an eternal night.

—From *The Garden of Proserpine*
ALGERNON SWINBURNE

Let's talk of graves, of worms, and epitaphs,
Make dust our paper, and with rainy eyes
Write sorrow on the bosom of the earth.
Let's choose executors and talk of wills.
And yet not so—for what can we bequeath
Save our deposed bodies to the ground?
Our lands, our lives, and all, are Bolingbroke's,
And nothing can we call our own but death;
And that small model of the barren earth
Which serves as paste and cover to our bones.
For God's sake let us sit upon the ground
And tell sad stories of the death of kings:
How some have been depos'd, some slain in war,

219

GREAT OCCASIONS

Some haunted by the ghosts they have deposed,
Some poisoned by their wives, some sleeping kill'd,
All murthered—for within the hollow crown
That rounds the mortal temples of a king
Keeps Death his court, and there the antic sits,
Scoffing his state and grinning at his pomp,
Allowing him a breath, a little scene,
To monarchize, be fear'd, and kill with looks;
Infusing him with self and vain conceit,
As if this flesh which walls about our life
Were brass impregnable; and, humour'd this,
Comes at the last, and with a little pin
Bores through his castle wall, and farewell king!

—From *King Richard II*
WILLIAM SHAKESPEARE

I have finished my combat with the sun;
And my body, the old animal,
Knows nothing more.

The powerful seasons bred and killed,
And were themselves the genii
Of their own ends.

Oh, but the very self of the storm
Of sun and slaves, breeding and death,
The old animal,

The senses and feeling, the very sound
And sight, and all there was of the storm,
Knows nothing more.

—From *The Misery of Don Joost*
WALLACE STEVENS

DEATH

Our lives take their meaning from their interlacing with other lives, and when one life is ended those into which it was woven are also carried into darkness. Neither you nor I, but only the hand of time, slow-moving, yet sure and steady, can lift that blanket of blackness.

—Of Philip Murray
ADLAI STEVENSON

All things are gluttonously devoured by Time, all things are
    fleeting.
All things, though fixéd, are flowing, nothing abides long;
Rivers grow less in their banks, the great sea-bed is uncovered,
The mountain ranges vanish and their high pinnacles fall.
Why speak of so small a thing? For even the glorious masses
Of heaven must be consumed, at last, by their own fires.
Death waits for all, and to die is a law not a punishment:
A time will come when there will be no world here.

—SENECA
(tr. JOYCE PENNY)

We are always saying farewell in this world, always standing at the edge of a loss, attempting to retrieve some human meaning, from the silence, something which was precious and is gone. . . .

221

GREAT OCCASIONS

We are lonelier; someone has gone from one's own life who was like the certainty of refuge; and someone has gone from the world who was like a certainty of honor.

—Of Eleanor Roosevelt
ADLAI STEVENSON

Her life was touched with early frost,
About the April of her day,
Her hold on earth was lightly lost,
And like a leaf she went away.

—From Afterwards
DUNCAN CAMPBELL SCOTT

The edges of the summit still appall
When we brood on the dead or the beloved;
Nor can imagination do it all
In this last place of light: he dares to live
Who stops being a bird, yet beats his wings
Against the immense immeasurable emptiness of things.

—From The Dying Man
THEODORE ROETHKE

DEATH

Life and death are brothers that dwell together; they cling to each other and cannot be separated. They are joined by the two extremes of a frail bridge over which all created beings travel. Life is the entrance; death is the exit. Life builds, death demolishes; life sows, death reaps; life plants, and death uproots.

—From *Duties of the Heart*
BAHYA IBN PAKUDA

The creature is born, it fades away, it dies,
And comes then the great cold.
It is the great cold of night, it is the dark.

The bird comes, it flies, it dies,
And comes then the great cold.
It is the great cold of night, it is the dark.

The fish swims away, it goes, it dies,
And comes then the great cold.
It is the great cold of night, it is the dark.

Man is born, he eats and sleeps. He fades away,
And comes then the great cold.
It is the great cold of night, it is the dark.

And the sky lights up, the eyes are closed,
The star shines.
The cold down here, the light up there.

Man is gone, the prisoner is freed,
The shadow has disappeared.
The shadow has disappeared.

—PYGMY FUNERAL HYMN
(tr. REX BENEDICT)

GREAT OCCASIONS

No human being should ever wake without looking at the sun with grateful recognition of the liberty of another day; nor give himself to sleep without casting his mind, like a merlin, into the gulfs between the furthest stars. We are all of us grossly constituted. To listen for a moment to the wind as it stirs the leaves of our garden trees, and to realize that this murmur was troubling earth vegetation before men were, and will be troubling it when they have gone, is to take knowledge of the breath of the infinite. It is a mystery, a sign for everyone, this movement of the planet's atmosphere. It dislodges the dust in the belfry where the owl stares and a loose board rattles. The nettles grouped by the farmyard wall sway to it, and in wide open spaces its music is not lost. No message comes through our senses but is full of worship.

—From *Earth Memories*
LLEWELYN POWYS

I am old and had forgotten
the benediction of the earth.
A warm amnesia wraps like cotton
packing down my bones to rest.

I am old and years are peeling
petal-wise, undone.
I am old, and feeling
presses dry and fever-sprung.

Bless me now, Earth, warm me deep.
I am old, would sleep.

—From *Old Woman in the Sun*
SHEILA PRITCHARD

224

DEATH

Drop of dew on green bowl fostered
on leaf green bowl grows under the lamp
        without flesh or colour;
under the lamp into stream of
        song, streamsong,
in flight into the infinite—
        a blinded heron
thrown against the infinite—
        where solitude
weaves her interminable mystery
        under the lamp.

The moonman has gone under the sea:
the singer has gone under the shade.

—Transition
CHRISTOPHER OKIGBO

Man's life is like a sojourning,
His longevity lacks the firmness of stone and metal.
For ever it has been that mourners in their turn were mourned,
Saint and Sage,—all alike are trapped.
Seeking by food to obtain Immortality
Many have been the dupes of strange drugs.
Better far to drink good wine
And clothe our bodies in robes of satin and silk.
The dead are gone and with them we cannot converse.
The living are here and ought to have our love.

—MEI SHĒNG
(tr. ARTHUR WALEY)

225

There is a limit to human suffering. When one thinks: "Now I have touched the bottom of the sea—now I can go no deeper," one goes deeper. . . . [But] suffering can be overcome. . . . What must one do? One must *submit*. Do not resist. Take it. Be overwhelmed. Accept it fully. Make it *part of life*. Everything in life that we really accept undergoes a change. So suffering must become Love.

—*The Journal*
KATHERINE MANSFIELD

When by-which-I-came-to-be
Shall uncreate as deftly me,
Where my irrelevant ashes lie
Write only this: THAT WHICH WAS I
NO LONGER HOLDS ITS LITTLE PLACE
AGAINST THE PUSHING LEAGUES OF SPACE.

—From *Journal*
EDNA ST. VINCENT MILLAY

The living is a passing traveler;
The dead, a man come home.
One brief journey betwixt heaven and earth,

226

DEATH

Then, alas! we are the same old dust of ten
     thousand ages.

. . .

Man dies, his white bones are dumb without a word
When the green pines feel the coming of the spring.
Looking back, I sigh; looking before, I sigh again.
What is there to prize in the life's vaporous glory?

              —From a selection by
              LI PO
              (tr. SHIGEYOSHI OBATA)

Our day is over, night comes up
shadows steal out of the earth.
Shadows, shadows
wash over our knees and splash between our thighs,
our day is done;
we wade, we wade, we stagger, darkness rushes between
                our stones,
we shall drown.

Our day is over
night comes up.

              —*Our Day Is Over*
              D. H. LAWRENCE

There is no conclusion. What has concluded that we might conclude in regard to it? There are no fortunes to be told and no advice to be given. Farewell.

              —WILLIAM JAMES

GREAT OCCASIONS

Goodnight; ensured release,
Imperishable peace,
   Have these for yours,
While sea abides, and land,
And earth's foundations stand,
   And heaven endures.

When earth's foundations flee,
Nor sky nor land nor sea
   At all is found,
Content you, let them burn:
It is not your concern;
   Sleep on, sleep sound.

                    —*Parta Quies*
                 A. E. HOUSMAN

Lie you easy, dream you light,
   And sleep you fast for aye;
And luckier may you find the night
   Than ever you found the day.

               —From *The Isle of Portland*
              A. E. HOUSMAN

Death this year has taken men
Whose kind we shall not see again.

DEATH

Pride and skill and friendliness,
Wrath and wisdom and delight,
Are shining still, but shining less,
And clouded to the common sight.
Time will show them clear again.
Time will give us other men
With names to write in burning gold
When they are great and we are old,
But these were royal-hearted, rare
Memory keeps with loving care
Deeds they did and tales they told.
But living men are hard to spare.

—Death This Year
JOHN HOLMES

Give up to the grass.
It forgives you wholly.
Where your father drowned,
After all the men
Before him, and women,
You not last in that line,
Flung and gone down
To the grassy underlands,
You wash in that green,
That grass in your hands.

—From *Grass*
JOHN HOLMES

GREAT OCCASIONS

A body remains. But the painful
Disquiet has left it, and this heart
Is nothing but dead muscle now . . .

I have extinguished the world,
Exchanged being for nothingness,
I have drowned time in eternity.

—From *Last Letter*
HANS EGON HOLTHUSEN
(tr. MARIANNE LEIBHOLZ)

Like the leaves in their generations, such is the
    race of men.
For the wind casts the leaves from their branches
    to earthward, and again
Others the budding greenwood each springtide brings
    to birth,
So do man's generations spring up and fade from
    earth.

—From *The Iliad*
HOMER
(tr. F. L. LUCAS)

You needn't pretend to be so clever. You have seen people die;
there's nothing very funny about it. You try to joke so as to hide
your fear; but your voice trembles and your sham poem is frightful.

DEATH

Perhaps. . . . Yes, I have seen people die. In most cases it seemed to me that just before death and once the crisis was past, the sharpness of the sting was in a way blunted. Death puts on velvet gloves to take us. He does not strangle us without first lulling us to sleep, and the things he robs us of have already lost their distinctness, their presence, and, as it were, their reality. The universe becomes so colorless that it is no longer very difficult to leave it, and nothing is left to regret.

So I say to myself that it can't be so difficult to die since, as a matter of fact, everybody manages it. And, after all, it would perhaps be nothing but a habit to fall into if only one died more than once.

But death is dreadful to those who have not filled their lives. In their case it is only too easy for religion to say: "Never mind! It's in the other world that things begin; you'll get your reward there."

It is *now* and in *this* world that we must live.

—From *Fruits of the Earth*
ANDRÉ GIDE
(tr. DOROTHY BUSSY)

Man cometh forth like a flower from concealment, and of a sudden shews himself in open day, and in a moment is by death withdrawn from open view into concealment again. The greenness of the flesh exhibits us to view, but the dryness of dust withdraws us from men's eyes. For whereas infancy is going on to childhood, childhood to youth, youth to manhood, and manhood to old age, and old age to death, in the course of the present life he is forced by the very steps of his increase upon those of decrease, and is ever wasting from the very cause whence he thinks himself to be gaining ground in the space of his life. For we cannot have a fixed stay here, whither we are come only to pass on.

—GREGORY THE GREAT

231

What an absurd conception of the world and of life it is that causes three quarters of our misery! Out of attachment to the past we refuse to understand that tomorrow's happiness is only possible if today's makes room for it, that every wave owes the beauty of its curve to the retreat of the one that precedes it, that every flower must fade in order to bear its fruit, and unless the fruit falls and dies, it cannot produce future flowerings, so that spring itself is founded upon winter's loss.

—From *Fruits of the Earth*
ANDRÉ GIDE
(tr. DOROTHY BUSSY)

Death asks us for our identity. Confronted by death, man is compelled to provide in some form a response to the question: Who am I?

The manner in which this question has been asked and the replies that it has received have varied from era to era and have reflected the personal aspirations and the social consensus of the time and place.

It is only the implacable and challenging presence of death itself which has remained constant.

—ROBERT FULTON

DEATH

When the spent sun throws up its rays on cloud
And goes down burning into the gulf below,
No voice in nature is heard to cry aloud
At what has happened. Birds, at least, must know
It is the change to darkness in the sky.
Murmuring something quiet in her breast,
One bird begins to close a faded eye;
Or overtaken too far from his nest,
Hurrying low above the grove, some waif
Swoops just in time to his remembered tree.
At most he thinks or twitters softly, "Safe!
Now let the night be dark for all of me.
Let the night be too dark for me to see
Into the future. Let what will be, be."

—Acceptance
ROBERT FROST

Death is before me today
Like the odor of myrrh
Like sitting under a tree on a windy day.

Death is before me today
Like the clearing of the sky
Like a man sailing towards that which he knows not.

Death is before me today
As a man longs to see his house
When he has spent many years in captivity.

—EGYPTIAN
(tr. JAMES H. BREASTED)

This death of the body, is it not in the natural order of things in the physical universe? Behold the flowers of the field! They bloom for a brief season and then wither away. The birds of the air, they ascend for their last flight, then descend to fold their wings and find peace in their nest, even the peace of death.

So it is with the beasts of the forest. When their time is come, they seek out some quiet, secluded spot, make their last lair and lay them down there to die; unafraid, they, and unashamed. Yea, the very stars in their courses, though they glow for centuries and centuries, lose their radiance at last; they grow cold and crumble away into cosmic ashes.

What is man that he should think to escape this common destiny of all earthly things, or the son of man that he should resent this final blow of fate called death?

—From a selection by
FRANK CARLETON DOAN

All, all of a piece throughout;
Thy chace had a beast in view:—
Thy wars brought nothing about;—
Thy lovers were all untrue:—
'Tis well an old age is out,
And time to begin anew.

—JOHN DRYDEN

Our hard entrance into the world, our miserable going out of it, our sicknesses, disturbances, and sad encounters in it, do clamorously tell us we come not into the world to run a race of delight, but to perform the sober acts and serious purposes of man; which to omit were foully to miscarry in the advantage of humanity.

—From *Christian Morals*
THOMAS BROWNE

The day we die
Then the wind comes
To wipe us out,
The traces of our feet.
The wind creates dust
Which covers
The traces that were
Where we had walked,
For otherwise
It would be
As if we were
Still alive.
That is why it is the wind
That comes
To wipe out
The traces of our feet.

—AFRICAN BUSHMAN

A word, a phrase—: from cyphers rise
Life recognized, a sudden sense,

GREAT OCCASIONS

The sun stands still, mute are the skies,
And all compacts it, stark and dense.

A word—a gleam, a flight, a spark,
A thrust of flames, a stellar trace—
And then again—immense—the dark
Round world and I in empty space.

—*A Word*
GOTTFRIED BENN
(tr. RICHARD EXNER)

What else is our life but a light vapor, which is driven away and disappears with the wind—a blade of grass which is dried up in the heat of the sun?

—From *The Way of Salvation*
ST. ALPHONSUS DE LIGUORI

Every summary has a trend
Every question has an answer
Every event has an hour
Every action has its account
Every ascent has its limit
Every man has his book of fate.

Every guarantee is a symbol of death
Every building a promise of destruction
Every king and his domain the original of dust.

—ABU AL-ATAHIYAH
(tr. HERBERT HOWARTH
and IBRAHIM SHUKRALLAH)

236

DEATH

You are dead—
You, the kindly, courteous,
You whom we loved,
You who harmed no man
Yet were brave to death
And died that other men might live.

Far purer, braver lips than mine shall praise you,
Far nobler hands than mine record your loss,
Yet since your courteous high valour scorned no man,
I, who but loved you from the ranks, can greet you,
Salute your grave, and murmur: "Brother,
Hail and farewell."

—*Epitaph, H.S.R. Killed April 1917*
RICHARD ALDINGTON

Praise to our faring hearts

—DYLAN THOMAS

All times I have enjoy'd
Greatly, have suffer'd greatly, both with those
That loved me, and alone; . . .
Much have I seen and known: cities of men,
And manners, climates, councils, governments,
Myself not least, but honour'd of them all; . . .
I am a part of all that I have met;
Yet all experience is an arch wherethro'
Gleams that untravell'd world, whose margin fades
For ever and for ever when I move.
How dull it is to pause, to make an end,
To rust unburnish'd, not to shine in use!
As tho' to breathe were life. Life piled on life
Were all too little . . . and vile it were
For some three suns to store and hoard myself,
And this gray spirit yearning in desire
To follow knowledge like a sinking star,
Beyond the utmost bound of human thought. . . .
Death closes all; . . .
The light begins to twinkle from the rocks;
The long day wanes: the slow moon climbs: the deep
Moans round with many voices. Come, my friends,
'Tis not too late to seek a newer world.
  . . .   My purpose holds

DEATH

To sail beyond the sunset, and the baths
Of all the western stars . . .
It may be that the gulfs will wash us down:
It may be we shall touch the Happy Isles
And see the great Achilles . . .
Tho' much is taken, much abides; and tho'
We are not now that strength which in old days
Moved earth and heaven; that which we are, we are;
One equal temper of heroic hearts,
Made weak by time and fate, but strong in will
To strive, to seek, to find, and not to yield.

—From *Ulysses*
ALFRED TENNYSON

Take him, earth, for cherishing,
    To thy tender breast receive him.
Body of a man I bring thee,
    Noble even in its ruin.

Not though ancient time decaying
    Wear away these bones to sand,
Ashes that a man might measure
    In the hollow of his hand;

Not though wandering winds and idle,
    Drifting through the empty sky,
Scatter dust was nerve and sinew,
    Is it given man to die.

But for us, heap earth about him,
    Earth with leaves and violets strewn,
Grave his name, and pour the fragrant
    Balm upon the icy stone.

—From *Prudentius*
HELEN WADDELL

GREAT OCCASIONS

Let me die, working.
Still tackling plans unfinished, tasks undone!
Clean to its end, swift may my race be run.
No laggard steps, no faltering, no shirking;
Let me die, working!

Let me die, thinking.
Let me fare forth still with an open mind,
Fresh secrets to unfold, new truths to find,
My soul undimmed, alert, no question blinking;
Let me die, thinking!

Let me die, giving.
The substance of life for life's enriching;
Time, things, and self on heaven converging,
No selfish thought, loving, redeeming, living;
Let me die, giving!

—From *Into the Sunset*
S. HALL YOUNG

Now I have lost you, I must scatter
All of you on the air henceforth;
Not that to me it can even matter
But it's only fair to the rest of earth.

Now especially, when it is Winter
And the sun's not half so bright as he was,
Who wouldn't be glad to find a splinter
That once was you, in the frozen grass?

Snowflakes, too, will be softer feathered,
Clouds, perhaps, will be whiter plumed;

DEATH

Rain, whose brilliance you caught and gathered,
Purer silver have reassumed.

Farewell, sweet dust; I was never a miser:
Once, for a minute, I made you mine:
Now you are gone, I am none the wiser,
But the leaves of the willow are bright as wine.

—*Farewell Sweet Dust*
ELINOR WYLIE

The hour must come to return into the night,
To do the seemingly impossible—
Unself the self, surrender all,
Be as at first in the blackness of that night:
Seed-bed of all delight,
Darkness from which the white blossom draws its
    flowering white,
Source of all light.
The fiery sword of fear and pain,
Turning this side and that to bar the way,
Once overcome, can harm no more.
Time will have fallen away,
Terror have done its worst;
The agony passed,
We may return into our peace at last,
Be as we were before,
Till love summon us from the night again.

—From *Return into the Night*
JOHN HALL WHEELOCK

GREAT OCCASIONS

Life, where your lone candle burns
In the darkness of the night,
Mothlike my lost spirit turns
Toward you, in its circling flight.

Steadily your beauty draws
Onward, with each hurrying breath—
Till I flutter, till I pause
In the radiance of death.

I am flaming, I am fled—
All around you reigns the night;
But my agony has fed
You, a moment, holy light.

—*Holy Light*
JOHN HALL WHEELOCK

I see what was, and is, and will abide;
Still glides the stream, and shall forever glide;
The form remains, the function never dies;
While we, the brave, the mighty, and the wise,
We men, who in the morn of youth defied
The elements, must vanish;—be it so!
Enough, if something from our hands have power
To live, and act, and serve the future hour;
And if, as toward the silent tomb we go,
Through love, through hope, and faith's transcendent dower,
We feel that we are greater than we know.

—From *After-Thought*
WILLIAM WORDSWORTH

DEATH

After the dazzle of day is gone,
Only the dark, dark night shows to my eyes the stars;
After the clangor of organ majestic, or chorus, or
      perfect band,
Silent, athwart my soul, moves the symphony true.

—After the Dazzle of Day
WALT WHITMAN

Give me your hand
By these grey waters—
The day is ending.

Already the first
Faint star pierces
The veil of heaven.

Oh, the long way
We two have come,
In joy, together,

To these grey shores
And quiet waters
And the day's ending!

The day is ending.
The journey is ended.
Give me your hand.

—Telos
JOHN HALL WHEELOCK

GREAT OCCASIONS

Life that stays for none,
Must now flow on in others, shall we demur
That had such bounty of happiness from her,
In years together and hours that made us one!
Blessed be they in whom life's ardors run—
Great life, whose temporary abode we were.

—From *So Dark, So True*
JOHN HALL WHEELOCK

The seed that is to grow
    must lose itself as seed;
And they that creep
    may graduate through
chrysalis to wings.

Wilt thou then, O mortal,
    cling to husks which
    falsely seem to you
        the self?

—WU MING FU

Now finalè to the shore,
Now land and life finalè and farewell,
Now Voyager depart, (much, much for thee is yet in store,)
Often enough hast thou adventur'd o'er the seas,
Cautiously cruising, studying the charts,
Duly again to port and hawser's tie returning;

244

DEATH

But now obey thy cherish'd secret wish,
Embrace thy friends, leave all in order,
To port and hawser's tie no more returning,
Depart upon thy endless cruise old Sailor.

—Now Finalè to the Shore
WALT WHITMAN

Our life is closed, our life begins,
The long, long anchorage we leave,
The ship is clear at last, she leaps!
She swiftly courses from the shore,
Joy, shipmate, joy!

—Joy, Shipmate, Joy!
WALT WHITMAN

Old, old is the earth,
the small stars dreaming over the hills;
old are the sorrowing seas
whose burden is heartbreak;
and the dead under sun or snow
are old with the world's age,
the fallen years and the lost.

Lost to our change, unknowing of the falling
leaf, the weathering hills, the river's flowing,
They dream of no fabulous city of the heart
for these have come
into the only equitable kingdom.

245

GREAT OCCASIONS

Kind is that sleep in which love has no voices,
where the hands carry no meaning of love or prayer,
when is forgotten the wind in the hair, the rain
beating on winter windows, the still
midnight of pain.

Old, old is the earth,
and shall be kind to us at least.

—From *Now Against Winter*
FREDERIC VANSON

What are we bound for? What's the yield
   Of all this energy and waste?
Why do we spend ourselves and build
   With such an empty haste?

Wherefore the bravery we boast?
   How can we spend the laughing breath
When at the end all things are lost
   In ignorance and death?

The stars have found a blazing course
   In a vast curve that cuts through space;
Enough for us to feel that force
   Swinging us through the days.

Enough that we have strength to sing
   And fight and somehow scorn the grave;
That life's too bold and bright a thing
   To question or to save.

—*What Are We Bound For?*
LOUIS UNTERMEYER

DEATH

Life as a whole never takes death seriously. It laughs, dances and plays, it builds, hoards and loves in death's face. Only when we detach one individual fact of death do we see its blankness and become dismayed. We lose sight of the wholeness of a life of which death is part. It is like looking at a piece of cloth through a microscope. It appears like a net; we gaze at the big holes and shiver in imagination. But the truth is, death is not the ultimate reality. It looks black, as the sky looks blue; but it does not blacken existence, just as the sky does not leave its stain upon the wings of the bird.

—From *Sādhanā*
RABINDRANATH TAGORE

How plain that death is only the phenomenon of the individual or class. Nature does not recognize it, she finds her own again under new forms without loss. Yet death is beautiful when seen to be a law, and not an accident—It is as common as life. Men die in Tartary, in Ethiopia—in England—in Wisconsin. And after all what portion of this so serene and living nature can be said to be alive? Do this year's grasses and foliage outnumber all the past?

Every blade in the field—every leaf in the forest—lays down its life in its season as beautifully as it was taken up. It is the pastime of a full quarter of the year. Dead trees—sere leaves—dried grass and herbs—are not these a good part of our life? And what is that pride of our autumnal scenery but the hectic flush—the sallow and cadaverous countenance of vegetation—its painted throes—with the November air for canvas—

When we look over the fields are we not saddened because the particular flowers or grasses will wither—for the law of their death is the law of new life? Will not the land be in good heart *because* the crops die down from year to year? The herbage cheerfully consents to bloom, and wither, and give place to a new.

So it is with the human plant. We are partial and selfish when we lament the death of an individual, unless our plaint be a paean to the departed soul, and a sigh as the wind sighs over the fields, which no shrub interprets into its private grief.

—Letter, March 11, 1842
HENRY DAVID THOREAU

I share with you the agony of your grief,
 The anguish of your heart finds echo in my own.
 I know I cannot enter all you feel
 Nor bear with you the burden of your pain;
I can but offer what my love does give:
 The strength of caring,
 The warmth of one who seeks to understand
 The silent storm-swept barrenness of so great a loss.
This I do in quiet ways,
 That on your lonely path
 You may not walk alone.

—From *Meditations of the Heart*
HOWARD THURMAN

On the day when death will knock at thy door what wilt thou offer to him?

Oh, I will set before my guest the full vessel of my life—I will never let him go with empty hands.

248

DEATH

All the sweet vintage of all my autumn days and summer
nights, all the earnings and gleanings of my busy life
will I place before him at the close of my days when
death will knock at my door.

—From *Gitanjali No. 90*
RABINDRANATH TAGORE

It is not that we are singled out for a special judgment; when we
give up our dead, we but enter into a common sorrow, a sorrow
that visits the proudest and humblest, that has entered into unnumbered hearts before us and will enter into innumerable ones after
us, a sorrow that should make the world one, and dissolve all
other feelings into sympathy and love.

—W. M. SALTER

Next to the encounter of death in our own bodies, the most
sensible calamity to an honest man is the death of a friend. The
comfort of having a friend may be taken away, but not that of
having had one. It is an ill construction of providence to reflect
only upon my friend's being taken away, without any regard to the
benefit of his once being given me. He that has lost a friend has
more cause of joy that once he had him, than of grief that he is
taken away. Shall a man bury his friendship with his friend?

—From *On Death*
SENECA

GREAT OCCASIONS

Death is sweet when it comes in its time and in its place, when it is part of the order of things. For a mother death is only half a death. Each life in turn bursts like a pod and sends forth its seed. When a mother dies, for a second time the umbilical cord is cut. For a second time the knot is loosened, the knot that bound one generation to another.

And now the mother lies broken but at rest, a vein from which the gold has been extracted. In their turn, her sons and daughters will bring forth young from their mould. So simple is this image of a generation dropping one by one its white-haired members as it makes its way through time and through its metamorphoses towards a truth that is its own.

This is life that is handed on here from generation to generation with the slow progress of a tree's growth, but it is also fulfilment. What a mysterious ascension! From a little bubbling lava, from the vague pulp of a star, from a living cell miraculously fertilized, we have issued forth and have bit by bit raised ourselves to the writing of cantatas and the weighing of nebulae.

—From *Wind, Sand, and Stars*
ANTOINE DE SAINT-EXUPÉRY)
(tr. LEWIS GALANTIÈRE)

Now voyager, lay here your dazzled head.
Come back to earth from air, be nourishèd,
Not with that light on light, but with this bread.

Here close to earth be cherished, mortal heart,
Hold your way deep as roots push rocks apart
To bring the spurt of green up from the dark.

DEATH

Where music thundered let the mind be still,
Where the will triumphed let there be no will,
What light revealed, now let the dark fulfill.

Here close to earth the deeper pulse is stirred,
Here where no wings rush and no sudden bird,
But only heart-beat upon beat is heard.

Here let the fiery burden be all spilled,
The passionate voice at last be calmed and stilled
And the long yearning of the blood fulfilled.

Now voyager, come home, come home to rest,
Here on the long-lost country of earth's breast
Lay down the fiery vision, and be blest, be blest.

—Now Voyager
MAY SARTON

Calm was the sea to which your course you kept,
Oh, how much calmer than all southern seas!
Many your nameless mates, whom the keen breeze
Wafted from mothers that of old have wept.
All souls of children taken as they slept
Are your companions, partners of your ease,
And the green souls of all these autumn trees
Are with you through the silent spaces swept.

Your virgin body gave its gentle breath
Untainted to the gods. Why should we grieve,
But that we merit not your holy death?
We shall not loiter long, your friends and I;
Living, you made it goodlier to live,
Dead, you will make it easier to die.

—To W. P. I
GEORGE SANTAYANA

251

GREAT OCCASIONS

Content thee, howsoe'er, whose days are done;
   There lies not any troublous thing before,
   Nor sight nor sound to war against thee more,
For whom all winds are quiet as the sun,
   All waters as the shore.

          —From *Ave Atque Vale*
          ALGERNON SWINBURNE

Gather the stars if you wish it so.
Gather the songs and keep them.
Gather the faces of women.
Gather for keeping years and years.
     And then . . .
Loosen your hands, let go and say good-by.
     Let the stars and songs go.
     Let the faces and years go.
     Loosen your hands and say good-by.

          —*Stars, Songs, Faces*
          CARL SANDBURG

It was much stronger than they said. Noisier.
Everything in it more colored. Wilder.
More at the center calm.

DEATH

Everything was more violent than ever they said,
Who tried to guard us from suicide and life.
We in our wars were more than they had told us.
Now that descent figures stand about the horizon,
I have begun to see the living faces,
The storm, the morning, all more than they ever said.
Of the new dead, that friend who died today,
Angel of suicides, gather him in now.
Defend us from doing what he had to do
Who threw himself away.

—F. O. M.
MURIEL RUKEYSER

In an old man who has known human joys and sorrows, and has achieved whatever work it was in him to do, the fear of death is somewhat abject and ignoble. The best way to overcome it—so at least it seems to me—is to make your interests gradually wider and more impersonal, until bit by bit the walls of the ego recede, and your life becomes increasingly merged in the universal life. An individual human existence should be like a river—small at first, narrowly contained within its banks, and rushing passionately past boulders and over waterfalls. Gradually the river grows wider, the banks recede, the waters flow more quietly, and in the end, without any visible break, they become merged in the sea, and painlessly lose their individual being. The man who, in old age, can see his life in this way, will not suffer from the fear of death, since the things he cares for will continue. And if, with the decay of vitality, weariness increases, the thought of rest will be not unwelcome. The wise man should wish to die while still at work, knowing that others will carry on what he can no longer do, and content in the thought that what was possible has been done.

—From *New Hopes for a Changing World*
BERTRAND RUSSELL

GREAT OCCASIONS

I died a mineral, and became a plant.
I died a plant, and rose an animal.
I died an animal, and I was man.
Why should I fear? When was I less by dying?

—From a selection by
JALAL-UDDIN RUMI
(tr. E. H. WHINFIELD)

Corpuscle, skin,
cell, and membrane,
each has its minute seasons
clocked within the bones.

Millions grow lean and fall away
in the hourly autumn of the body.
But fertile in fall, ending as others begin,
to the naivete of death they run.

From the complexity
of reasons gyring within reasons,
of co-extensive spring and autumn,

into the soil as soil we come,
to find for a while a simplicity
in larger, external seasons.

—*Towards Simplicity*
A. K. RAMANUJAN

DEATH

When mine hour is come
Let no teardrop fall
And no darkness hover
Round me where I lie.
Let the vastness call
One who was its lover,
Let me breathe the sky.

Where the lordly light
Walks along the world,
And its silent tread
Leaves the grasses bright,
Leaves the flowers uncurled,
Let me to the dead
Breathe a gay goodnight.

—When
GEORGE RUSSELL ("A.E.")

Brief and powerless is Man's life; on him and all his race the slow, sure doom falls pitiless and dark. Blind to good and evil, reckless of destruction, omnipotent matter rolls on its relentless way; for Man, condemned to-day to lose his dearest, to-morrow himself to pass through the gate of darkness, it remains only to cherish, ere yet the blow falls, the lofty thoughts that ennoble his little day; disdaining the coward terrors of the slave of Fate, to worship at the shrine that his own hands have built; undismayed by the empire of chance, to preserve a mind free from the wanton tyranny that rules his outward life; proudly defiant of the irresistible forces that tolerate, for a moment, his knowledge and his condemnation, to sustain alone, a weary but unyielding Atlas, the world that his own ideals have fashioned despite the trampling march of unconscious power.

—From *A Free Man's Worship*
BERTRAND RUSSELL

Why, when this span of life might be fleeted away,
Why *have* to be human, and, shunning Destiny,
long for Destiny? . . .
                    Not because happiness really
exists, that premature profit of imminent loss.
Not out of curiosity, not just to practise the heart,
But because being here amounts to so much, because all
this Here and Now, so fleeting, seems to require us
                    and strangely
concerns us. Us, the most fleeting of all. Just once,
everything, only for once. Once and no more. And we, too,
once. And never again. But this
having been once, though only once,
having been once on earth—can it ever be cancelled?

—From *Duino Elegies*
RAINER MARIA RILKE
(tr. LEISHMAN and SPENDER)

We come here bearing our grief and perhaps feeling bruised by
this death and what we might have done to prevent it.

Remember that no single act of desperation can portray a life.
No matter how stalked by hurt, this life also had its moments of
delight and happiness, caring and friendship, sharing and love. Let
us be daring enough never to forget these.

Let us admit the deep truth that none of us carries enough concern for his brother upon this earth. We try with our best resources, with what we can bring to bear, with what we can lavish
out of self at the time. But it may not be enough, though our failures are not through callousness.

DEATH

Self-death does not mean life denial, but it is the cry of despair for more life. It is the refusal to crawl forever through the yawning caverns of the absurd. The battle may be long and arduous, but the sense of alienation within this choice is personal, is taken alone, after an epic conflict within the self.

Whenever a death cuts across life, we are left with a certain incompleteness. We know that he leaves much unfinished, unfulfilled, unsaid. There are yet other things we wanted to share with him, and he with us. But what has been must not suffice. What is and cannot be changed must be accepted. We are simply thankful that we could know and partake in the journey of life with him, for it has enriched us all.

—PETER RAIBLE

Death is a daily event. Your life, my life, anybody's, is a succession of deaths and resurrections. These deaths-in-life are a perishing out of smaller worlds and a being reborn into larger. Another name for them is growth—growth, which is life, and often as painful as death, yet "Except a seed fall into the ground and die, it cannot bring forth fruit."

Not until we let go our tense, rigid mortal grasp of the beloved object is the secret revealed: that another Paradise lies just outside the Garden. These, life's dress rehearsals for death, are a testing of the soul's mettle, of its willingness to die out of the life that was—beautiful, rich and useful though it may have been—and to be born into another, of molten gold from which the soul may smith what masterpiece it will.

—From *Litany for All Souls*
LUCIEN PRICE

GREAT OCCASIONS

The hills have something to say,
And this sky and the trees.
They saw this man born,
And now he is laid away
At their still feet.
They do not care or know,
And yet they say, "Snow has not won
For more than a winter over the sun."

—Country Burial
HARRIET PLIMPTON

Man is like a breath,
    His days are as a fleeting shadow.
In the morning he flourishes and grows up like grass,
In the evening he is cut down and withers.
    So teach us to number our days,
    That we may get us a heart of wisdom.
Mark the man of integrity, and behold the upright,
For there is a future for the man of peace.

—Psalms
(SABBATH PRAYER BOOK)

Man is brought to the dust;
To dust must man return.
A thousand years are
A day that has passed

DEATH

As a watch in the night.
Men are consigned to sleep;
Like grass, we are fresh
In the morning, in the morning
We sprout, blossom forth;
In the evening we wither and fade.
Our days decline
And end as a sigh;
Destined for seventy,
With strength for eighty,
Most of them toil and travail,
Soon they pass as we fail.

Let us, then, value our days,
Hallowing each with grace
As a trust bestowed upon men,
Acquiring a heart full of wisdom
And love for the living of earth.
Through all the days though we suffer
And all the years though we sorrow,
Rejoice and be glad alway,
For the precious gift give thanks:
Live for the good each day.

—An adaptation of Psalm 90
(EMIL WEITZNER)

It is the same at the end as it was in the beginning.
We come out of the womb of the mother to open our eyes, and we
return to the grave with our eyes closed.
The world that gave us forth in magnificent motherhood, receives
us back to her disconsolate bosom.
The world is the rejoicing mother and the grieving woman, giving
birth and suffering the death of all her beloved offspring.

Mankind is one when as infants they are held to the breast.
Mankind is one when as corpses they are given back to the flames
and the dust.
If we would learn it, mankind is also one during the few years of
breath we call life.
When will we live as one humanity, even as we are now born one,
and die one?

—From *This World, My Home*
KENNETH L. PATTON

Men have a terrible tendency to institutionalize life. Fear of life,
born from their own willful estrangement from it, makes men build
fortresses to hold what they have chosen to select from life. Instead
of striving to make permanent the passing forms and shapes of
meaning it would be more creative if men entrusted themselves to
the natural processes of change and so refused to become ensnared
in surface patterns. Man cannot bend life to his own narrow will.

—From *The Seed and the Sower*
LAURENS VAN DER POST

The dead are not dead if we have loved them truly. In our own
lives we give them immortality.

Let us arise and take up the work they have left unfinished,
and preserve the treasures they have won, and round out the cir-
cuit of their being to the fullness of an ampler orbit in our own.

—FELIX ADLER

DEATH

To our friends and loved ones we shall give the most worthy honour and tribute, if we never say nor remember that they are dead, but contrariwise that they have lived.

That hereby the brotherly force and flow of their action and work may be carried over the gulfs of death and made immortal in the true and healthy life which they worthily had and used.

—W. K. CLIFFORD

Leaves should not fall in early summer. Winter should not follow on the heels of spring, yet, when they do, man can and must still speak for life. For there is no answer to death but to live vigorously and beautifully. We give respect and dignity to the one we mourn only when we respect and dignify life and move towards its richest fulfillment.

—ANGUS H. MAC LEAN

Time cannot break the bird's wing from the bird.
Bird and wing together
Go down, one feather.

No thing that ever flew,
Not the lark, not you,
Can die as others do.

—To a Young Poet
EDNA ST. VINCENT MILLAY

GREAT OCCASIONS

The sunlicht still on me, you row'd in clood,
We look upon each ither noo like hills
Across a valley. I'm nae mair your son.
It is my mind, nae son o'yours, that looks,
And the great darkness o'your death comes up
And equals it across the way.
A livin' man upon a deid man thinks
And ony sma'er thocht's impossible.

—At My Father's Grave
HUGH MAC DIARMID

His laughter was better than birds in the morning: his smile
Turned the edge of the wind: his memory
Disarms death and charms the surly grave.
Early he went to bed, too early we
Saw his light put out: yet we could not grieve
More than a little while,
For he lives in the earth around us, laughs from the sky.

—From a selection by
C. DAY LEWIS

Although it is premature death that is most tragic, the final parting signified by death is bound to bring shock and sorrow whenever
the ties of love and friendship are involved. Those who feel deeply

262

will grieve deeply. No philosophy or religion ever taught can prevent this wholly natural reaction of the human heart.

Yet whatever relationships and enterprises death may break in upon, we can feel sure that those who have passed on are finally and eternally at peace. And whatever length of time we have had a friend, we always remain grateful for his having lived and for our having known him in the full richness of his personality.

Nothing now can detract from the joy and beauty that we shared with ——————; nothing can possibly affect the happiness and depth of experience that he himself knew. What has been, has been—forever. The past, with all its meanings, is sacred and secure. Our love for him and his love for us, his friends and family, cannot be altered by time or circumstance.

We rejoice that —————— was and still is part of our lives. His influence endures in the unending consequences flowing from his character and deeds; it endures in our own acts and thoughts. We shall remember him as a living, vital presence. And that memory will bring refreshment to our hearts and strengthen us in times of trouble. These are reflections that we treasure; for there can never be too much friendship in the world, too much human warmth and affection.

—Meditation
CORLISS LAMONT

When we are very young Death seems a dreadful thing, not to be dwelt upon; when it comes into the mind it is hurriedly thrust out again. But life is one long process of getting tired, as Samuel Butler said, and midway of the process we cease to regard Death as the fantastical figure in the morality play and come to think of him as a grave and sweet companion, whose hand we shall not shrink from when it is laid upon our arm. And if it is spring when we go with others to a graveside, the birth in death that is all about us, tempers the sadness of the hour. The green of the turf is deepening, life is coursing through the stark limbs of the trees; if there come a flow of rain, each drop means life to a seed that waits the moisture. It is a kindly earth to which the loved friend is committed—the great mother who was never far [away].

—From *The East Window*
BERT LESTON TAYLOR

It is Nature's way to affirm life through death. She has decreed death for all the higher forms of life in order that life may rise to greater heights. Instead of retaining indefinitely the same instruments for the evolutionary upsurge, she discards them at a certain stage and produces new and more vigorous ones. We die to make room for newborn and lustier vitality. Generation after generation of youths and maidens, men and women, have their chance to taste the joys of living and to make their own particular contribution to the never-ending human adventure. Such is the meaning of death.

—From *Man Against Death*
CORLISS LAMONT

A man's basic and essential faith is faith in himself, in the validity of the dreams he has had in his greatest moments, and in his ability to meet proudly and bravely both whatever life may bring to him and death at its end.

—ROBERT KILLAM

DEATH

The mountains, and the lonely death at last
Upon the lonely mountains: O strong friend!
The wandering over, and the labour passed,
      Thou art indeed at rest,
      Earth gave thee of her best,
      That labour and this end.

Earth was thy mother, and her true son thou:
Earth called thee to a knowledge of her ways,
Upon the great hills, up the great streams: now
      Upon earth's kindly breast
      Thou art indeed at rest:
      Thou, and thine arduous days.

Fare thee well, O strong heart! The tranquil night
Looks calmly on thee: and the sun pours down
His glory over thee, O heart of might!
      Earth gives thee perfect rest:
      Earth, whom thy swift feet pressed:
      Earth, whom the vast stars crown.

—To a Traveller
LIONEL JOHNSON

Though man, the fiery element, sink like fire
With winter on the world, and go out black,
He flames again, a new light leaping higher,
A human warmth that drives the winter back.

His is the burning, variously bright,
Now tall as love is tall, now low as shame,

GREAT OCCASIONS

That breaks earth's shadow with a human light,
Himself the fuel and ash, himself the flame.

—From *The Fiery Element*
JOHN HOLMES

A late lark twitters from the quiet skies,
   and from the west,
Where the sun, his day's work ended,
   Lingers as in content,
There falls on the old gray city
   An influence luminous and serene,
   A shining peace.

The smoke ascends in a rosy and golden haze.
The spires shine and are changed.
In the valley shadows rise.
The lark sings on.
   The sun
Closing his benediction,
   Sinks, and the darkening air
Thrills with a sense of the triumphant night.
   Night, with her train of stars
   And her great gift of sleep.
So be my passing!
My task accomplished and the long day done,
   My wages taken, and in my heart
   Some late lark singing,
Let me be gathered to the quiet west,
   The sundown splendid and serene,
     Death.

—*Margaritae Sorori*
WILLIAM E. HENLEY

DEATH

Happy the man, and happy he alone,
He, who can call today his own:
He who, secure within, can say,
Tomorrow do thy worst, for I have liv'd today.
Be fair or foul, or rain or shine,
The joys I have possess'd, in spite of fate, are mine.
Not Heaven itself upon the past has power,
But what has been, has been, and I have had my hour.

—HORACE
(tr. JOHN DRYDEN)

The people I respect most behave as if they were immortal and as if society was eternal. Both assumptions are false: both of them must be accepted as true if we are to go on eating and working and loving, and are to keep open a few breathing holes for the human spirit.

—From *Two Cheers for Democracy*
E. M. FORSTER

I had not taken the first step in knowledge;
I had not learned to let go with the hands,
As still I have not learned to let go with the heart,
And have no wish to with the heart—nor need,

GREAT OCCASIONS

That I can see. The mind—is not the heart.
I may yet live, as I know others live,
To wish in vain to let go with the mind—
Of cares, at night, to sleep; but nothing tells me
That I need learn to let go with the heart.

—From *Wild Grapes*
ROBERT FROST

Death is an essential part of this ceaseless process of growth and
change and decay which characterizes all life. Though its random
blow may bring bitter loss to individuals, or though, with equal
disregard, it may postpone too long the welcome surcease from
pain and weakness which it alone can bring, it is nevertheless the
friend and not the enemy of the continuous on-going of life upon
this planet.

The universe has its darker aspects which bid us move with
circumspection, but they are more like over-shadowing warnings
against carelessness than like threats to our well-being. In the
measure in which we have learned to meet the conditions which
it imposes upon all living things, we find it friendly to the life with
which earth overflows, else life would disappear.

—From *The Religion of an Inquiring Mind*
HENRY WILDER FOOTE

And if he die? He for an hour has been
Alive, aware of what it is to be.
The high majestic hills, the shining sea,
He has looked upon, and meadows golden-green.

DEATH

The stars in all their glory he has seen.
Love he has felt. This poor dust that is he
Has stirred with pulse of inward liberty,
And touched the extremes of hope, and all between.
Can the small pain of death-beds, can the sting
Of parting from the accustomed haunts of earth,
Make him forget the bounty of his birth
And cancel out his grateful wondering
That he has known exultance and the worth
Of being himself a song the dark powers sing?

—From *Tumultuous Shore*
ARTHUR FICKE

Let us be thankful that our sorrow lives in us as an indestructible
force, only changing in form, as forces do, and passing from pain
to sympathy. To have suffered much is like knowing many lan-
guages. Thou hast learned to understand all.

—From *Adam Bede*
GEORGE ELIOT

We tell of life, we take it by the hands
We look into its eyes and it returns our look
And if this which makes us drunk is a magnet, we know it
And if this which gives us pain is bad, we have felt it
We tell of life, we go ahead
And say farewell to its birds, which are migrating

—From a selection by
ODYSSEUS ELYTIS
(tr. E. KEELEY and P. SHERRARD)

Ego integrity is the acceptance of one's one and only life cycle as something that had to be and that, by necessity, permitted of no substitutions: it thus means a new, a different love of one's parents. It is a comradeship with the ordering ways of distant times and different pursuits, as expressed in the simple products and sayings of such times and pursuits. Although aware of the relativity of all the various life styles which have given meaning to human striving, the possessor of integrity is ready to defend the dignity of his own life style against all physical and economic threats. For he knows that an individual life is the accidental coincidence of but one life cycle with but one segment of history; and that for him all human integrity stands or falls with the one style of integrity of which he partakes. The style of integrity developed by his culture or civilization thus becomes the "patrimony of his soul," the seal of his moral paternity of himself. Before this final solution, death loses its sting.

—From *Childhood and Society*
ERIK H. ERIKSON

For the first sharp pangs there is no comfort; whatever goodness may surround us, darkness and silence still hang about our pain. But slowly, the clinging companionship with the dead is linked with our living affections and duties, and we begin to feel our sorrow as a solemn initiation, preparing us for that sense of loving, pitying fellowship with the fullest human lot, which, I think, no one who has tasted it will deny to be the chief blessedness of our life. And especially to know what the last parting is, seems needful to give the utmost sanctity of tenderness to our relations with each other.

—From her *Letters*
GEORGE ELIOT

DEATH

We grow accustomed to the Dark—
When Light is put away—
As when the Neighbor holds the Lamp
To witness her Goodbye—

A Moment—We uncertain step
For newness of the night—
Then—fit our Vision to the Dark—
And meet the Road—erect—

And so of larger—Darknesses—
Those Evenings of the Brain—
When not a Moon disclose a sign—
Or Star—come out—within—

The Bravest—grope a little—
And sometimes hit a Tree
Directly in the Forehead—
But as they learn to see—

Either the Darkness alters—
Or something in the sight
Adjusts itself to Midnight—
And Life steps almost straight.

—EMILY DICKINSON

Take death for granted. It is a good thing. The world could not move on without it. Live with that particular reckoning behind you. You will grow old much more cheerfully, if you are willing to die when the time comes.

—A. POWELL DAVIES

GREAT OCCASIONS

Pass to thy Rendezvous of Light,
Pangless except for us—
Who slowly ford the Mystery
Which thou hast leaped across!

—EMILY DICKINSON

We commit the body of our beloved to the keeping of Mother
Earth which bears us all. We are glad that he lived, that we saw
his face, knew his friendship, and walked the way of life with him.
We deeply cherish the memory of his words and deeds and character. We leave our dead in peace. With respect we bid him farewell. In love we remember his companionship, his kindly ways.
And thinking of him in this manner, let us go in quietness of
spirit and live in charity, one with the other.

—ALFRED S. COLE

The only joy I ever found
Was the tread of my feet on forest ground.
The only time my eye could see
Was when it held a flowering tree.
My ear could keep no sound at all,
Until it heard a wild loon call.

DEATH

Chisel my name and mark my birth,
I sleep content with my lover, Earth.

—Epitaph for an Earth Lover
JOSEPH PAYNE BRENNAN

When Chuang Tzu was about to die, his disciples expressed a wish to give him a splendid funeral. But Chuang Tzu said: "With heaven and earth for my coffin and shell; with the sun, moon, and stars as my burial regalia; and with all creation to escort me to the grave—are not my funeral paraphernalia ready to hand?"

—CHUANG TZU
(tr. LIONEL GILES)

As a white candle
In a holy place,
So is the beauty
Of an aged face.

As the spent radiance
Of the winter sun,
So is a woman
With her travail done.

Her brood gone from her,
And her thoughts as still
As the waters
Under a ruined mill.

—The Old Woman
JOSEPH CAMPBELL

GREAT OCCASIONS

In a little while I will be gone from you, my people, and whither I cannot tell. From nowhere we come, into nowhere we go. What is life? It is the flash of a firefly in the night. It is the breath of a buffalo in the wintertime. It is the shadow that runs across the grass and loses itself in the sunset.

—CHIEF CROWFOOT

In death no strange new fate befalls us. In the beginning we lack not life only, but form. Not form only, but spirit. We are blent in the one great featureless, indistinguishable mass. Then a time came when the mass evolved spirit, spirit evolved form, form evolved life. And now life in its turn has evolved death. For not nature only but man's being has its seasons, its sequence of spring and summer, summer and winter. If someone is tired and has gone to lie down, we do not pursue him with shouting and bawling. She whom I have lost has lain down to sleep for a while in the Great Inner Room. To break in upon her rest with the noise of lamentation would but show that I knew nothing of nature's Sovereign law.

—CHUANG TZU

He goes free of the earth.
The sun of his last day sets
clear in the sweetness of his liberty.

DEATH

The earth recovers from his dying,
the hallow of his life remaining
in all his death leaves.

Radiance knows him. Grown lighter
than breath, he is set free
in our remembering. Grown brighter

than vision, he goes dark
into the life of the hill
that holds his peace.

He's hidden among all that is,
and cannot be lost.

—*Elegy for Harry Erdman Perry*
WENDELL BERRY

The laws of life and death are as they should be. The laws of matter and force are as they should be; and if death ends my consciousness, still is death good. I have had life on those terms, and somewhere, somehow, the course of nature is justified. I shall not be imprisoned in that grave where you are to bury my body. I shall be diffused in great Nature, in the soil, in the air, in the sunshine, in the hearts of those who love me, in all the living and flowing currents of the world, though I may never again in my entirety be embodied in a single human being. My elements and my forces go back into the original sources out of which they came, and these sources are perennial in this vast, wonderful, divine cosmos.

—From *Accepting the Universe*
JOHN BURROUGHS

GREAT OCCASIONS

Time is the root of all this earth;
These creatures, who from Time had birth,
　Within his bosom at the end
Shall sleep; Time hath nor enemy nor friend.

All we in one long caravan
Are journeying since the world began;
　We know not whither, but we know
Time guideth at the front, and all must go.

Like as the wind upon the field
Bows every herb, and all must yield,
　So we beneath Time's passing breath
Bow each in turn,—why tears for birth or death?

　　　　　　　　—Time
　　　　　　　　BHARTRIHARI
　　　　　　　　(tr. PAUL ELMER MORE)

When Death to either shall come,—
　I pray it be first to me,—
Be happy as ever at home,
　If so, as I wish, it be.

Possess thy heart, my own;
　And sing to the child on thy knee,
Or read to thyself alone
　The songs that I made for thee.

　　　　　　　　—ROBERT BRIDGES

DEATH

This small, unseeing figure looked,
    And, powerless, stood up.
She could not feel but still took hold,
    And thirstless drank her cup.

The power and the right to guess
    A purpose in it all
Belong to those who helped her stand
    And later saw her fall,

And if their probing finds no more
    Than fingers and a face
That searched into the darkness,
    So briefly finding space,

We have kept faith with Nature
    If we say a quiet "Amen,"
And try no more to justify
    The ways of God to man.

—*This Small, Unseeing Figure Looked*
WILLIAM BROWER

An honest man here lies at rest,
The friend of man, the friend of truth,
The friend of age, and guide of youth:
Few hearts like his, with virtue warm'd,
Few heads with knowledge so inform'd;
If there's another world, he lives in bliss;
If there is none, he made the best of this.

—From *Epitaph on a Friend*
ROBERT BURNS

277

GREAT OCCASIONS

Little of brilliance did they write or say.
They bore the battle of living, and were gay.
Little of wealth or fame they left behind.
They were merely honorable, brave, and kind.

—From *The Stricken Average*
WILLIAM ROSE BENÉT

Clouds come from time to time—
and bring to men a chance to rest
from looking at the moon.

—MATSUO BASHŌ
(tr. HAROLD E. HENDERSON)

There will come a supreme moment in which there will be care neither for ourselves nor for others, but a complete abandon, a *sans souci* of unspeakable indifference, and this moment will never be taken from us; time cannot rob us of it but, as far as we are concerned, it will last for ever and ever without flying. So that, even for the most wretched and most guilty, there is a heaven at last where neither moth nor rust doth corrupt and where thieves do not break through and steal. To himself every one is an immortal; he may know that he is going to die, but he can never know that he is dead.

If life is an illusion, then so is death—the greatest of all illusions. If life must not be taken too seriously—then so neither must death.

DEATH

The dead are often just as living to us as the living are, only we cannot get them to believe it. They can come to us, but till we die we cannot go to them. To be dead is to be unable to understand that one is alive.

—From *The Notebooks*
SAMUEL BUTLER

Mourn not our dead this day,
Who poured their lavish youth,
Their hopes and dreams away;
Mourn that men still betray
Their country and their truth.

Mourn honor bought and sold;
Mourn fear and apathy;
Mourn faith turned faint and cold . . .
These dead will not grow old
As we, alas, as we.

The world they died to save
May by God's grace be found
This side the hero's grave;
Break, heart, without a sound,
For here is holy ground.

—*Holy Ground*
JOSEPH AUSLANDER

The future is worth expecting

—HENRY DAVID THOREAU

Who shall be brave enough to sing
When this, the tired leaf ‌as fallen?
  We shall, the living
  For whom death, dark mother,
  Waits in turn beyond the sighing
  Of the wind.
Who shall be brave enough to fling
Remembrance, for the taking,
In the face of happiness bereft?
  We shall, in giving
  Of our love—in garlands and in loyalty—
  To all our bright tomorrows
  And to her.
Who shall be brave enough to ring
The high and holy bells
When all the world's amourn for him
Who's crucified?
  We shall, forgiving
  Naught; no sacredness more deep
  Or holiness more rare than human kinship
  Soft within the heart,
Who then shall mourn? the robins cry,
Who then shall grieve among the willows budding by the brook?
Who then shall bear the tender burden of the mourners passing by?

DEATH

Who shall make sorrow plain?
  And all the rich and fragrant Spring responds
  Wherever grasses nod their eager heads,
  Wherever flowers shake away their winter sleep,
  Wherever water races down from waking hills,
  Wherever heartbeats leap:
Perceive, that sun and chemistry of life
Have now, in me, outwon the frost—
There's nothing lost
  For this was April's child
  Come home again.

—GEORGE C. WHITNEY

Child, though the years divide us till the rust
Of time has tarnished memory, and you, too
Seem but a voice from some forgotten shore,
It shall not be for long. O quiet dust,
Sleep unafraid, I journey on to you,
Though you, indeed, to me may come no more.

—*Epitaph*
JOHN HALL WHEELOCK

Passage, immediate passage! the blood burns in my veins!
Away O soul! hoist instantly the anchor!
Cut the hawsers—haul out—shake out every sail!
Have we not stood here like trees in the ground long enough?
Have we not grovel'd here long enough, eating and drinking
  like mere brutes?

Have we not darken'd and dazed ourselves with books long
  enough?

Sail forth—steer for the deep waters only,
Reckless, O soul, exploring, I with thee, and thou with me,
For we are bound where mariner has not yet dared to go,
And we will risk the ship, ourselves and all.

O my brave soul!
O farther, farther sail!
O daring joy, but safe! are they not all the seas of God?
O farther, farther, farther sail!

—From *Passage to India*
WALT WHITMAN

Darest thou now O soul,
Walk out with me toward the unknown region,
Where neither ground is for the feet nor any path to follow?

No map there, nor guide,
Nor voice sounding, nor touch of human hand,
Nor face with blooming flesh, nor lips, nor eyes, are in that land.

I know it not O soul,
Nor dost thou, all is a blank before us,
All waits undream'd of in that region, that inaccessible land.

Till when the ties loosen,
All but the ties eternal, Time and Space,
Nor darkness, gravitation, sense, nor any bounds bounding us.

Then we burst forth, we float,
In Time and Space O soul, prepared for them,
Equal, equipt at last (O joy! O fruit of all!) them to fulfil O soul.

—*Darest Thou Now O Soul*
WALT WHITMAN

DEATH

Beautiful are the youth whose rich emotions flash and burn, whose lithe bodies filled with energy and grace sway in their happy dance of life; and beautiful likewise are the mature who have learned compassion and patience, charity and wisdom, though they be rarer far than beautiful youth. But most beautiful and most rare is a gracious old age which has drawn from life the skill to take its varied strands: the harsh advance of age, the pang of grief, the passing of dear friends, the loss of strength, and with fresh insight weave them into a rich and gracious pattern all its own. This is the greatest skill of all, to take the bitter with the 'sweet and make it beautiful, to take the whole of life in all its moods, its strengths and weaknesses, and of the whole make one great and celestial harmony.

—ROBERT TERRY WESTON

The closer I move
To death, one man through his sundered hulks,
　　The louder the sun blooms
And the tusked, ramshackling sea exults;
　　And every wave of the way
And gale I tackle, the whole world then,
　　With more triumphant faith
Than ever was since the world was said,
　　Spins its morning of praise,

　　I hear the bouncing hills
Grow larked and greener at berry brown
　　Fall and the dew larks sing
Taller this thunderclap spring, and how

GREAT OCCASIONS

More spanned with angels ride
The mansouled fiery islands! Oh,
    Holier than their eyes,
And my shining men no more alone
    As I sail out to die.

—From *Poem on His Birthday*
DYLAN THOMAS

Awake, my sleeper, to the sun,
A worker in the morning town,
And leave the poppied pickthank where he lies;
The fences of the light are down,
All but the briskest riders thrown,
And worlds hang on the trees.

—From *When Once the Twilight*
Locks No Longer
DYLAN THOMAS

Contemplate all this work of Time,
    The giant labouring in his youth;
    Nor dream of human love and truth,
As dying Nature's earth and lime;

But trust that those we call the dead
    Are breathers of an ampler day
    For ever nobler ends. They say
The solid earth whereon we tread

DEATH

In tracts of fluent heat began,
   And grew to seeming-random forms,
   The seeming prey of cyclic storms,
Till at the last arose the man;

Who throve and branch'd from clime to clime,
   The herald of a higher race,
   And of himself in higher place,
If so he type this work of Time

Within himself, from more to more;
   Or, crown'd with attributes of woe
   Like glories, move his course, and show
That life is not as idle ore,

But, iron dug from central gloom,
   And heated hot with burning fears,
   And dipt in baths of hissing tears,
And batter'd with the shocks of doom

To shape and use. Arise and fly
   The reeling Faun, the sensual feast;
   Move upward, working out the beast,
And let the ape and tiger die.

—From *In Memoriam*
ALFRED TENNYSON

Leave me, O Love, which reachest but to dust;
And thou, my mind, aspire to higher things;
Grow rich in that which never taketh rust;
Whatever fades, but fading pleasures brings.
Draw in thy beams, and humble all thy might
To that sweet yoke, where lasting freedoms be;
Which breaks the clouds, and opens forth the light

GREAT OCCASIONS

That doth both shine, and give us sight to see.
O take fast hold; let that light be thy guide
In this small course which birth draws out to death,
And think how evil becometh him to slide,
Who seeketh heav'n, and comes of heav'nly breath.
Then farewell, world; thy uttermost I see:
Eternal Love, maintain thy Life in me.

—Leave Me, O Love
PHILIP SIDNEY

I learned not to fear infinity,
The far field, the windy cliffs of forever,
The dying of time in the white light of tomorrow,
The wheel turning away from itself,
The sprawl of the wave,
The on-coming water.

What I love is near at hand,
Always, in earth and air.

A man faced with his own immensity
Wakes all the waves, all their loose wandering fire.
The murmur of the absolute, the why
Of being born fails on his naked ears.
His spirit moves like monumental wind
That gentles on a sunny blue plateau.
He is the end of things, the final man.

All finite things reveal infinitude:
The pure serene of memory in one man,—
A ripple widening from a single stone
Winding around the waters of the world.

—From The Far Field
THEODORE ROETHKE

DEATH

I will lift up mine eyes unto the hills from whence cometh my strength. My help cometh from the heavens and the earth, from good neighbors and the spirit of the hills and the valleys which I cannot make my own.

My help cometh from outside and from inside. It waits when I am impatient; it goads me when I hesitate from fear. When I am strong with courage and with faith, the sun and rain shall not smite me by day, and sorrow will not haunt me by night; goodness and mercy shall follow me all the days of my life.

I will lift up mine eyes unto the hills. They will keep my coming in and my going out. They look from afar like the inscrutable heights of the soul.

—*Psalm 121*
(adapted by ROBERT ZOERHEIDE)

Her life was like a splendid day. The morning is fair; noon is radiant; the afternoon is mellow-golden; the sunset is beauteous. Is this the end? No. After sunset, the afterglow, aloft in the Western sky, and below in the heart of memory. And when the afterglow has failed, lo! in the East over the illimitable sea is rising the moon, the clear, pure light of a just soul resting like a benediction upon the world.

Looking on the peace of the night, I asked myself, "In what lies beyond, can any harm come to that clear and aspiring spirit?" And my soul answered, "No." And I asked, "Where shall I find her again?" And my soul answered, "Seek, and ye shall find."

—From *Mater Gloriosa*
LUCIEN PRICE

GREAT OCCASIONS

In a man who goes to the beyond for strength
there is a silence as deep and sure
as the utter silence of a Summer sky
when the winds are quiet.
And it is this silence we need,
it is this silence we cleave to
after the confusion of shallow tongues
preaching the shallow doctrines of the hour.

*   *   *

Everything else shall go to dust: everything—
in the shipwreck of eternal change
he only shall be safe
who has ceased to make of his barbarous will
the center of his life,
but removing to the lap of his imagination
and gathering about him
tender and apprehensive thoughts of his beloveds,
enters the great silence of the moment.

—ANONYMOUS

Life is only possible for all of us because, in our past, there have
been those who put the claims of life itself before all else. Does
it really matter whether the end of life comes from the crab within
or the hyena without? We will have the courage to meet it and give
meaning to the manner of our dying, provided we have not set
a part of ourselves above the wholeness of life.

—From *The Lost World of the Kalahari*
LAURENS VAN DER POST

DEATH

I shall die, but that is all that I shall do for Death.
I hear him leading his horse out of the stall: I hear the clatter on
 the barn-floor.
He is in haste; he has business in Cuba, business in the Balkans,
 many calls to make this morning.
But I will not hold the bridle while he cinches the girth.
And he may mount by himself: I will not give him a leg up.

Though he flick my shoulders with his whip, I will not tell him
 which way the fox ran.
With his hoof on my breast, I will not tell him where the black
 boy hides in the swamp.
I shall die, but that is all that I shall do for Death;
I am not on his pay-roll.

I will not tell him the whereabouts of my friends nor of my enemies
 either.
Though he promise me much, I will not map him the route to any
 man's door.
Am I a spy in the land of the living, that I should deliver men to
 Death?
Brother, the password and the plans of our city are safe with
 me; never through me
Shall you be overcome.

       —Conscientious Objector
       EDNA·ST. VINCENT MILLAY

The blue hen's chickens,* the salt of the world,
lying out there in two hundred fathoms

* The blue hen's chickens—"an old American idiom denoting rare and
wonderful things—or persons."

dead out there: gone out there
lost out there
finished

Gone, gone, the good ones:
the ones who tore a hole in the sky and climbed through it
the ones who could do anything
the big ones, the blue hen's chickens, the salt of the world

—*The Blue Hen's Chickens*
VINCENT MCHUGH

Fairest one, folded in flowers,
Wrapped in the warmth of the hidden heart of the rose,
While the cold hand traces the edges of empty hours,
And the light comes and goes.
Help us, in this final meeting
In a room blessed with the echo of words you have spoken,
Discover our peace in your knowledge that life, though fleeting,
Leaves love unbroken.
Here, among friends, in sorrow,
Let the Living Love in the silence reveal the seed
Of your strength, that we may share it in facing tomorrow,
The time of our need.

—*Quaker Funeral*
W. H. MATCHETT

DEATH

I must warn you that being an individual is a high-priced privilege. Sometimes it demands everything. The person who actually succeeds in being an individual, who does make up his own mind and speaks it, who does achieve self-realization and self-expression may acquire in life a knowledge, a courage, and a faith that will help him when he leaves it, when he *must* go alone.

—ROBERT KILLAM

Heaps of shards and shambles far and wide:
Thus ends the world, thus ends this life of mine.
And I wished but to cry and to resign—
If there were not this stubbornness inside,

This stubbornness to ward off and to fight,
Defiance deep, deep in my heart below,
And then my faith: that what torments me so
Must, must one day turn into light.

—HERMANN HESSE

I have lived; it is your turn now. It is in you that my youth will be prolonged. I pass you my powers. If I feel that you are my successor, I shall resign myself more easily to dying. I hand on my hopes to you.

The knowledge that you are brave and strong enables me to leave life without regret. Take my joy. Let your happiness be to increase that of others. Work and strive and accept no evil that you might change. Keep saying to yourself: "It lies with me." One cannot resign oneself to the evils that come from men without baseness. Cease believing, if you ever believed it, that wisdom consists in resignation; or else cease laying claim to wisdom.

My son, do not accept the life that is offered you by men. Never cease to be convinced that life might be better—your own and others'; not a future life that might console us for the present one and help us to accept its misery, but this one of ours. Do not accept. As soon as you begin to understand that it is not God but man who is responsible for nearly all the ills of life, from that moment you will no longer resign yourself to bearing them.

Do not sacrifice to idols.

—From *The Fruits of the Earth*
ANDRÉ GIDE
(tr. DOROTHY BUSSY)

No more delay! No more delay! O obstructed road! I push on. It is my turn. The sunbeam has signed to me; my desire is the surest of guides and this morning I am in love with the whole world.

A thousand luminous threads cross and intertwine on my heart. Out of thousands of fragile perceptions I weave a miraculous garment. Through it the god laughs and I smile back to the god. Who was it said that great Pan was dead? I saw him through the mist of my breath. My lips are stretched toward him. Was it not he I heard whisper this morning: "What are you waiting for?"

With mind and hand I brush aside all veils, so that there shall be nothing before me but what is brilliant and bare.

—From *The Fruits of the Earth*
ANDRÉ GIDE
(tr. DOROTHY BUSSY)

DEATH

Death, be not proud, though some have callèd thee
Mighty and dreadful, for thou art not so:
For those whom thou think'st thou dost overthrow
Die not, poor Death; nor yet canst thou kill me.
From Rest and Sleep, which but thy pictures be,
Much pleasure, then from thee much more must flow;
And soonest our best men with thee do go—
Rest of their bones and souls' delivery!
Thou'rt slave to Fate, Chance, kings, and desperate men,
And dost with poison, war, and sickness dwell;
And poppy or charms can make us sleep as well
And better than thy stroke. Why swell'st thou then?
    One short sleep past, we wake eternally,
    And Death shall be no more: Death, thou shalt die!

—A Defiance of Death
JOHN DONNE

They gave us tomorrow! The tomorrow they themselves would not return to share. They left us bright dreams! Dreams that for them could not come true. Paid for in blood: the blood of youth with pulse and passion; and in the grief of vainly waiting, who were told that those they loved would not come back. This was the cost: the cost unspeakable! O God, be with us! Make us worthy! Lift us up in high resolve.

—A. POWELL DAVIES

293

Man shares with all complex forms of life the necessity of dying. He inherits this condition as a child of nature. Yet, he is separated from nature by the fact that, so far as we know, only man faces life with the certain knowledge of having to die. This knowledge leads him to the edge of the abyss and threatens all his actions with meaninglessness and partiality.

To avoid this some will seek a bridge that will stretch through the shroud of fog and span the chasm. Others, however, will look deeply into the abyss and will draw back to contemplate the earth on which they stand; they will see the rocks and the mud, with the flowers poking through, they will feel the sensuous warmth of the sun and the cleansing breath of the wind, they will touch the comrades with whom they work, and laugh, and weep, and love. Let such be my lot.

Man is the being who dies, but who in dying can defy death with courage and, standing at the edge of the abyss, can affirm those things which gave him life.

—PAUL N. CARNES

We ourselves must, in spite of an indifferent universe, keep alive the fire of our own intelligence and insight. Although the universe cares not particularly about our mortality and our ideals, we must care for them. Upon our shoulders is being carried the ark of life through the wilderness. All the virtues, all there is of goodness, kindliness, courtesy, is of our own creation, and we must sustain them; otherwise they will go out of existence into darkness, as a star goes out. Apart from us, they are not. They are children born to humanity in its climb out of the valley of brutality, and we humans must give them color and zest.

We can be builders of a beautiful home for mankind on this temporary earth. We can be crusaders for human loveliness, for after all we are life's pilgrims out of the infinite and bound for a port unknown. We are really more than businessmen, housewives, lawyers, mechanics, laborers, physicians. These are the things that keep us busy. We are also priests and prophets who carry the torch of life in "the proud procession of eternal things." We have come out of the darkness and bleakness of eternity as dreamers, lovers, creators, haters, despisers, companions to forest ferns, seabirds, and evening stars—all joined together by a universe that travels onward into the unknown.

—From *The Universe of Humanism*
EARL F. COOK

The soul that loves and works will need no praise;
But, fed with sunlight and with morning breath,
Will make our common days eternal days,
And fearless greet the mild and gracious death.

—W. M. W. CALL

We have gathered here at this time and in this place to pay our tribute of affection and respect. May these moments together be filled with memories of a mutual friend and loved one, who only such a short time ago walked the way with us, blessing us with his presence and departing, leaving us saddened but uplifted in spirit because of the many memories and the quality of his living. Poet, singer, and writer alike have looked squarely into the face of this greatest of life's mysteries, and all through the ages have sung their messages and songs of faith and courage.

GREAT OCCASIONS

In an hour like this, nothing can take the place of the out-stretched hands of human sympathy and understanding, the spoken or the silent assurance given by friends—"We have walked this way of sorrow also in times past and tasted its bitterness and sense of loss. We stand ready to help you through your valley of sorrow until that time comes when you emerge again into the light, and to continually assure you that you do not walk alone."

—ALFRED S. COLE

Come, Death, old captain! Time to put to sea!
   Up anchor! Earth grows dull. Let us be gone.
Though black as ink both wave and heaven be,
   Deep in the hearts you know, the light shines on.

Pour us your poison's comfort. For—so hot
   The fire beats on our brains—we will pursue
Through the abyss—Hell, Heaven, it matters not—
   Of the Unknown, the quest of what is *New*.

—From *The Voyage*
CHARLES BAUDELAIRE
(tr. F. L. LUCAS)

Being
One who never turned his back but marched breast forward,
   Never doubted clouds would break,
Never dreamed, though right were worsted, wrong
      would triumph,

DEATH

Held we fall to rise, are baffled to fight better,
  Sleep to wake.

No, at noonday in the bustle of man's work-time
  Greet the unseen with a cheer!
Bid him forward, breast and back as either should be,
"Strive and thrive!" cry "Speed,—fight on, fare ever
    There as here!"

—*Epilogue to Asolando*
ROBERT BROWNING

For day is stone and night is stone
Save she has made them bright,
Now she knows all that may be known
Of day and night.

Courage like hers we have from her,
Strength to be straight and brave,
And noble memories that recur
And heal and save.

—From *Perpetual Light*
WILLIAM ROSE BENÉT

Where are the shattering horns of Nineveh,
where the armies which marched through Babylon's gates,
against what enemy?
Where are the graves of the conquerors and the conquered?

297

GREAT OCCASIONS

Like ships the nations pass over the seas of time—
to what destination?
To perish and leave behind as jetsam
a few broken doors, tablets, statues.
And they all wanted to go on forever.
O let us so live
that we go out laughing
to have been here, to have loved each other,
to have wanted nothing as long as we lay together.
Let us wake up with joy on this earth
which is full of dead nations and perished races.
Let's scatter the big names with a light hand into the air
like ashes.

—*Being Here*
WALTER BAUER
(tr. CHRISTOPHER MIDDLETON)

What the grave says, the nest denies

—THEODORE ROETHKE

Do not weep for me,
This is not my true country,
I have lived banish'd from my true country,
I now go back there,
I have returned to the celestial sphere
Where every one goes in his turn.

—From *Salut Au Monde*
WALT WHITMAN

What do you think has become of the young and old men?
And what do you think has become of the women and children?

They are alive and well somewhere,
The smallest sprout shows there is really no death,
And if ever there was it led forward life, and does not wait at the
    end to arrest it,
And ceas'd the moment life appear'd.

299

GREAT OCCASIONS

All goes outward and outward, nothing collapses,
And to die is different from what any one supposed, and luckier.

—From *Song of Myself*
WALT WHITMAN

If all came but to ashes of dung,
If maggots and rats ended us, then Alarum! for we are betray'd,
Then indeed suspicion of death.

Do you suspect death? if I were to suspect death I should die now,
Do you think I could walk pleasantly and well-suited toward
annihilation?

Pleasantly and well-suited I walk,
Whither I walk I cannot define, but I know it is good,
The whole universe indicates that it is good,
The past and the present indicate that it is good.

How beautiful and perfect are the animals!
How perfect the earth, and the minutest thing upon it!
What is called good is perfect, and what is called bad is just as
perfect,
The vegetables and minerals are all perfect, and the imponderable
fluids perfect;
Slowly and surely they have pass'd on to this, and slowly and
surely they yet pass on.

I swear I think now that every thing without exception has an
eternal soul!
The trees have, rooted in the ground; the weeds of the sea have!
the animals!
I swear I think there is nothing but immortality!
That the exquisite scheme is for it, and the nebulous float is for
it, and the cohering is for it!

DEATH

And all preparation is for it—and the identity is for it—and life and materials are altogether for it!

—*To Think of Time*
WALT WHITMAN

I planted a ripe seed, and it split, and where it had been a green sprout appeared; but the seed disintegrated.

The green sprout grew, a thing of beauty, sent down roots, sent out leaves, budded, flowered, bore fruit, decayed and was itself a withered thing. I could not even keep the ripe seed.

Each in its time had its own peculiar beauty. All things change; nothing remains the same.

So, each in its time, each life in its every moment—the baby, the child, the youth, the lover, the parent, the aged—is at its ultimate state in each moment and passes on.

Pluck this moment as you would a precious flower; share it as if it were love, and let it go. Beauty and wonder lie all about you even now; they too, even as you, are never final, but always in process of being and becoming. Take, then, each moment as the perfect gift of life, knowing that you shall no more be able to hold it as it is than what is already past.

Even as you let go, another and yet different moment comes . . .

—From a selection by
ROBERT T. WESTON

GREAT OCCASIONS

They shall have stars at elbow and foot;
Though they go mad they shall be sane,
Though they sink through the sea they shall rise again;
Though lovers be lost love shall not;
And death shall have no dominion.

Faith in their hands shall snap in two,
And the unicorn evils run them through;
Split all ends up they shan't crack;
And death shall have no dominion.

Though they be mad and dead as nails,
Heads of the characters hammer through daisies;
Break in the sun till the sun breaks down,
And death shall have no dominion.

—From *And Death Shall Have No Dominion*
DYLAN THOMAS

I am attired for the future so, as the sun setting presumes all men at leisure and in contemplative mood,—and am thankful that it is thus presented blank and indistinct. It still o'ertops my hope. My future deeds bestir themselves within me and move grandly towards a consummation, as ships go down the Thames. A steady onward motion I feel in me, as still as that, or like some vast, snowy cloud, whose shadow first is seen across the fields. It is the material of all things loose and set afloat that makes my sea.

—*Journal, February 27, 1841*
HENRY DAVID THOREAU

DEATH

What fills the heart of man
Is not that his life must fade,
But that out of his dark there can
A light like a rose be made,
That seeing a snow-flake fall
His heart is lifted up,
That hearing a meadow-lark call
For a moment he will stop
To rejoice in the musical air
To delight in the fertile earth
And the flourishing everywhere
Of spring and spring's rebirth.
And never a woman or man
Walked through their quickening hours
But found for some brief span
An intervale of flowers,
Where love for a man or a woman
So captured the heart's beat
That they and all things human
Danced on rapturous feet.
And though, for each man, love dies,
And the rose has flowered in vain,
The rose to his children's eyes
Will flower again, again,
Will flower again out of shadow
To make the brief heart sing,
And the meadow-lark from the meadow
Will call again in spring.

—From *An Act of Life*
THEODORE SPENCER

Spirit has nothing to do with infinity. Infinity is something physical
and ambiguous; there is no scale in it and no center. The depths

303

of the human heart are finite, and they are dark only to ignorance. Deep and dark as a soul may be when you look down into it from outside, it is something perfectly natural; and the same understanding that can unearth our suppressed young passions, and dispel our stubborn bad habits, can show us where our true good lies. Nature has marked out the path for us beforehand; there are snares in it, but also primroses, and it leads to peace.

—GEORGE SANTAYANA

The dark has its own light.
A son has many fathers.
Stand by a slow stream:
Hear the sigh of what is.
Be a pleased rock
On a plain day.
Waking's
Kissing.
Yes.

—From *O, Thou Opening, O*
THEODORE ROETHKE

Sleep? Eternal rest? But is it that which we desire for our dead? For the old, perhaps; or for those who have fulfilled a life purpose. But what of those who were frustrated; what of those who were splendidly aflame with the fire of living; what of those cut off in the blossom of their powers with all their best work undone?

DEATH

What could we wish them better than another life in which to do it? Then how if that life be our own?

—From *Litany for All Souls*
LUCIEN PRICE

Ride, ride through the day,
Ride through the moonlight,
Ride, ride through the night,
For far in the distance burns the fire,
For someone who has waited long.

I rode all through the day,
I rode through the moonlight,
I rode all through the night
To the fire in the distance burning
And beside the fire found
He who had waited for so long.

—From *The Seed and the Sower*
LAURENS VAN DER POST

The rugged old Norsemen spoke of death as *Heimgang*—home-going. So the snow-flowers go home when they melt and flow to the sea, and the rock-ferns, after unrolling their fronds to the light and beautifying the rocks, roll them up close again in the autumn and blend with the soil. Myriads of rejoicing living creatures, daily, hourly, perhaps every moment sink into death's arms, dust to dust, spirit to spirit—waited on, watched over, noticed only by their

Maker, each arriving at its own Heaven-dealt destiny. All the
merry dwellers of the trees and streams, and the myriad swarms
of the air, called into life by the sunbeam of a summer morning,
go home through death, wings folded perhaps in the last red rays
of sunset of the day they were first tried. Trees towering in the sky,
braving storms of centuries, flowers turning faces to the light for a
single day or hour, having enjoyed their share of life's feast—all
alike pass on and away under the law of death and love. Yet all
are our brothers and they enjoy life as we do, share Heaven's
blessings with us, die and are buried in hallowed ground, come
with us out of eternity and return into eternity. "Our lives are
rounded with a sleep."

—JOHN MUIR

Shall hearts that beat no base retreat
   In youth's magnanimous years—
Ignoble hold it, if discreet
   When interest tames to fears;
Shall spirits that worship light
   Perfidious deem its sacred glow,
   Recant, and trudge where worldlings go,
Conform and own them right?

Shall Time with creeping influence cold
   Unnerve and cow? the heart
Pine for the heartless ones enrolled
   With palterers of the mart?
Shall faith abjure her skies,
   Or pale probation blench her down
   To shrink from Truth so still, so lone
Mid loud gregarious lies?

Each burning boat in Caesar's rear,
   Flames—No return through me!

DEATH

So put the torch to ties though dear,
   If ties but tempters be.
Nor cringe if come the night:
   Walk through the cloud to meet the pall,
   Though light forsake thee, never fall
From fealty to light.

—The Enthusiast
HERMAN MELVILLE

Now we face a paradox: on the one hand nothing in the world is more precious than one single human person; on the other hand nothing in the world is more squandered, more exposed to all kinds of dangers, than the human being—and this condition must be. What is the meaning of this paradox? It is perfectly clear. We have here a sign that man knows very well that death is not an end, but a beginning. He knows very well, in the secret depths of his own being, that he can run all risks, spend his life and scatter his possessions here below, because he is immortal. The chant of the Christian liturgy before the body of the deceased is significant: Life is changed, life is not taken away.

—From The Immortality of Man
JACQUES MARITAIN

I have always loved this solitary hill,
This hedge as well, which takes so large a share
Of the far-flung horizon from my view;

307

GREAT OCCASIONS

But seated here, in contemplation lost,
My thought discovers vaster space beyond,
Supernal silence and unfathomed peace;
Almost I am afraid; then, since I hear
The murmur of the wind among the leaves,
I match that infinite calm unto this sound
And with my mind embrace eternity,
The vivid, speaking present and dead past;
In such immensity my spirit drowns,
And sweet to me is shipwreck in this sea.

—*Infinity*
GIACOMO LEOPARDI
(tr. LORNA DE' LUCCHI)

The universe is deathless,
Is deathless because, having no finite self,
It stays infinite.
A sound man by not advancing himself
Stays the further ahead of himself,
By not confining himself to himself
Sustains himself outside himself:
By never being an end in himself
He endlessly becomes himself.

—LAO-TSE
(tr. WITTER BYNNER)

DEATH

We leave the here below
And build beyond instead.
The land of the Great Yes

—PAUL KLEE

Here we are, you and I, and the millions of men and animals about us: the innumerable atoms which make our bodies, blown as it were by mysterious processes together, so that there has happened, just now, for every one of us, the wonder of wonders, we have come to life. And here we stand, our senses, our keen intellects, our infinite desires, our nerves quivering to the touch of joy or pain: beacons of brief fire, burning between two unexplored eternities.

To be is a wonderful thing. It is a miracle itself enough to stagger the mind, should we ever really contemplate it. It is to sense within us the creative power of life, of growth, of being. It is to take the world that is given us into our own hands and to climb the mountain of excellence. It is to know the higher levels of experience not only in our full powers but also in suffering. It is to understand, to know, to appreciate, to feel, to think, to wonder, to roll back the darkness and despair by faith and courage. It is to glimpse the new morning. It is the renewal of life.

—ROBERT KILLAM

The world we know is always passing, and yet it is always the same. Our lives and loves are temporal affairs and yet how great

309

a thing is living! Man is a pilgrim born into a kind of wilderness no metropolis will ever populate. The heart is a lone stranger on this journey. Each man treads a path in solitude—through the evil, the tragedy, the heartbreak, the sunrise, the accomplishment, the thrill—and beyond and oft times in the most difficult part of it, a green and pleasant path that has a kind of tomorrow in it. Nothing is ever of itself fully contained and sufficient; it relates to the elements we have come from. For in our living clay bloom the hopes that give courage to the soul.

—From *Impassioned Clay*
RALPH N. HELVERSON

Sweet day, so cool, so calm, so bright,
The bridall of the earth and skie:
The dew shall weep thy fall to night;
  For thou must die.

Sweet rose, whose hue angrie and brave
Bids the rash gazer wipe his eye:
Thy root is ever in its grave,
  And thou must die.

Sweet spring, full of sweet dayes and roses,
A box where sweets compacted lie;
My musick shows ye have your closes,
  And all must die.

Onlly a sweet and vertuous soul,
Like season'd timber, never gives;
But though the whole world turn to coal,
  Then chiefly lives.

—*Vertue*
GEORGE HERBERT

DEATH

You shall not get the better of me, sadness! Through lamentations and sobs, I can hear the sweet sounds of singing. The words are my own invention and they bring courage to my heart when it begins to fail me. I fill that song with your name, friend, and with an appeal to those undaunted hearts who will answer it.

Up! Up then, bowed heads! Look up, eyes bent down toward the grave! Look up! Not to the empty heavens, but to the earth's horizon. Wherever your steps lead you, friend, let your hope bear you on, regenerate, valiant, ready to leave these places of the dead. Let no love of the past hold you back. Hasten forward to the future.

> —From *The Fruits of the Earth*
> ANDRÉ GIDE
> (tr. DOROTHY BUSSY)

> He is that fallen lance that lies as hurled,
> That lies unlifted now, come dew, come rust,
> But still lies pointed as it plowed the dust.
> If we who sight along it round the world,
> See nothing worthy to have been its mark,
> It is because like men we look too near,
> Forgetting that as fitted to the sphere,
> Our missiles always make too short an arc.
> They fall, they rip the grass, they intersect
> The curve of earth, and striking, break their own;
> They make us cringe for metal-point on stone.
> But this we know, the obstacle that checked
> And tripped the body, shot the spirit on
> Further than target ever showed or shone.

> —*A Soldier*
> ROBERT FROST

GREAT OCCASIONS

Old servant Death, with solving rite,
Pours finite into infinite.
Wilt thou freeze love's tidal flow,
Whose streams through Nature circling go?
Nail the wild star to its track
On the half-climbed Zodiac?
Light is light which radiates,
Blood is blood which circulates,
Life is life which generates,
And many-seeming life is one,—
Wilt thou transfix and make it none?
Its onward force too starkly pent
In figure, bone and lineament?
Hearts are dust, heart's loves remain;
Heart's love will meet thee again.

—From *Threnody*
RALPH WALDO EMERSON

The sun set, but set not his hope:
Stars rose; his faith was earlier up:
Fixed on the enormous galaxy,
Deeper and older seemed his eye;
And matched his sufferance sublime
The taciturnity of time.
He spoke, and words more soft than rain
Brought the Age of Gold again:
His action won such reverence sweet
As hid all measure of the feat.

—*Character*
RALPH WALDO EMERSON

DEATH

The world we know is passing: all things grow strange;
all but the stout heart's courage;
all but the undiminished lustre of an ancient dream—
which we shall dream again as men have dreamed before us,
pilgrims forever of a world forever new.

And what we loved and lost
we lose to find how great a thing
is loving
and the power of it to make a dream come true.

For us, there is no haven of refuge;
for us, there is the wilderness, wild and trackless,
where we shall build a road and sing a song.

But after us there is the Promised Land,
strong from our sorrows and shining from our joys,
our gift to those who follow us
along the road we build
singing our song.

—A. POWELL DAVIES

Superiority to Fate
Is difficult to gain
'Tis not conferred of Any
But possible to earn

A pittance at a time
Until to Her surprise
The Soul with strict economy
Subsist till Paradise.

—EMILY DICKINSON

GREAT OCCASIONS

This World is not Conclusion.
A Species stands beyond—
Invisible, as Music—
But positive, as Sound—
It beckons, and it baffles—
Philosophy—don't know—
And through a Riddle, at the last—
Sagacity, must go—
To guess it, puzzles scholars—
To gain it, Men have borne
Contempt of Generations
And Crucifixion, shown—
Faith slips—and laughs, and rallies—
Blushes, if any see—
Plucks at a twig of Evidence—
And asks a Vane, the way—
Much Gesture, from the Pulpit—
Strong Hallelujahs roll—
Narcotics cannot still the Tooth
That nibbles at the soul—

—EMILY DICKINSON

life is more true than reason will deceive
(more secret or than madness did reveal)
deeper is life than lose:higher than have
—but beauty is more each than living's all

multiplied with infinity sans if
the mightiest meditations of mankind

DEATH

cancelled are by one merely opening leaf
(beyond whose nearness there is no beyond)

or does some littler bird than eyes can learn
look up to silence and completely sing?
futures are obsolete;pasts are unborn
(here less than nothing's more than everything)

death,as men call him,ends what they call men
—but beauty is more now than dying's when

> *—life is more true than reason will deceive*
> E. E. CUMMINGS

A hush of peace—a soundless calm descends;
The struggle of distress, and fierce impatience ends;
Mute music soothes my breast—unuttered harmony,
That I could never dream till Earth was lost to me.

Then dawns the Invisible; the Unseen its truth reveals;
My outward sense is gone, my inward essence feels:
Its wings are almost free—its home, its harbor found,
Measuring the gulf, it stoops and dates the final
bound.

> —From *The Prisoner*
> EMILY BRONTË

Now, like withdrawing music
Where pillared aisles implore,

GREAT OCCASIONS

You are a vanished choir,
A soft-closed door.

Victorious voices blended
Fade, and I kneel still-hearted.
Sudden my life is ended.
We have parted.

Lost in the vault's vast splendor
My ghost goes rising, thinning.
Can heartbreak be an end, or
Some strange beginning?

—*The Adoration*
WILLIAM ROSE BENÉT

Absence becomes the greatest presence

—MAY SARTON

O my collapsed brother,
the body
does bring us
down
     The images
have to be
contradicted
        The metamorphoses
are to be
undone
The stick
and the ear
are to be no more than
they are: the cedar
and the lebanon
of this impossible
life.
I give you no visit
to your mother.
What you have left us
is what you did
It is enough

317

GREAT OCCASIONS

It is what we
praise
I take back
the stick.
I open my hand
to throw dirt
into your grave
I praise you
who watched the riding
on the horse's back
It was your glory to know
that we must mount
O that the Earth
had to be given to you
this way!

O friend, rest
in the false
peace

Let us who live
try

—From *The Death of Europe*
CHARLES OLSON

Death alone can bring us affection's true summary. Who can tell a man? Only the invisible chemistry of one personality, when it has been made complete, can tell, and know; and then by the wings of love, whose movements reveal us to ourselves in death, life has declared itself eternal, and, knowing the gift of one we loved, we know ourselves a little better. And tomorrow returns the promise of today: a promise made new and sure, honest and comforting, by one we will not see again but never be without, where love and honor have come to stay.

—ROBERT ZOERHEIDE

DEATH

Life burns us up like fire,
And song goes up in flame;
The body returns in ashes
To the ashes whence it came.

Out of things it rises,
And laughs, and loves, and sings;
Slowly it subsides
Into the char of things.

Yet a voice soars above it—
Love is great and strong;
The best of us forever
Escapes, in love and song.

—Song VII
JOHN HALL WHEELOCK

Bury me east or west, when you come I will rise to greet you;
I will rise to greet you with love if you come where I lie
in the south;
If you come to my grave in the north, with love I will rise
to greet you—
And a song on my mouth.

—Song V
JOHN HALL WHEELOCK

GREAT OCCASIONS

Thy soul was like a Star, and dwelt apart;
Thou hadst a voice whose sound was like the sea:
Pure as the naked heavens, majestic, free,
So didst thou travel on life's common way,
In cheerful godliness; and yet thy heart
The lowliest duties on herself did lay.

—From *London 1802*
WILLIAM WORDSWORTH

The fragile network of love that binds together
Spirit and spirit, over the whole earth,
Love—that by the very nature of things
Is doomed, is destined to heartbreak, mortal love,
Which is a form of suffering—here and now,
In its brief moment, yes even in its defeat,
Triumphs over the very nature of things,
And is the only answer, the only atonement,
Redeeming all.

—From *The Part Called Age*
JOHN HALL WHEELOCK

The old inexorable mysteries
Transcend our sorrow; no mere discord jars
That music, which no lesser music mars—
It was enough to have made peace with these:
To have kept high hearts among the galaxies,
Love's faith amid this wilderness of stars.

—From *In This Green Nook*
JOHN HALL WHEELOCK

DEATH

The dead in this war—there they lie, strewing the fields and woods and valleys and battle-fields—the numberless battles, camps, hospitals everywhere—the crop reap'd by the mighty reapers, typhoid, dysentery, inflammations—and blackest and loathsomest of all, the dead and living burial-pits, the prison-pens—the dead, the dead, the dead—*our* dead—somewhere they crawl'd to die, alone, in bushes, low gullies, or on the sides of hills—our young men, once so handsome and so joyous, taken from us—the son from the mother, the husband from the wife, the dear friend from the dear friend—the clusters of camp graves—the single graves left in the woods or by the road-side—the corpses floated down the rivers, and caught and lodged—some lie at the bottom of the sea—the general million—the infinite dead—(the land entire saturated, perfumed with their impalpable ashes' exhalation in Nature's chemistry distill'd, and shall be so forever, in every future grain of wheat and ear of corn, and every flower that grows, and every breath we draw).

—From *Specimen Days*
WALT WHITMAN

How do we take the measure of a man? By inch of waist, or length of leg, or size of shoe or span of arm? Perhaps by all these things, but more: Within the corners of the mind, the broad dimensions of the soul, and precious heritage of the heart.
And so, our task for love and friendship's sake, to capture and make plain the quiet strength of him who was and is our friend.
And in the gentleness that like a wreath about his brow we take to make it ours, we feel the patient virtues of a life well-lived, bequeathed to us.

The mark of such a man, above all else, is honesty. If nothing more than this we learned from him, our lives and all the future of the world would stand assured.

The falsehoods of this world stand shamed and shattered on the rock of truth; the shabby and the pompous and the mean are scattered by the brightness of integrity.

We need such darting wit to pierce the sham of pettiness and strike, with certain aim, the center of an issue; we need to cast aside the artifice more clever but without the stern demand of principle.

We cannot let such honor perish and, if praise from us would less than empty tribute be, we must take up such valiant purpose with the will to bind it to our hearts.

—From a selection by
GEORGE C. WHITNEY

We remember gratefully the courage and faith and love which she manifested to the end.

Neither infirmity nor age availed to break her spirit. Her pride was in the family she reared and in the spirit she instilled in them. She hath taught us that in the midst of trouble and pain one can yet smile, that the abundant life is not of possession of things but of the full spirit; the cheerful fulfillment of duty, the maintenance of faith and love and self-forgetting service; that we should seek our happiness not in what we may get for ourselves but in the spirit we may share with our fellowmen and in the fellowship of that spirit as we find it, whether in the church which she loved, the neighborhood which was warmed by her goodness of heart, or the community of all great souls.

—From *A Cup of Strength*
ROBERT TERRY WESTON

DEATH

We stand today in the presence of unfathomable mystery; with humble hearts we bow before the veil which has fallen between us and one we loved.

Let none fear: for greater than sorrow is love, which endureth through pain and conquereth even grief. Love bindeth all hearts in bonds of fellowship and courage. They who love unselfishly face even the depths with courage, for their strength is the strength of many, and their courage resteth upon the love of friends.

—From *A Cup of Strength*
ROBERT TERRY WESTON

Although he was too proud to die, he *did* die, blind, the most agonizing way but he did not flinch from death & was brave in his pride.

In his innocence, & thinking he was God-hating, he never knew that what he was was: an old kind man in his burning pride.

Now he will not leave my side, though he is dead.

His mother said that as a baby he never cried; nor did he, as an old man; he just cried to his secret wound & his blindness, never aloud.

—DYLAN THOMAS

GREAT OCCASIONS

Time flies,
Suns rise
And shadows fall.
Let time go by.
Love is forever over all.

—FROM AN OLD ENGLISH SUNDIAL
ANONYMOUS

Love, I thought, is stronger than death or the fear of death. Only by it, by love, life holds together and advances.

—From *The Sparrow*
IVAN TURGENEV
(tr. CONSTANCE GARNETT)

When they told us that you had died quietly in your sleep we saw your face and the unbelievable became believable. We saw your face quietly, gladly, generously alive and the believable became bearable. The moment was one for our philosophies to turn to dust, as you forewarned, an ashed dust from which the Phoenix, life, rises, given time, but now waiting the confirmation of your name.

When they told us that you had died, we heard your voice as one hears music, beyond the meaning of the words to the intent. The burdened moment goes beyond explanations, lament, or eloquence, goes to the reaches of the music of your voice and the clarity of your face.

When they told us that you had died afar, we found your presence near, answering to our need, more friend than you could have guessed, more than we ourselves had known.

—ERNEST H. SOMMERFELD

DEATH

There are people who so live that they give to us a quality of human life. They show us what it is to be man at his best in some particular. They cheer us even when our own lives do not dwell on that particular. We who are not composers hear the music and are moved because that music is in us also. We have a talent for recognition. So it is that our lives are enriched in so many ways by so many people.

How fortunate to be one of those who has opportunity for craftsmanship and who uses that opportunity with both love and integrity. For fine craftsmanship comes out of fine men. And every good workman, every artist and craftsman, brings us the gift of form. The dream brought to reality. The word made flesh and sometimes made iron or glass or fabric or wood. How can love speak at all except it speak to us through form? This is love's ultimate gift.

—From a selection by
ERNEST H. SOMMERFELD

Though dwelling here, I still am yours
and you, though there, are mine;
for they, dear husband, whose hearts are joined,
not they whose bodies only join,
are truly joined.

—From the Sanskrit
(tr. DANIEL INGALLS)

GREAT OCCASIONS

Man does not die. Man imagines that it is death he fears; but what he fears is the unforeseen, the explosion. What man fears is himself, not death. There is no death when you meet death. When the body sinks into death, the essence of man is revealed. Man is a knot, a web, a mesh into which relationships are tied. Only these relationships matter. The body is an old crock that nobody will miss. I have never known a man to think of himself when dying. Never.

—From *Flight to Arras*
ANTOINE DE SAINT-EXUPÉRY
(tr. LEWIS GALANTIÈRE)

When a good man dies his friends gather together for many reasons. Life has touched them with a deep grief and they need one another's company for their own comfort. Just to be together, to look in friends' faces and see the common expression of hurt takes away the loneliness of their feeling and draws their hearts together in the blessed healing that men can do for one another.

At such a time the various faiths which sustain us separately come together in a harmony which acts across all creeds and assures us of the permanence of goodness, the inspiration of dedication, the value of a serviceable life.

It is well for us to speak of those qualities which we treasured in our friend, for by speaking of them they somehow become vital and enduring and grow into us so that we take on what was noble and become more noble ourselves.

—WILLIAM B. RICE

DEATH

Throatfuls of life, arms crammed with brilliant days,
the colored years beat strength upon her youth,
pain-bombs exploded her body, joy rocketed in her,
the stranger forests, the books, the bitter times,
preluded college in a sheltered town.
This was my friend of whom I knew the face
the steel-straight intellect, broidered fantastic dreams
the quarrel by the lake
and knew the hopes
                She died.   And must be dead.
and is not dead where memory prevails.

Cut the stone, deepen her name.
Her mother did not know her.
Her friends were not enough, we missed essentials.
Love was enough and its blossoms.   Behind her life
stands a tall flower-tree, around her life
are worked her valid words into her testament
of love and writing and a ring of love.
        Upon what skies are these ambitions written?
        across what field lies scattered the young wish,
        beneath what seas toll all those fallen dreams—?

—From *For Memory*
MURIEL RUKEYSER

They say you have left me, but it is not true.
My eyes are liars, and my reaching hands
Are become traitors when they reach for you.
Only the heart within me understands.

It's true the body you built so long ago,
A house to live in, houses you no more.
Your voice is still, your steps no longer go
About their business, quiet across the floor.

GREAT OCCASIONS

But you and I have lived so long together
We have no further need of sound and sight
And outward touch to recognize each other.
You have long lived within me, like a light.

Still like a light you're there to lead me on
When those who understand not say you're gone.

—DONALD F. ROBINSON

Beneath the canopy of the infinite heavens and in this place of peace, set apart from the world's stresses and griefs, we pray for an understanding of the age-long mystery of death and mystery of life.

Into the friendly earth which has served as a final resting-place of innumerable bodies of those who have lived before us and left the stage, we commit the body of this child, her coming welcomed with ready love, her earthly span so brief, her departure so sudden.

Like a nascent particle she arrived, she flashed across our vision, she was gone, and we are left with but a photographic trace in the clouded chamber of our minds.

But through the eons of time, from which we glean the story of our world, our lives also are but a momentary flash, giving scarcely time to ask: Why are we here and whither bound?

Let us then be not overly concerned with the length of our lives. Let us rather take thought for their quality.

Since it has been given to us to live under the guidance of our own dedication to some noble purpose, may the death of this little one recall us to our own destiny and strengthen us in our loyal commitment to those who remain with us.

328

DEATH

As we sometimes think of her and what she might have become, may we think of ourselves and the kind of lives she would have wished us to live for her.

Thus may her life, though brief, be an eternal influence upon those whom she did not linger to meet.

—ELMO A. ROBINSON

Joy, how far can you go?
  "As far as the shade
  Where my flowers fade;
  In the light, by the light
  For the light was I made."

Grief, how far can you go?
  "As far as the dawn
  Where hope is born.
  That night is mine
  Where no stars shine,
  But I die with the dawn."

Love, how far can you go?
  "Through all light and all shade,
  Past all things made,
  And deep beyond death:
  After these tears
  And failure of breath,
  In other spheres, and other years,—
  Deep beyond, deep beyond, deep beyond death!"

—Limitless
ARCHIBALD RUTLEDGE

GREAT OCCASIONS

When a life has been supremely well lived and brought to a fitting close, it is not a time for mourning. It is a time for rejoicing. And such was the life that has ended.

The common debts of wifehood and motherhood she paid willingly, and more. She bore the children gladly. The endless cares of rearing a brood, the tedious and often unpleasant offices of the sick room, the drudgery of housework, she never shirked. The bearing of these common burdens is, of course, a first condition to self-respect, but out of her abundant zest for life she added the one thing more which transforms the humblest work into an art-form, and that is joy. And yet, well as all this was done, it was only half her work. First she fed her children the bread of the body. That done, she fed them the bread of the spirit.

All the years when as wife and mother she was bearing her share of the universal burden of one generation's rearing of the next, amid all the cares and distractions of household and children, with only the meagerest opportunities, she kept on reading and studying. The beauty of youth is of the body. The beauty of age is of the spirit.

And so in whatsoever place she is, that place is filled with the music of her voice and spirit. Such lives are the strength of the world and the hope of it. Of such is the Kingdom.

—From *Mater Gloriosa*
LUCIEN PRICE

Dwell in thought with the dear departed, continue the communion that you were privileged to have while he was still here on earth. Sadly, we often do not take the time out of the haste and press of daily life to commune with those who have gone. We form unconsciously the habit of silence with regard to them, so that their image in our hearts grows steadily fainter and threatens to disappear. And yet it is quite possible, without the slightest touch of

330

superstition, to hold intercourse with the beloved dead. For whenever there is a movement of our mind toward the outgoings of
another there is real intercourse even though retroactive response
be suspended. They can still benefit us though we can do nothing
for them, except indirectly, by transmitting to others the spiritual
gains received from them.

Thus the light of their countenance will still continue to shine down
upon us, and we will walk, work, and grow in that high light,
sanctifying daily life through the sense of that hallowing presence.

—From a selection by
ALFRED W. MARTIN

He was for children and whisky and flowers
or anything warm. His name was Tim
Warm heart, go find your rest
Death, be good to him

—From *The Pacific Suite #5*
VINCENT MCHUGH

Love is but a promise. I would not for all the world that you
should fall in the depths of inert despair if I died. If love is not an
empty word, a passionate, passive movement, but rather a state of
progression for the soul, you would feel yourself bound to worship
with a renewed enthusiasm all that you found good in me, and all
that I loved, yourself, the Beautiful, the Good, the True.

—From a selection by
GIUSEPPE MAZZINI

We come to this place, that we may give expression to the depth of loneliness and the longing-after-new-life which the death of —————————— has brought upon us.

Thus do we share sights and sounds of loss and comfort, of fear and courage, of bitterness and love.

But especially of love—a love which can triumph over all pain, bringing us again to the font from which all meaning, beauty, and truth doth eternally flow.

—DAVID H. MACPHERSON

Let us have tenderly in our minds and hearts him in whose memory we are gathered here, having in mind the wonder and the mystery of life and death, cherishing his generous impulses and his good deeds in love, remembering the strong and beautiful meanings of his life.

In a world where our most precious goods are perishable, let us resolve to honor the dead by being so good in our living, so kindly, so understanding, so forgiving, so transcendent of pettiness, that in our love for those who remain and who need us and our strength we shall partly make good our loss and in the beauty of our lives erect the noblest monument to our dead.

May we go back to the daily round of our duties, more eager to be helpful and kind, as though in the presence of death itself we had learned to know the deeper meanings of life. Thankful for this fine life, in whose company we walked these short years on earth, may we be better people, now that it has been taken away.

—ROBERT KILLAM

DEATH

He was a worshipper of liberty, a friend of the oppressed. A thousand times I have heard him quote these words: "For Justice all place a temple, and all season, summer." He believed that happiness was the only good, reason was the only torch, justice the only worship, humanity the only religion, and love the only priest. He added to the sum of human joy; and were everyone to whom he did some loving service to bring a blossom to his grave, he would sleep tonight beneath a wilderness of flowers.

—On His Brother
ROBERT G. INGERSOLL

Green be the turf above thee,
Friend of my better days!
None knew thee but to love thee,
None named thee but to praise.

—On His Friend, Joseph Rodman Drake
FITZ-GREENE HALLECK

We have come here this day to commit to the preciousness of memory a life that was mingled with our own, the strength and loveliness of which remain to bless us. Those whom we love do indeed leave us, and when we lose them no spoken words can lessen our grief. But what they were can never leave us. The

333

strength of their presence, the gentleness of their sympathy, the warmth of their love—these are ours always, interfused with our thought and blended with our lives.

Last week this brave and beautiful spirit was caught up into the greater life it had been seeking. And so today we commit her to the joy of memory and the peace of God. And we ask ourselves, what is it that moves the world forward if it be not such lives as hers? The great words that are spoken—truth, justice, love —what would they mean to us if no one ever lived them into life? What would kindness mean if we had never felt it? And sympathy? —what would we know of it if it were just a word? And God?— the greatest word of all? The spirit of God—if we are to find it —must first be found in ourselves and in one another. And we find it best in those whose lives remind us that God's other name is Love.

—From a selection by
A. POWELL DAVIES

Your death will not prevent future wars, will not make the world safe for your children. Your death means no more than if you had died in your bed, full of years and respectability, having begotten a tribe of young. Yet by your courage in tribulation, by your cheerfulness before the dirty devices of this world, you have won the love of those who have watched you. All we remember is your living face, and that we loved you for being of our clay and our spirit.

—From *A Passionate Prodigality*
GUY CHAPMAN

DEATH

Wherever you go now I go with you:
I am the wind—I tousle your hair,
Fling it away from brow and temple,
Back from your cheek and your small ear bare,
Wherever you go now.

I am the sunlight that wakens with you,
I am your shadow along the grass,
In the quickset hedges when you go walking
I dance on the leaves to see you pass
Wherever you go now.

. . .

In autumn that scatters rain on your windows,
In winter that brings the silent snow
To lift long night from earth's laden shoulders,
My step by your side you still may know
Wherever you go now.

Stare in the fire, at the corded moulding
That holds the ash on the fire-back there.
Do you not hear me? I am with you.
My hands are stroking your firelit hair,
And you may rest now.

—From *Wherever You Go Now*
JOHN BUXTON

Time is too slow for those who wait; too swift
for those who fear; too long for those who grieve;
too short for those who rejoice. But for those
who live, Time is Eternity. Hours fly, flowers
die, new days, new ways pass by. Love stays.

—*Inscription on sundial,*
University of Virginia
ANONYMOUS

We must not part, as others do,
With sighs and tears, as we were two,
Though with these outward forms, we part;
We keep each other in our heart.
What search hath found a being, where
I am not, if that thou be there?

True love hath wings, and can as soon
Survey the world, as sun and moon;
And everywhere our triumphs keep
Over absence, which makes others weep:
By which alone a power is given
To live on earth, as they in heaven.

—ANONYMOUS

Woods where the woodthrush forever sings

—*Journal, June 22, 1853*
Henry David Thoreau

In this solemn hour consecrated to our beloved dead, we ponder over the flight of time, the frailty and uncertainty of human life. We ask ourselves: What are we? What is our life? To what purpose our wisdom and knowledge? Wherein is our strength, our power, our fame? Alas, man seems born to trouble, and his years are few and full of travail.

But our great teachers have taught us to penetrate beneath appearances and see the higher worth, the deeper meaning, and the abiding glory of human life.

Implanted in man is the faith to overcome disillusionment and despair, the power to resist evil, the wisdom to use his gifts nobly, and the will to transform chaos and misery into harmony and happiness. When we free the oppressed, feed the hungry, clothe the naked, bring cheer into the lives of those, in distress, when we strive for justice and the coming of the beloved community, we invest our life with high significance.

In this hour sacred to memory, when the past and the future merge, we are grateful for the blessings that have come to us through the love and devotion of our dear ones.

For many of us this hour recalls the memory of beloved parents now removed from their earthly tasks. We are ever mindful of the devotion with which they tended and guided us, the sacrifices they made, the comforts and joys they brought us, the teachings and

337

traditions they sought to impart unto us. They are forever bound to us by undying love.

There are those among us who call to mind a departed husband or wife. They recall the affectionate bonds formed, the faith and understanding, the struggles and hopes, the trials and griefs, the fears and joys they shared together.

There are parents in our midst who mourn a beloved child taken from them in the freshness and vigor of youth, for whom they had planned and hoped, upon whom they lavished care and affection. There are those who recall a sister or brother, now no longer among the living, with whom they grew up in happy fellowship, loyal and devoted companions who shared with them the experience of childhood and youth.

With tender emotions we all recall friends and companions who were dear to us in life and whose friendship and understanding were a constant benediction to us. Though our departed are no longer with us, their memories are forever enshrined in our hearts and their influence abides with us, directing our thoughts and deeds toward the lofty purposes they cherished and for which they strived.

—Sabbath and Festival Prayer Book

Our meeting here today is to celebrate the fullness of life which we saw and loved in the brief days of his years. To say that he would want no show of mourning would be true, but grief does touch us deeply as his swift radiance passes and we are "left darkling." Surely his own eagerness against the adversary Fortune, his refusal to live timidly and hoard his hours should teach us to shake off grief and celebrate life.

To meet him was to find a man who gave no hint of the many battles of his few years. He made no show of sorrow over the several circumstances which would have made a weaker soul long

338

a coward. He could have followed a path of creeping caution, coddled himself, and wheedled a few more days or months out of life, but he could not live limping. The day was too short to waste time with petty anxiety for self.

And so he loved life much and spent it boldly, and he loved friends truly and gave them treasures which increase on recollection. This is what we must strengthen and increase in ourselves, this boldness and loving tenderness, that what had meaning and reality may continue undiminished by time and distance.

To say that a man has died is only to speak half a truth. There is more to us than the portion which is the prisoner of time. Part of us is free to live, to continue its joy and gentle whimsey, to grow deep and everlasting in loving hearts which hold in faithfulness the given love.

A man's voice may be stilled but his good words ever move us to daring adventure and eager sharing. All that came from deep within his heart is secure in the hearts of his loved ones and good friends.

Truly we are grateful for his living and we celebrate his being and stand strong as he would have us.

—WILLIAM B. RICE

What you have given me
Night, nor day,
Nor death, nor time
Can take away.

O most adored,
O my delight,
The day shall hear me,
And the night!

I will make this joy
Upon my lips

GREAT OCCASIONS

Your trumpet
To the Doom's eclipse.

—Song XIV
JOHN HALL WHEELOCK

✳

We are entered here into a House of Memory and Remembrance.
And here, within this House, when we remember a man, it is
more than the man who is remembered. We remember here what
a man was before he was born, and what he is after he has gone;
what we are because of what he was; and what he was because of
what we are.

—THEODORE A. WEBB

✳

The task is never finished, and there's never love enough. Take
then, unto thy heart, and steel thy will that in thy purpose and thy
forthright pledge to him, and memory and all that's yet to come,
that kindly strength may be about us still.

—From a selection by
GEORGE C. WHITNEY

340

This was the citizen articulate. There is a voice that all men hear,
but not all answer, bidding rectitude of deed as well as thought.
Our times are desperate enough, and if there should not live beyond the passing of the one some urgency to grasp the moment
as our own, and speak as conscience bids, we shall have failed
the promise destiny has brought.
This is our native land that stands in need—O may its sons be
strong in justice and in love; O may its daughters bear the
heritage of goodness and of faith.
There is a breadth and spirit knows, and in its vastness flies—
on wings that know no limits—above the walls of creed;
There is a patient dedication to the quietness of truth;
There is responsibility to man, that knows no fear;
There is a rugged and a free determination of the intellect and
heart;
There is a gentle laughter that can turn the cruel word;
There is a hope that keeps men free;
These things he knew; these things we cherish, to pass on, unsul-
lied, as inheritance.

—GEORGE C. WHITNEY

Her loyalty and courage,
　　Thoughtfulness and devotion—
Her friendliness, unselfishness
　　and understanding—
Were rare in one so young—
　　Like a rose that comes into the world full blown
And as the fragrance is born with the rose
　　So was she endowed with a loveliness and sweetness
　　That she shared with all who knew her.

She'll walk with you today and every day
　　You—who loved her much—

341

GREAT OCCASIONS

Her gallant spirit and her love
Are things immortal.

—For Lillian French
RUTH A. WOODMAN

Might it not be that in this great dream of time
In which we live and are the moving figures
There is no greater certitude than this:
That, having met, spoken,
Known each other for a moment,
As somewhere on this earth we were hurled onward
Through the darkness between two points of time,
It is well to be content with this,
To leave each other as we met,
Letting each one go alone to his appointed destination,
Sure of this only, needing only this—
That there will be silence for us all
And silence only,
Nothing but silence,
At the end?

—In Silence
THOMAS WOLFE

The thought of our past years in me doth breed
Perpetual benediction . . .
for those first affections,

DEATH

Those shadowy recollections,
    Which, be they what they may,
Are yet the fountain light of all our day,
Are yet a master light of all our seeing;
    Upholds us, cherish, and have power to make
Our noisy years seem moments in the being
Of the eternal Silence: truths that wake,
    To perish never;
Which neither listlessness, nor mad endeavour,
    Nor Man nor Boy,
Nor all that is at enmity with joy,
Can utterly abolish or destroy!

—From *Ode on Intimations
of Immortality*
WILLIAM WORDSWORTH

You could hurt and you could heal,
You could hide and still reveal,
You were lilies, lilies and steel.

You the near and you the far
Were as lamplight and a star.

I cannot tell them what you were;
Yet, Death, you have not all of her.

No, I, the passionate nondescript,
Have wine your lips have never sipped,

Have wine of her in my heart's blood
Whom I never understood.

You were tender and benign,
Trusting—and all fire divine
And a constellation's sign.

343

GREAT OCCASIONS

You the far and you the near,
You heaven high and heaven here,
You the quest, and closest dear.

Ah, God, you have not all of her,
For still my cause she can prefer
Where she goes, and where You were.

You could weep and you could rise
With the Word clear in your eyes,
With a strength beyond the wise.

Girl and goddess, will and love,
Struggling, battling, winged above
Memories I have memory of!

—The Woman
WILLIAM ROSE BENÉT

What lies beyond the grave remains a mystery not susceptible of proof. Whether death is the end or the beginning, none of us can ever know until we ourselves set upon that road which our friend took. Man's mind has envisioned everything from the shades beyond Styx to ineffable light. Whether individual consciousness survives, or whether, as the Buddhists would have it, the peace of limitless consciousness is unified with limitless will in Nirvana, no good man is ever dead when he is remembered in the minds of those who knew him with the affection we treasure for the memory of our friend. Of this degree of immortality there can be no doubt.

—On Jacob Wirth
WALTER MUIR WHITEHILL

DEATH

And not in grief or regret merely, but rather
With a love that is almost joy I think of them,
Of whom I am part, as they of me, and through whom
I am made more wholly one with pain and the glory,
The heartbreak at the heart of things.

—From *Dear Men and Women*
JOHN HALL WHEELOCK

Too proud to die; broken and blind he died
The darkest way, and did not turn away,
A cold kind man brave in his narrow pride

On that darkest day. Oh, forever may
He lie lightly, at last, on the last, crossed
Hill, under the grass, in love, and there grow

Young among the long flocks, and never lie lost
Or still all the numberless days of his death, though
Above all he longed for his mother's breast

Which was rest and dust, and in the kind ground
The darkest justice of death, blind and unblessed.
Let him find no rest but be fathered and found.

—From *Elegy*
DYLAN THOMAS

There will be stars over the place forever;
Though the house we loved and the street we loved are lost,

GREAT OCCASIONS

Every time the earth circles her orbit
   On the night the autumn equinox is crossed,
Two stars we knew, poised on the peak of midnight
   Will reach their zenith; stillness will be deep;
There will be stars over the place forever,
   There will be stars forever, while we sleep.

—There Will Be Stars
SARA TEASDALE

The monument of death will outlast the memory of the dead. The Pyramids do not tell the tale confided to them. The living fact commemorates itself. Why look in the dark for light? Look in the light rather.

—Journal, August 6, 1841
HENRY DAVID THOREAU

Music, when soft voices die,
Vibrates in the memory;
Odors, when sweet violets sicken,
Live within the sense they quicken.
Rose leaves, when the rose is dead,
Are heaped for the belovèd's bed;
And so thy thoughts, when thou art gone,
Love itself shall slumber on.

—To ———
PERCY BYSSHE SHELLEY

DEATH

Beauty is momentary in the mind—
The fitful tracing of a portal;
But in the flesh it is immortal.

The body dies; the body's beauty lives.
So evenings die, in their green going,
A wave, interminably flowing.
So gardens die, their meek breath scenting
The cowl of winter, done repenting.
So maidens die, to the auroral
Celebration of a maiden's choral.

Susanna's music touched the bawdy strings
Of those white elders; but, escaping,
Left only Death's ironic scraping.
Now, in its immortality, it plays
On the clear viol of her memory,
And makes a constant sacrament of praise.

> —From *Peter Quince*
> *at the Clavier*
> WALLACE STEVENS

As a perfume doth remain
In the folds where it hath lain,
So the thought of you, remaining
Deeply folded in my brain,
Will not leave me: all things leave me:
You remain.

Other thoughts may come and go,
Other moments I may know

That shall waft me, in their going,
As a breath blown to and fro,
Fragrant memories: fragrant memories
Come and go.

Only thoughts of you remain
In my heart where they have lain,
Perfumed thoughts of you, remaining,
A hid sweetness, in my brain.
Others leave me: all things leave me:
You remain.

—Memory
ARTHUR SYMONS

With you a part of me hath passed away;
For in the peopled forest of my mind
A tree made leafless by this wintry wind
Shall never don again its green array.

Chapel and fireside, country road and bay,
Have something of their friendliness resigned;
Another, if I would, I could not find,
And I am grown much older in a day.

But yet I treasure in my memory
Your gift of charity, and young heart's ease,
And the dear honor of your amity;
For these once mine, my life is rich with these.
   And I scarce know which part may greater be,—
   What I keep of you, or you rob from me.

—To W.P. II
GEORGE SANTAYANA

DEATH

So brilliant a moonshine:
if ever I am born again—
a hilltop pine!

—RYŌTA
(tr. HAROLD E. HENDERSON)

When I die! I am certain that I cannot take myself as a physical being into the mystery. This causes some regret for we are so made that we enjoy living with ourselves. We enjoy the music which pleases our ears, the color that touches our eyes, the hills that we have climbed and the work that our muscles and our training have brought into life. Yet in a way we do not leave this for we are part of these sounds and sights and objects and we shall be of them when the stuff of our bodies goes back to its less complex state.

I never was wholly separated from the nature which made me out of itself and my physical dissolution is never a destruction. I am living in a borrowed home which has given me much pleasure as well as pain and I see no sense in trying to pretend that my physical being should be kept in uniqueness. For I am rain and snow and clay and granite and salts and I belong with these things—the physical me.

—WILLIAM B. RICE

Warm summer sun, shine kindly here;
Warm western wind, blow softly here;

GREAT OCCASIONS

Green sod above, lie light, lie light—
Good-night, dear heart, good-night, good-night.

—For his daughter's gravestone
ROBERT RICHARDSON
(adapted by MARK TWAIN)

None but the callous will make little the sorrow of men and women at the death of their beloved.

There is no sure medicine for this ill, and the lover wishes none.

He knows his sorrow as the necessary penalty of the joy of love and possession; the heavier his sorrow, the more has been that which has been taken away.

He who embraces and affirms life willingly invites sorrow as the risk taken in owning the fullness of life and companionship.

We learn to possess our sorrows as the measure of our loves.

We will learn, in this parting, to dwell more constantly with him who is gone, bringing him into ourselves as the companion of our silence and solitude, even as he once was our outward companion.

The poignancy of these days, in deepening us, will draw us closer to him departed, not take him farther from us.

The words we say here will bring no final comfort; the condolences of friends and relatives will not fully heal.

Time will dull the pain and life and business will continue, but even the medicine of time is not sure.

The only final healing is to create our peace within ourselves by possessing our sorrows in our solitude, by possessing our memories, and finding in them strength.

—The Measure of Sorrow
KENNETH L. PATTON

DEATH

A man's life is not bounded by the frontiers of his body nor the days of his breathing; a man is what he does, and his doing goes on after the body's demise.

His was the length of years given by nature to man as his means of being. In those years he began and carried many projects by his labor; now these projects carry forward his meaning in their endurance.

Our neighbors lay upon us a responsibility of love, for we become the custodians of their memory; the portrait of their works and person is in our keeping.

For those who loved this man our fumbling commiserations are unneeded and futile; he is the ultimate source of their consolation, in the enduring rewards and the further outworkings of his labors.

Before their memories of him, before the engendering meaning of his presence, our words are thin and uninformative.

If the irrefragable body and self is no more, yet that which he loved better than himself, giving to it his energies and hours, persists beyond his leavetaking, through those who continue his tasks, in those whose lives have become his continuing existence.

—From *On Immortality*
KENNETH L. PATTON

Blessed are they that mourn for they shall be comforted. Our dead are lost only to be regained. When they lived they came and went, were with us and again were away from us. But when they died they came to lodge with us in our heart of hearts, eternally. When

351

they lived they could be had for cheer or comfort only in this hour or that. But dead, they live in every conscious thought and act of us, the living who hold them in loving memory.

—From *Litany For All Souls*
LUCIEN PRICE

❊

No person can sum up the life of another. Life is too precious to be passed over with mere words which ring empty. Rather, it must remain as it is remembered by those who loved and watched and shared. For such memories are alive, unbound by events of birth or death. And as living memories, we possess the greatest gift one person can give to another.

—CHARLES GAINES

❊

When the rose is faded,
   Memory may still dwell on
Her beauty shadowed,
   And the sweet smell gone.

That vanishing loveliness,
   That burdening breath,
No bond of life hath then
   Nor grief of death.

'Tis the immortal thought
   Whose passion still
Makes of the changing
   The unchangeable.

352

DEATH

Oh, thus thy beauty,
  Loveliest on earth to me,
Dark with no sorrow, shines
  And burns, with Thee.

—When the Rose Is Faded
WALTER DE LA MARE

Slowly receding surf,
tide going down.

A time ago
you taught my eyes to see.

And you are here
alive
within my memory.

No sliding world takes you.

You're here
as sure as sea
        as sun.

I trust this slippery world
because of you.

We're time and tide
and life and love
and linked
with moving stars.

—From *Sound of Silence*
RAYMOND J. BAUGHAN

Out of the white immensities always young

—JAMES M. BARRIE

It was these men and their like who made Athens great. With them, as with few among Greeks, words cannot exaggerate the deeds that they have done. Such an end as we have here seems indeed to show us what a good life is, from its first signs of power to its final consummation. For even where life's previous record showed faults and failures it is just to weigh the last brave hour of devotion against them all. There they wiped out evil with good and did the city more service as soldiers than they did her harm in private life. There no hearts grew faint because they loved riches more than honor; none shirked the issue in the poor man's dream of wealth. All these they put aside to strike a blow for the city. Counting the quest to avenge her honor as the most glorious of all ventures, and leaving Hope, the uncertain goddess, to send them what she would, they faced the foe as they drew near him in the strength of their own manhood; and when the shock of battle came, they chose rather to suffer the uttermost than to win life by weakness. So their memory has escaped the reproaches of men's lips, but they bore instead on their bodies the marks of men's hands, and in a moment of time, at the climax of their lives, were rapt away from a world filled, for their dying eyes, not with terror but with glory.

Such were the men who lie here and such the city that inspired them. We survivors may pray to be spared their bitter hour, but must disdain to meet the foe with a spirit less triumphant. Let us

DEATH

draw strength, not merely from twice-told arguments—how fair and noble a thing it is to show courage in battle—but from the busy spectacle of our great city's life as we have it before us day by day, falling in love with her as we see her, and remembering that all this greatness she owes to men with the fighter's daring, the wise man's understanding of his duty, and the good man's self-discipline in its performance—to men who sacrificed their lives as the best offerings on her behalf. So they gave their bodies to the commonwealth and received each for his own memory, praise that will never die, and with it the grandest of all sepulchres, not that in which their mortal bones are laid, but a home in the minds of men, where their glory remains fresh to stir to speech or action as the occasion comes by. For the whole earth is the sepulchre of famous men; and their story is not graven only on stone over their native earth, but lives on far away, without visible symbol, woven into the stuff of the lives of other men.

—Funeral Oration of Pericles
THUCYDIDES
(tr. A. E. ZIMMERN)

With the immortality of memory from one who was quiet, gentle, and kind, go gently into the days ahead. Use gifts to the full that have been shared before. Remember, that you are a child of the universe and of life, no less than the trees and the stars. May your shortened dreams be made full in use. For this is still a beautiful world.

—ROBERT ZOERHEIDE

GREAT OCCASIONS

It is not we who come to consecrate the dead—we reverently come to receive, if so it may be, some consecration to ourselves and daily work from him.

—From *Specimen Days*
WALT WHITMAN

Thankfulness should be the tenor of this occasion, as we realize how many lives have been touched and tenderly lifted and encouraged, enlightened by the fine mind and patient merit of a Master Teacher. There are teachers and teachers. Some impart only knowledge. From others we learn more than prescribed lessons. We learn kindness and integrity.

Out over the rows of desks, through the thick-paged books, into the receptive minds and spirits of growing boys and girls, our teacher has cast his influence. It far exceeded in importance the specific knowledge he was paid to impart. And today, let us learn from him his final lesson for us: to face each day, however unpromising, with hope and happiness and gratitude.

—THEODORE A. WEBB

Spirit of Life, remove from us all fear,
Walk softly, for thy footsteps are on holy ground.
He sought the laughter of the stars and left
To us a legacy of loveliness and taught us
That the heart of life is in the interplay
Of mind and friendship shared. The world was his

DEATH

And limitless. In seeking
He gave more than anything he found.
Beneath a springtime sky, where cactus shyly shows
Its flower, and grass defies the sun to bind
The desert in its green embrace,
We leave him, to the everlasting grace
Of wild and untamed things and free
That, for his presence timeless,
There will always be
A touch of joy within this tender place.

—GEORGE C. WHITNEY

She lived and died, as we say, obscure. Would she have served her fellowmen better had she been famous? I do not think so. The heavenly fire is as needful on the hearth as in the lighthouse. And once kindled there is no quenching it. It is an irresistible force of life which will find an outlet, if not here, then there. Her life spent itself in a multitude of channels, hidden, unknown, obscure, in humble places, yet none of it has been lost or wasted, for it is these humble places and not the great which count. It is only out of the humble that greatness comes: out of that choir invisible whose music is the gladness of the world, and in that choir she is singing and will sing eternally.

It would be a poor vaunt of life indeed if we were born perfect. A character without faults would be a battle without an enemy. We cannot have brilliant lights without shadow. Such a positive personality is bound to have faults, often grave ones. To speak of her virtues without admitting faults would be a piece of disingenuousness of which she would have been the first to disapprove. No one saw the faults more clearly than she. No one could have lamented them more sincerely. No one could have combatted them more valiantly. In one sort or another, her whole life was

357

a battle and a gradually winning one. But winning or not, the point of the matter is that the battle went on: that she never gave up her efforts at a stern self-discipline. "For the refiner's pot is for silver, and the furnace for gold, but the Lord trieth the heart."

How cold and feeble words are in the presence of such a radiant personality. The artist cannot dip his brush in light. He must be content with painting the shadow of light. Words avail little. The saying is nothing. The doing is all. The utmost words can do is recall a memory of the once-seen splendor, and say: "Such a life has been lived. See ye to it that others are lived in a like spirit."

—From *Mater Gloriosa*
LUCIEN PRICE

Let us not mourn for him, the valiant one,
Who rests beyond the hushed and shadowed sea,
He, who saw visions in the rising sun
Of radiant years to be!

Let us rejoice that he lived and fought
Throughout his life's courageous span
To bear the torch of truth, and that he sought
To help his fellow-man.

Let us not mourn for him, the valiant one,
But guard the faith he held so manfully,
Seeking his visions in the rising sun
Of radiant years to be.

—*Robert M. La Follette*
LUCIA TRENT

DEATH

When I lie down, worn out, other men will stand young and fresh. By the steps that I have cut they will climb; by the stairs I have built, they will mount. They will never know the name of the man who made them. At the clumsy work they will laugh; when the stones roll, they will curse me. But they will mount, and on my work: they will climb, and by my stair! And no man liveth to himself, and no man dieth to himself.

—From *The Story of an African Farm*
OLIVE SCHREINER

He has outsoared the shadow of our night;
Envy and calumny and hate and pain,
And that unrest which men miscall delight,
Can touch him not and torture not again;
From the contagion of the world's slow stain
He is secure, and now can never mourn
A heart grown cold, a head grown gray in vain;

He is made one with Nature; there is heard
His voice in all her music, from the moan
Of thunder, to the song of night's sweet bird;
He is a presence to be felt and known
In darkness and in light . . .

He is a portion of the loveliness
Which once he made more lovely . . .

The splendors of the firmament of time
May be eclipsed, but are extinguished not;
Like stars to their appointed height they climb
And death is a low mist which cannot blot
The brightness it may veil. . . .

The One remains, the many change and pass;
Heaven's light forever shines, Earth's shadows fly;

GREAT OCCASIONS

Life, like a dome of many colored glass,
Stains the white radiance of Eternity,
Until Death tramples it to fragments. . . .

—From *Adonais*
PERCY BYSSHE SHELLEY

Under the wide and starry sky,
Dig the grave and let me lie.
Glad did I live and gladly die,
   And I laid me down with a will.

This be the verse you grave for me:
Here he lies where he longed to be;
Home is the sailor, home from the sea,
   And the hunter home from the hill.

—*Requiem*
ROBERT LOUIS STEVENSON

It is better to lose health like a spendthrift than to waste it like a miser. It is better to live and be done with it, than to die daily in the sickroom. It is not only in finished undertakings that we ought to honor useful labor. A spirit goes out of the man who means execution, which outlives the most untimely ending. All who have meant good work with their whole hearts, have done good work, although they may die before they have the time to sign it. Every heart that has beat strong and cheerfully has left a hopeful impulse behind it in the world, and bettered the tradition of mankind.

And even if death catch people, like an open pitfall, and in mid-career, laying out vast projects, and planning monstrous foundations, flushed with hope, and their mouths full of boastful language, they should be at once tripped up and silenced: is there not something brave and spirited in such a termination? and does not life go down with a better grace, foaming in full body over a precipice, than miserably straggling to an end in sandy deltas? When the Greeks made their fine saying that those whom the gods love die young, I cannot help believing they had this sort of death also in their eye. For surely, at whatever age it overtake the man, this is to die young. Death has not been suffered to take so much as an illusion from his heart. In the hot-fit of life, a-tiptoe on the highest point of being, he passes at a bound on to the other side. The noise of the mallet and chisel is scarcely quenched, the trumpets are hardly done blowing, when, trailing with him clouds of glory, this happy-starred, full-blooded spirit shoots into the spiritual land.

—From *Aes Triplex*
ROBERT LOUIS STEVENSON

I think continually of those who were truly great.
The names of those who in their lives fought for life,
Who wore at their hearts the fire's centre.
Born of the sun, they travelled a short while toward the sun
And left the vivid air signed with their honour.

—From a selection by
STEPHEN SPENDER

GREAT OCCASIONS

These dead are not done
Though they rust in the sun
While we play "Run Life Run"

These dead are not dead
Though we bone them to bed
Yet they hurt in our head

These dead are the strong
They bleed away the wrong
And die the truth along

—To the African Dead
CARL SEABURG

We know nothing of what happened, or where or when it was,
We can imagine very little of the final disastrous hour,
Yet we know one thing; of one thing we are certain,
Just as his own knowledge was always quietly certain.
For if, before the last violence, there was something right to say,
We who knew him, know he was sure to say it;
And if at the last there was anything brave to do,
We who knew him, know it was done by him.

—From *Colleague*
THEODORE SPENCER

Many astounds before, I lost my identity to a pebble;
The minnows love me, and the humped and spitting creatures.

DEATH

I believe! I believe!—
In the sparrow, happy on gravel;
In the winter-wasp, pulsing its wings in the sunlight;
I have been somewhere else; I remember the sea-faced uncles.
I hear, clearly, the heart of another singing,
Lighter than bells,
Softer than water.

Wherefore, O birds and small fish, surround me.
Lave me, ultimate waters.
The dark showed me a face.
My ghosts are all gay.
The light becomes me.

—From Praise to the End
THEODORE ROETHKE

For what we owe to other days,
Before we poisoned him with praise,
May we who shrank to find him weak
Remember that he cannot speak.

For envy that we may recall,
And for our faith before the fall,
May we who are alive be slow '
To tell what we shall never know.

For penance he would not confess,
And for the fateful emptiness
Of early triumph undermined,
May we now venture to be kind.

—Exit
EDWIN ARLINGTON ROBINSON

GREAT OCCASIONS

We to your story, game and smugness, do add
This death, our death. We to the clown commit
The glory given us; we to the further, after-breath
Of fame declare our dividend of fire, our mite
Of trampled ash. We to that cavernous place
You call "our time," commend an anger charged
To rip the face of worlds so simply snuggling in
Above our rotted heads; we to the wily saviors
Send warning, sound a war's depth
That shall be a stop to their stuttering guns,
That shall be a sound which no battle's strut can scare.

We were your only decent war; we were answer, aim.
We were that rooted story, Man's game. We to your bare lands
Lend prestige, dead. We to others' sons spell glory.

—*Tomorrow*
KENNETH PATCHEN

We have lost a fellow worker; he was one of the quiet laborers of the world, taking more than his share of the burden of our common lot, and acquitting his tasks with dignity and skill.

He sought not the honor of the high seat, but the place where the needed tasks were to be done; he was a willing servant, knowing the honor and the reward in being used.

Beneath the convenience of life are men and women who labor while we sleep and play; we forget them at the cost of our own shallowness and ingratitude.

It is from the courageous that we learn courage; from the patience of our companions we are taught patience.

DEATH

Those who accept adversity without self-pity, who stay at their jobs through the good days and the bad days, who quit their responsibilities with diligence, encourage and strengthen us in their example.

If he had been one to spare himself, or to let another do the task he had claimed as his own, he would not have been the man we loved.

He labored long and well; he was a tool of good steel that wore thin and broke at the work it was shaped to do.

He was loved by those with whom he worked, being just in his decisions and loving to see a job well done.

His person was to his family the warmth and surety of their days.

He was one of the foundation stones whose patient strength uphold the building of the world. He was a man.

—For a Worker
KENNETH L. PATTON

❋

Some, in their deaths, stand as symbols of life well lived, who have come to their end full of years and deeds. His going was halted even as he lifted his foot above the threshold of his labors.

Yet he knew the fresh and playful years, and the confident season of young strength and undefeated hopes. He will not suffer the dying of the generations, the ennui of the repeating days, and the crumbling of his vigor and comeliness. All his life was lived in the buoyancy of the young.

What is long and what is short? For a day can be longer than forever, and a year less than the blink of an eyelash when it is gone. Yet the death of the aged seems more easily borne, while the death of a youth is an affront to our need, and we say, "This should not be."

GREAT OCCASIONS

Even for one who has labored long, we are called to receive his tasks at his finishing. But here our charge is yet more deeply laid, for we must take upon us the work he was still preparing to do, and add to our retinue the unspent purposes of his dream.

—For a Youth
KENNETH L. PATTON

What else are we, we the living, but the Spring sowing of those myriad mortals whose Autumn harvest-time was death? From them we had our bodies, we are heirs to their passions and desires, from them are sprung many of our deepest thoughts and highest aspirations; they have bequeathed to us their sacred flame, and we shall do the same for others. We the living are enjoined to fulfill the lives of the dead. On a vast scale this is what all existence is— fulfillment by us who are, of all those who have been.

The vanished life can never be fulfilled, the vacant place never supplied? In the flesh, no; in the specific talent, no; in the spirit, yes. What else are our hospitals, colleges, museums, laboratories, libraries, and a host of other memorial foundations than the souls of those long since dead in the flesh living on in the spirit of beneficent action, and that vital spark of dedicated memory can burn as nobly in the breasts of obscure persons whose monument to their beloved dead is not an institution but an heroic life. The force which animates this continuing immortality of all souls is love, for it is because they loved us and we them that they live on in us. And this is true not alone of persons, but also of peoples, of centuries, and of whole epochs: they are reincarnate in us, and men of genius who have left their souls on earth are only this universal process raised in excelsis.

—From Litany for All Souls
LUCIEN PRICE

366

DEATH

Death in our time has changed its face. Never before has life meant so little or death so much. For most of those lives which war is reaping are the wrong ones—young men, forced to die for a way of life which they have not had time to enjoy. We are losing our best.

The only spirit which is worthy of their broken bodies, of their shattered minds, their blasted hopes, their thwarted talents, is the prevention of this frightful and recurrent scourge, the Plague of the First-Born. Who dare say that we who live are worthy of those who have died? Who dare say that our society is yet worthy of such human sacrifices? On us who survive is laid the solemn accountability to build a world-order that can live guiltless of innocent blood.

—From *Litany for All Souls*
LUCIEN PRICE

Young men whom we have known
   We bear in mind to-day,
Men who have never grown
   Like us so stiff and grey.

Young men of merry speech,
   Seeming of obscure lives.
Yet it is due to each
   That liberty survives.

The little we can pay
   To them who kept us free
We offer them to-day,
   Gratitude, memory.

—*1949*
EDWARD PLUNKETT

GREAT OCCASIONS

And Death itself, to her, was but
The wider opening of the door
That had been opening, more and more,
Through all her life, and ne'er was shut.

—And never shall be shut. She left
The door ajar for you and me,
And, looking after her, we see
The glory shining through the cleft.

—From *E.A., November 6, 1900*
JOHN OXENHAM

With pencil and palette hitherto
  You made your art high Nature's paragon;
  Nay more, from Nature her own prize you won
  Making what she made more fair to view.
Now that your learned hand with labor new
  Of pen and ink a worthier work hath done,
  What erst you lacked, what still remained her own,
  The power of giving life, is gained for you.
If men in any age with Nature vied
  In beauteous workmanship, they had to yield
  When to the fated end years brought their name.
You, reilluming memories that died,
  In spite of Time and Nature have revealed
  For them and for yourself eternal fame.

—*Sonnet XI*
MICHELANGELO
(tr. J. A. SYMONDS)

DEATH

We were young. We have died. Remember us.
We have done what we could but until it is finished
  it is not done.
We have given our lives, but until it is finished no
  one can know what our lives gave.
Our deaths are not ours; they are yours; they will
  mean what you make them.
Whether our lives and our deaths were for peace and
  a new hope or for nothing we cannot say; it is
  you who must say this.
We leave you our deaths. Give them meaning.
We were young. We have died. Remember us.

—From *The Young Dead Soldiers*
ARCHIBALD MAC LEISH

Happy the dead!
If we do ill,
They will not know we lied.
Happy the dead!
If we do well,
Their death is justified.

—*Consolation in Time of War*
LEWIS MUMFORD

GREAT OCCASIONS

There are gallant and fortunate deaths. I have seen death bring a wonderfully brilliant career, and that in its flower, to such a splendid end that in my opinion the dead man's ambitions and courageous designs had nothing so lofty about them as their interruption. He arrived where he aspired to without going there, more grandly and gloriously than he had desired or hoped. And by his fall he went beyond the power and the fame to which he had aspired by his career.

—From *The Essays*
MICHEL DE MONTAIGNE
(tr. DONALD M. FRAME)

All worlds lie folded in the arms of Power:
The live seed lifts its earth-load and is free:
The filmy moon lifts the eternal sea.
Armed with this might, the insect builds its tower
And lives its little epoch of an hour.
Man's giant thought, in ever-daring flight,
Explores the universe, the Ancient Night,
And finds infinity even in a flower.

But there is something that is greater still,
The strength that slumbers in Heroic Will.
Yes, there is something greater than them all:
It is the high translunar strength that streams
Downward on man at some imperious call,
And gives him power to perish for his dreams.

—*Power*
EDWIN MARKHAM

DEATH

Refresh thy heart, where heart can ache no more,
    What is it we deplore?
He leaves behind him, freed from griefs and years,
    Far worthier things than tears,
The love of friends without a single foe:
    Unequalled lot below!
His gentle soul, his goodness, these are thine;
    For these dost thou repine?
He may have left the lowly walks of men;
    Left them he has; what then?
Are not his footsteps followed by the eyes
    Of all the good and wise?
Tho' the warm day is over, yet they seek
    Upon the lofty peak
Of his pure mind the roseate light that glows
    O'er death's perennial snows.

—To the Sister of Elia
WALTER SAVAGE LANDOR

No power can die that ever wrought for Truth;
    Thereby a law of Nature it became,
And lives unwithered in its blithesome youth,
    When he who called it forth is but a name.

Therefore I cannot think thee wholly gone;
    The better part of thee is with us still;
Thy soul its hampering clay aside hath thrown,
    And only freer wrestles with the Ill.

Thou livest in the life of all good things;
    What words thou spak'st for Freedom shall not die;
Thou sleepest not, for now thy Love hath wings
    To soar where hence thy Hope could hardly fly.

—From Elegy for William Ellery Channing
JAMES RUSSELL LOWELL

371

GREAT OCCASIONS

Praised be youth forever,
　　Lay wreaths where they lie—
They died in their finest hour
　　Who choose this hour to die.

—From *Praised Be Youth*
SCHARMEL IRIS

Someone grabbed three dreams of twisted youth and shook
Them into nothing.
Someone blew the ripe, rich horn of the angel of death
And he laughed at its throat and winked in its face
But it took him along nevertheless.
Nevertheless they had a funeral.
Nevertheless four bands played glowingly out of tune.
Nevertheless fifty fellow orphans lined up in the rain
To take their hats off;
To kiss him goodbye across the bridge of night.
Nevertheless the polished senator with the bulging
Toupee spoke rapturously about sacrifice,
About glory,
About the wonderful horsemen who would come on
Strong white chargers and lead him home.
Nevertheless the grass grew brighter in the morning
Sun of dying twilight;
The birds who knew death intimately;
Who pipe organ music over stilted meadows wept in
Their beaks.
They remembered him for he pulled their tails and
Made them cry.

DEATH

Someone put a bullet through his orphan brain
Somewhere in the smiling eastern evening.

—From *Play the Last March Slowly*
RICHARD DAVIDSON

He was willing to perish in the using. He sacrificed the future to
the present, was willing to spend and be spent; felt himself to belong to the day he lived in, and had too much to do than that he
should be careful for fame. He used every day, hour, and minute;
he lived to the latest moment, and his character appeared in the
last moments with the same firm control as in the day of strength.

—*Journal, June 1861*
(*On the death of Theodore Parker*)
RALPH WALDO EMERSON

We learn in the Retreating
How vast an one
Was recently among us—
A Perished Sun

Endear in the departure
How doubly more
Than all the Golden presence
It was—before—

—EMILY DICKINSON

GREAT OCCASIONS

Men of character are the conscience of the society to which they belong. As one lamp lights another, nor grows less, so nobleness enkindleth nobleness. No life can be pure in its purpose and strong in its strife, and all life not be purer and stronger thereby.

Great men are the fire pillars in this dark pilgrimage of mankind: they stand as everlasting witnesses of what has been, prophetic tokens of what may still be, the revealed, embodied possibilities of human nature. Great deeds cannot die; they with the sun and moon renew their light for ever, blessing those that look on them.

Ethics are thought not to satisfy affection. But all the religion we have is the ethics of one or another holy person; as soon as character appears, be sure love will, and veneration, and anecdotes and fables about him, and delight of good men and women in him.

> More sweet than odours caught by him who sails,
> Near spicy shores of Araby the blest,
> A thousand times more exquisitely sweet,
> The freight of holy feeling which we meet,
> In thoughtful moments, wafted by the gales
> From fields where good men walk, or bowers
>   wherein they rest.

—Arranged by STANTON COIT

> Brief, brave, and glorious was his young career,—
>   His mourners were two hosts, his friends and foes;
>   And fitly may the stranger lingering here
>   Pray for his gallant spirit's bright repose;
>   For he was freedom's champion, one of those,

DEATH

The few in number, who had not o'erstept
The charter to chastise which she bestows
On such as wield her weapons; he had kept
The whiteness of his soul, and thus men o'er him wept.

—From *Childe Harold*
GEORGE BYRON

Our roll of honour is long, but it holds no nobler figure. He will stand to those of us who are left as an incarnation of the spirit of the land he loved. . . . He loved his youth, and his youth has become eternal. Debonair and brilliant and brave, he is now part of that immortal England which knows not age or weariness or defeat.

—From *Pilgrim's Way*
JOHN BUCHAN

The sun bursts through in unlooked-for directions

—WALT WHITMAN

We are gathered here in memory of ——————. Looking across a span of human years, as we do now, is like looking out on the expanse of the seas. The years roll by with the regularity of the waves, reminding each one that life is a long voyage into the known and the unknown. Along the way there will be tenderness and trouble, long labor and short sweetness, ideals, defeats and sickness. There will be sparkling joy and cavernous sorrow, the molehill of misunderstanding against the mountain of true accord, puddles of regret beside the beautiful lakes of love and companionship.

Each one of us is somewhere along the way of this great journey. Birth is but awakening, life is dedication, death is the change which comes between where we are and where the universe is; when that change is filled with the understanding that envelops all differences and distinctions, life has renewed itself with that from which it cannot be removed. And we are forever at home on a vast but friendly shore.

—ROBERT ZOERHEIDE

376

DEATH

This day before dawn I ascended a hill and look'd at the crowded heaven,
And I said to my spirit *When we become the enfolders of those orbs, and the pleasure and knowledge of every thing in them, shall we be fill'd and satisfied then?*
And my spirit said *No, we but level that lift to pass and continue beyond.*

—From *Song of Myself*
WALT WHITMAN

I too pass from the night,
I stay a while away O night, but I return to you again and love you.

Why should I be afraid to trust myself to you?
I am not afraid, I have been well brought forward by you,
I love the rich running day, but I do not desert her in whom I lay so long,
I know not how I came of you and I know not where I go with you, but I know I came well and shall go well.

I will stop only a time with the night, and rise betimes,
I will duly pass the day O my mother, and duly return to you.

—From *The Sleepers*
WALT WHITMAN

I depart as air, I shake my white locks at the runaway sun,
I effuse my flesh in eddies, and drift it in lacy jags.

GREAT OCCASIONS

I bequeath myself to the dirt to grow from the grass I love,
If you want me again look for me under your boot-soles.

You will hardly know who I am or what I mean,
But I shall be good health to you nevertheless,
And filter and fibre your blood.

Failing to fetch me at first keep encouraged,
Missing me one place search another,
I stop somewhere waiting for you.

—From *Song of Myself*
WALT WHITMAN

Nothing is ever really lost, or can be lost,
No birth, identity, form—no object of the world,
Nor life, nor force, nor any visible thing;
Appearance must not foil, nor shifted sphere confuse
    thy brain.
Ample are time and space—ample the fields of Nature.
The body, sluggish, aged, cold—the embers left from
    earlier fires,
The light in the eye grown dim, shall duly flame again;
The sun now low in the west rises for mornings and for
    noons continual;
To frozen clods ever the spring's invisible law returns,
With grass and flowers and summer fruits and corn.

—*Continuities*
WALT WHITMAN

DEATH

So I pass, a little time vocal, visible, contrary,
Afterward a melodious echo, passionately bent for,
   (death making me really undying,)
The best of me then when no longer visible, for
   toward that I have been incessantly preparing.

Remember my words, I may again return,
I love you, I depart from materials,
I am as one disembodied, triumphant, dead.

               —From *So Long*
               WALT WHITMAN

Thou hast left behind
Powers that will work for thee; air, earth, and skies;
There's not a breathing of the common wind
That will forget thee; thou hast great allies;
Thy friends are exultations, agonies,
And love, and Man's unconquerable mind.

          —From *Sonnet to Toussaint L'Ouverture*
          WILLIAM WORDSWORTH

Something has spoken to me in the night,
Burning the tapers of the waning year;
Something has spoken in the night,
And told me I shall die, I know not where.

Saying:
"To lose the earth you know, for greater knowing;

GREAT OCCASIONS

To lose the life you have, for greater life;
To leave the friends you loved, for greater loving;
To find a land more kind than home, more large than earth—

"—Whereon the pillars of this earth are founded,
Toward which the conscience of the world is tending—
A wind is rising, and the rivers flow."

—*Toward Which*
THOMAS WOLFE

Time and space, succession and extension, are merely accidental conditions of thought. The imagination can transcend them, and move in a free sphere of ideal existence. Things, also, are in their essence what we choose to make them. A thing *is,* according to the mode in which one looks at it. "Where others," says Blake, "see but the Dawn coming over the hill, I see the Sons of God shouting for joy."

—From *De Profundis*
OSCAR WILDE

O Fire, my brother, I sing victory to you.
    You are the bright red image of fearful freedom.
    You swing your arms in the sky, you sweep your impetuous fingers across the harp-string, your dance music is beautiful.

    When my days are ended and the gates are opened you will burn to ashes this cordage of hands and feet.

DEATH

My body will be one with you, my heart will be caught in the whirls of your frenzy, and the burning heat that was my life will flash up and mingle itself in your flame.

—Fruit-Gathering, No. 40
RABINDRANATH TAGORE

We shall see but little way if we require to understand what we see. How few things can a man measure with the tape of his understanding! How many greater things might he be seeing in the meanwhile!

—Journal, February 14, 1851
HENRY DAVID THOREAU

We live in an old chaos of the sun,
Or old dependency of day and night,
Or island solitude, unsponsored, free,
Of that wide water, inescapable.
Deer walk upon our mountains, and the quail
Whistle about us their spontaneous cries;
Sweet berries ripen in the wilderness;
And in the isolation of the sky,
At evening, casual flocks of pigeons make
Ambiguous undulations as they sink
Downward to darkness, on extended wings.

—From Sunday Morning
WALLACE STEVENS

GREAT OCCASIONS

To suffer woes which Hope thinks infinite;
To forgive wrongs darker than death or night;
   To defy Power, which seems omnipotent;
To love and bear; to hope till Hope creates
From its own wreck the thing it contemplates;
   Neither to change, nor falter, nor repent;—
This, like thy glory, Titan, is to be
Good, great and joyous, beautiful and free;
This is alone Life, Joy, Empire, and Victory!

—From *Prometheus Unbound*
PERCY BYSSHE SHELLEY

We meet to celebrate the life of ——————. This is a moment to remember again the wise and the good who have blessed our lives. This is a time to be grateful for men who seek for liberty and justice for all, to be thankful for men who labor for a world in which every man may reach his highest good. This is a day to know again that when a man of stature enters our midst, life has given more than death can take away.

—ERNEST H. SOMMERFELD

After the laboring birth, the clean stripped hull
Glides down the ways and is gently set free,

DEATH

The landlocked, launched; the cramped made bountiful—
Oh, grave great moment when ships take the sea!
Alone now in my life, no longer child,
This hour and its flood of mystery,
Where death and love are wholly reconciled,
Launches the ship of all my history.
Accomplished now is the last struggling birth,
I have slipped out from the embracing shore
Nor look for comfort to maternal earth.
I shall not be a daughter any more,
But through this final parting, all stripped down,
Launched on the tide of love, go out full grown.

—My Father's Death
MAY SARTON

To enter the great continent of death
Through the hard or easy door
Is to surrender the country of breath
For the kingdom of the core

—CARL SEABURG

I give back to the earth what the earth gave,
All to the furrow, nothing to the grave,
The candle's out, the spirit's vigil spent;
Sight may not follow where the vision went.

I leave you but the sound of many a word
In mocking echoes haply overheard,

GREAT OCCASIONS

I sang to heaven. My exile made me free,
From world to world, from all worlds carried me.

Spared by the Furies, for the Fates were kind,
I paced the pillared cloisters of the mind;
All times my present, everywhere my place,
Nor fear, nor hope, nor envy saw my face.

Blow what winds would, the ancient truth was mine,
And friendship mellowed in the flush of wine,
And heavenly laughter, shaking from its wings
Atoms of light and tears for mortal things.

To trembling harmonies of field and cloud,
Of flesh and spirit was my worship vowed.
Let form, let music, let all-quickening air
Fulfill in beauty my imperfect prayer.

—*The Poet's Testament*
GEORGE SANTAYANA

Down gently down
Softer to sleep
Than bed of night
From the littleness
Go

Down gently down
Wider to wake
Than need of sun
Into the greatness
Go

—From *Destinations*
CARL SEABURG

DEATH

The sun! The sun! And all we can become!
And the time ripe for running to the moon!
In the long fields, I leave my father's eye;
And shake the secrets from my deepest bones;
My spirit rises with the rising wind;
I'm thick with leaves and tender as a dove,
I take the liberties a short life permits—
I seek my own meekness;
I recover my tenderness by long looking.
By midnight I love everything alive.
Who took the darkness from the air?
I'm wet with another life.
Yea, I have gone and stayed.

—From *What Can I Tell My Bones?*
THEODORE ROETHKE

Affirmation of life *and* affirmation of death reveal themselves as one. To concede the one without the other is a restriction that finally excludes all infinity. Death is our reverted, our unilluminated, side of life; we must try to achieve the greatest possible consciousness of our existence, which is at home in both of these unlimited provinces, which is inexhaustibly nourished out of both. The true form of life extends through both regions, the blood of the mightiest circulation pulses through both: there is neither a here nor a beyond, but only the great unity, in which those beings that surpass us are at home.

—*Notes to Duino Elegies*
RAINER MARIA RILKE
(tr. LEISHMAN and SPENDER)

385

GREAT OCCASIONS

How much every one of our deepest raptures makes itself independent of duration and passage; indeed, they stand vertically upon the courses of life, just as death, too, stands vertically upon them; they have more in common with death than with all the aims and movements of our vitality. Only from the side of death (when death is not accepted as extinction, but imagined as an altogether surpassing intensity), only from the side of death is it possible to do justice to love.

—From *Duino Elegies*
RAINER MARIA RILKE
(tr. LEISHMAN and SPENDER)

Up into the boundless skies
Rose whirlwinds of gray patches:
Flocks of pigeons taking off
In fast flight from dovecotes.

Just as if some drowsy soul
Bestirred himself to set loose
Birds with wishes for long life
To overtake the wedding.

For life, too, is only an instant,
Only the dissolving of ourselves
In the selves of all others
As if bestowing a gift—

Only the wedding noises
Soaring in through a window;

DEATH

Only a song, only a dream,
Only a gray pigeon.

—From *Wedding*
BORIS PASTERNAK
(tr. BERNARD GUILBERT GUERNEY)

There is a mysterious coming and going between the quick and the dead. Those who know most about it say the least. For they are fearful lest revealing it in speech should break the contact.

But even in this life there is a life not of the body. What is this magic by which our thoughts can be leagues away, wide over land, far over sea, companioning the absent? What are the enchanted carpets of Arabian tales compared to this inner wizardry of the human imagination? What is this magic by which we can whisk ourselves back across the years to the hour and the place and the person; to the moonlit garden, the scent of roses, the touch of hands? The memory can be as fresh and as vivid as the reality. What, then, is the meaning which speaks in this—that the reality fades, but that the memory endures?

In such moments, when our minds are free and ranging the illimitable universe without and within, our bodies are seen in public places. People speak to us and we reply. But we are not there. Who shall say where we are? Who, then, shall say where our dead are? Why are they not all about us always? What if we let their souls go laughing and singing in our own, and ours in theirs, eternally?

—From *Litany for All Souls*
LUCIEN PRICE

GREAT OCCASIONS

The hour of love and dignity and peace
Is surely not dead.
With more splendor than these sombre lives
The gates within us
Open on the brilliant gardens of the sun.
Then do these inscrutable soldiers rise upward,
Nourished and flowering
On the battleslopes of the Unseen. For Victory,
Unlike the sponsored madness in these undertakings,
Is not diminished by what is mortal; but on its peaks
Grows until the dark caverns are alight
With the ordained radiance of all mankind.

—From *The Climate of War*
KENNETH PATCHEN

Nothing is lost; be still; the universe is honest.
Time, like the sea, gives all back in the end,
But only in its own way, on its own conditions:
Empires as grains of sand, forests as coal,
Mountains as pebbles. Be still, be still, I say;
You were never the water, only a wave;
Not substance, but a form substance assumed.

—From *The Exegesis*
ELDER OLSON

Not one death but many,
not accumulation but change, the feed-back proves, the
    feed-back is the law

DEATH

Into the same river no man steps twice
When fire dies air dies
No one remains, or is, one

—From *In Cold Hell, In Thicket*
CHARLES OLSON

All things pass, all things return; eternally turns the wheel of Being. All things die, all things blossom again, eternal is the year of Being. All things break, all things are joined anew; eternally the house of Being builds itself the same. All things part, all things welcome each other again; eternally the ring of Being abides by itself. In each Now, Being begins; round each Here turns the sphere of There. The center is everywhere. Bent is the path of eternity.

—From *Thus Spake Zarathustra*
FRIEDRICH NIETZSCHE

The day on which a great man dies is better than the day on which he was born, because no one knows on the day of the child's birth what deeds he will perform; but at his death, his good deeds are acclaimed by all. This may well be compared to two ocean-going ships—one leaving the harbor and the other entering. Everybody seemed to rejoice over the one setting out on her voyage, while only few greeted with pleasure the one arriving. Upon seeing this, a wise man reflected: People should not rejoice at the ship leaving the harbor, since they do not know what seas she may traverse and what winds she may have to face. On the other hand, everybody should rejoice for the ship that has safely returned to the harbor. When a man is born, every year of his life brings the day of his death nearer, and he is constantly haunted by the certainty of death; but when he dies, he is solaced by the hope of immortality and he looks forward to his revival.

—MIDRASH

Today we honor the memory of —————, and once again we know how keenly the passing of friends and loved ones affects us, and how deeply our own eventual passing enters into all that we are and do. Man's few days have for long been described as like the grass of the fields in their brevity, but they also represent the flowering of some great cosmic urge that brings forth intelligence, a sense of law and order, of love and duty and responsibility, and a sense of creative beauty and song. Though days be brief they represent and reflect all time. Creation's wonders are in us, creation's tragedies, creation's miracles and secrets. Our comings and goings are the pulsations of eternity.

—ANGUS H. MACLEAN

Out of the earth to rest or range
Perpetual in perpetual change
The unknown passing through the strange.

For all things change, the darkness changes,
The wandering spirits change their ranges,
The corn is gathered to the granges.

390

DEATH

The corn is sown again, it grows;
The stars burn out, the darkness goes.
The rhythms change, they do not close.

They change, and we, who pass like foam,
Like dust blown through the streets of Rome,
Change ever, too; we have no home,

Only a beauty, only a power,
Sad in the fruit, bright in the flower,
Endlessly erring for its hour,

But gathering, as we stray, a sense
Of Life, so lovely and intense,
It lingers when we wander hence.

That those who follow feel behind
Their backs, when all before is blind,
Our joy, a rampart to the mind.

—From *The Passing Strange*
JOHN MASEFIELD

Many years hence, when I am a little heap of silent dust, play with me, with the earth of my heart and of my bones!

If a mason gathers me up, he will make me into a brick, and I shall remain fast forever in a wall; and I hate quiet niches. If they make me into a brick in a prison, I shall grow red with shame when I hear a man sob; and if I am a brick in a school, I shall suffer because I cannot sing with you in the early mornings.

I would rather be the dust with which you play on the country roads. Clasp me, for I have been yours; unmake me, for I made you; trample upon me, because I did not give you the whole of beauty and the whole of truth!

GREAT OCCASIONS

When you hold me in your hands recite some beautiful verse, and I shall rustle with delight between your fingers. I shall rise up to look at you, seeking among you the eyes, the hair of those whom I taught.

And when you make any image out of me, break it every moment; for every moment the children broke me, with tenderness and grief!

—From *To the Children*
GABRIELA MISTRAL

Throw all the little dreams away,
Scrap old philosophies and creeds.
Can visions of the truth climb higher
Than our own calculation leads?

Then why put limits of our own
On this illimitable power?
For we explore immensities
Beyond our little place and hour.

Yesterday's failure is today
The take-off for tomorrow's goal.
Let others tremble while we win
New spaces for the searching soul.

Why dream the same old idle dreams?
Move rather in the drift of years.
We count the spaces of the stars.
We hear the singing of the spheres.

—From *The Man of Science Speaks*
HARRIET MONROE

DEATH

Death that is the act
is a passing at the point of a possible beginning;

The world is constantly building
dying into beginning;

The world is enough
and that is enough.

—From *Apollinaire*
WALTER LOWENFELS

I cannot think that thou shouldst pass away,
Whose life to mine is an eternal law,
A piece of nature that can have no flaw,
A new and certain sunrise every day;
But, if thou art to be another ray
About the Sun of Life, 'and art to live
Free from what part of thee was fugitive,
The debt of Love I will more fully pay,
Not downcast with the thought of thee so high,
But rather raised to be a nobler man,
And more divine in my humanity,
As knowing that the waiting eyes which scan
My life are lighted by a purer being,
And ask high, calm-browed deeds, with it agreeing.

—*Sonnet X*
JAMES RUSSELL LOWELL

When the ripe fruit falls
its sweetness distils and trickles away into the veins of the
earth.

GREAT OCCASIONS

When fulfilled people die
the essential oil of their experience enters
the veins of living space, and adds a glisten
to the atom, to the body of immortal chaos.

For space is alive
and it stirs like a swan
whose feathers glisten
silky with oil of distilled experience.

—When the Ripe Fruit Falls
D. H. LAWRENCE

One came and said to the Prophet: My mother has died, what shall I do for the good of her soul?

The Prophet thought of the panting heat of the desert, and he replied: Dig a well, that the thirsty may have water to drink.

The man dug the well and said: This have I done for my mother.

—ISLAMIC

When someone whom we love dies we discover that our brittle defenses are broken and we stand defenseless in the face of a universe seemingly characterized only by the fragility of the precious, the mortality of achievement.

This is the intuition of futility, and it is easy to surrender to it, but when we do, we surrender everything that makes life worth living and that gives dignity to even a moment of time.

Life is worthwhile, worth our living with all our heart and mind

394

and strength, worth it in itself, whether or not we, as individuals, find final sleep, or more life, beyond death!

This is Eternity—now! You are sunk as deep in it, wrapped as close in it, as much a part of it, as you will ever be!

—ROBERT KILLAM

Inescapably in the course of our lives we must each sometime face the contradictions which threaten to undermine all sense of purpose or meaning. The loveliness of Spring is one glory; but in the very moment that we see it, we remember the horror of war, which has never been absent from the lifetime of many of us. Or we behold the natural wonder of growing lives, children whom we watch unfold into fine adults—then irrational disease works its senseless damage, and we are both pained and outraged. What kind of world is it? Is there anything really worthwhile?

Or we struggle to build a society of free men, based on respect for human personality, and employing the fruits of the mind and hand, working upon the resources of the earth. But one day, remote to be sure but inescapable, even if man does not stupidly destroy himself, our world and the universe seems doomed to "die," or at any rate undergo such drastic changes that life as we know it can hardly continue. Is the whole thing, then, a senseless joke that nature plays upon itself, without even knowing or caring that it is a joke?

It is when our spirits face such chasms of emptiness that we can begin to understand the meaning of despair. For we have seen destruction in a thousand forms. Yet never in our experience has destruction been so complete that there was nothing to survive. In the stream of time this may not always continue to be true. But the spirit finds a parable in the survivals we have seen: something there is, which is eternal. Something there is, about ourselves, about our living, about the things which are precious, which has a

395

setting in more than just this minute. Something there is which, no matter what occurs in nature or history, is ineradicable. In this faith in the life-renewing way, in that which does not perish, we too may find a ground to stand upon. Nothing can take away the beauty and significance of life.

—From *The Unconquerable Life*
WALTER ROYAL JONES

For what is life, if measured by the space
Not by the act?
It is not growing like a tree
In bulk, doth make men better be;
Or standing long an oak, three hundred year,
To fall a log at last, dry, bald, and sear:
A lily of a day,
Is fairer far in May,
Although it fall and die that night;
It was the plant, and flower of light.
In small proportions we just beauties see;
And in short measures, life may perfect be.

—From *A Pindaric Ode*
BEN JONSON

I am not dead, I have only become inhuman:
That is to say,
Undressed myself of laughable prides and infirmities,
But not as a man

DEATH

Undresses to creep into bed, but like an athlete
Stripping for the race.
The delicate ravel of nerves that made me a measurer
Of certain fictions
Called good and evil; that made me contract with pain
And expand with pleasure;
Fussily adjusted like a little electroscope:
That's gone, it is true;
(I never miss it; if the universe does,
How easily replaced!)
But all the rest is heightened, widened, set free.
I admired the beauty
While I was human. Now I am part of the beauty.
I wander in the air,
Being mostly gas and water, and flow in the ocean;
Touch you and Asia
At the same moment; have a hand in the sunrises
And the glow of this grass.
I left the light precipitate of ashes to earth
For a love-token.

—*Inscription for a Gravestone*
ROBINSON JEFFERS

O years! and Age! Farewell:
　　Behold I go,
　　Where I do know
Infinity to dwell.

And these mine eyes shall see
　　All times, how they
　　Are lost i' th' Sea
Of vast Eternity.

GREAT OCCASIONS

Where never Moon shall sway
The Stars; but she,
And Night, shall be
Drown'd in one endless Day.

—Eternity
ROBERT HERRICK

What must it be for a man as good as he to be able to push aside this fussy veil of the body and look unblinking at the Light, never again, maybe, to be distracted, unintentional, unaware, always concentrated.

—GERALD HEARD

A number of deaths, following each other like so many birds in a triangle going south, lured to other skies, and other waters with other air and other nourishment in them, like so many birds, swimming into the sundown, hastening, ere the gate should close, and leave them at a foolish portal.

They are over the edge of their chromatic selvages now, and we hear the sound of their voices, which they themselves no longer can hear.

They have left behind them their own life, which we weave into clothes that warm us, shut off too much harsh blowing of wind: and these clothes shelter us against too much north of earth's decisions.

—MARSDEN HARTLEY

DEATH

From Life to Death!
An eager breath,
A battle for the true and good,
An agony upon the rood;
A dark'ning of the light—
And night!

From Death to Life!
A peace from strife;
A voyage o'er an ocean wide
That moves from shore to shore its tide;
A passing of the night—
And light!

—From *I Speak for Myself*
JOHN HAYNES HOLMES

But for your Terror
Where would be Valour?
What is Love for
But to stand in your way?
Taker and Giver,
For all your endeavour
You leave us with more
Than you touch with decay!

—OLIVER ST. JOHN GOGARTY

GREAT OCCASIONS

The mind weighs and measures but it is the spirit that reaches the heart of life and embraces the secret; and the seed of the spirit is deathless.

The wind may blow and then cease, and the sea shall swell and then weary, but the heart of life is a sphere quiet and serene, and the star that shines therein is fixed for evermore.

—From *Jesus*
KAHLIL GIBRAN

There are no compensations when death enters the perfect round and leaves a broken arc. Something has gone which can never be regained. Memories are sweet and gratitude for what has been is a healing medicine, but the whole pattern of life is changed. Arguments kindly offered by those who do not know avail nothing. The attempt to light a little candle of argument does not bring the dawn.

But whatever the loss, whether it comes early or late, there is the unfinished adventure of life ahead; there are other people who have suffered and have needs which those who mourn can serve; there is work today, and there are the unborn for whom a kinder world may be provided; there are the counsels of our own hearts, counsels of self-respect and heroic living.

The reasons for living are not withdrawn when life is a broken arc. Follow those reasons; get back to the daily tasks; rejoin the circle of friends; remember to serve the people who crave what you, and perhaps you alone, can give. Then you will make a discovery: the loss has not grown less, but life has started anew. Scars remain, but health of spirit equal to the journey has been found. If there is darkness when you turn back or drop by the side of the road, there is also light when you go forward.

—From *Forward into Light*
FREDERICK R. GRIFFIN

DEATH

I found myself one day
cracking the shell of sky,
peering into a place
beyond mere universe.

I broke from egg of here
into anotherwhere
wider than worldly home
I was emerging from.

I breathed, I took a step,
I looked around, and up,
and saw another lining
inside a further sky.

—*The Hatch*
NORMA FARBER

I might see more if I were blind—
The sightless eyes, the illumined mind.
I might find what I've failed to find.

Sight can be a foe to sight.
Darkness can be friend to light
Even as stars are friends of night.

—*Sight*
ROBERT FRANCIS

GREAT OCCASIONS

In the singing sun where I am heading
    Will I have a brother tomorrow?

Over the fresh ruins
And wings of butterflies

The best thing about winter
Is the earth making believe it's asleep

        —From *The Poem That Can't Be Stopped*
        PAUL ELUARD
        (tr. WALTER LOWENFELS)

Oh may I join the choir invisible
Of those immortal dead who live again
In minds made better by their presence: live
In pulses stirred to generosity,
In deeds of daring rectitude, in scorn
For miserable aims that end with self,
In thoughts sublime that pierce the night like stars,
And with their mild persistence urge man's search
To vaster issues.
          So to live is heaven:
To make undying music in the world.

        —From *The Choir Invisible*
        GEORGE ELIOT

What need of Day—
To Those whose Dark—hath so—surpassing Sun—

DEATH

It deem it be—Continually—
At the Meridian?

—From a selection by
EMILY DICKINSON

So comes the next opening—the sense of being part of a universe, of a personal relatedness to all life, all growth, all creativity. Suddenly one senses that his life is not just his own little individual existence, but that he is bound in fact to all of life, from the first splitting off of the planets, through the beginning of animate life and on through the slow evolution of man. It is all in him and he is but one channel of it. What has flowed through him, flows on, through children, through works accomplished, through services rendered; it is not lost. Once given the vision of one's true place in the life stream, death is no longer complete or final, but an incident. Death is the way—the only way—life renews itself. When the individual has served his purpose as a channel, the flow transfers itself to other channels, but life goes on.

—From *Dear Gift of Life*
BRADFORD SMITH

Two Lengths has every Day—
Its absolute extent
And Area superior
By Hope or Horror lent—

Eternity will be
Velocity or Pause

GREAT OCCASIONS

At Fundamental Signals
From Fundamental Laws.

To die is not to go—
On Doom's consummate Chart
No Territory new is staked—
Remain thou as thou art.

—EMILY DICKINSON

The hallowing of Pain
Like hallowing of Heaven,
Obtains at corporeal cost—
The Summit is not given

To Him who strives severe
At middle of the Hill—
But He who has achieved the Top—
All—is the price of All—

—EMILY DICKINSON

As if the Sea should part
And show a further Sea—
And that—a further—and the Three
But a presumption be—

Of Periods of Seas—
Unvisited of Shores—
Themselves the Verge of Seas to be—
Eternity—is Those—

—EMILY DICKINSON

DEATH

Death is not without its sting, for we labor under the tribulation of this separation from him who was our father, husband, friend. But victory is not for the grave; it is, rather, for those who overcome their grief and adopt within their own lives the virtues of the life they mourn.

The sting of death! Can we give a balm to its pain? Can we quiet the troubled heart and give assurance to these who mourn? Here is a task not for religion alone, for they mourn their dead who are not religious at all, and they grieve their loss who know none of the accepted faiths of mankind. Here is a task for all humankind, for death reaches into the heart of all life, beyond the walls of faith, beyond piety, beyond class or condition.

Nor is our faith in any particular God the measure of our resourcefulness in times of grief. Believers are overcome, just as are the faithless. Death is a universal problem; its mystery is the concern of all. And it is the mystery that gives us the sting, for if we but *knew,* we could more readily accept consolation and find relief. Yet knowledge of the mystery would not lessen the pain of separation.

Life is the faithful keeping of the values by which we live when we think our noblest thoughts and dream our noblest dreams. We live best when we are building ideals into the fabric of all human relationships. Here then is the lesson we must learn as we stand in awe before the presence of death. Whatever it is that made him dear to us—his hopes, his noble intentions, his dreams— we ought to make real for others who depend on us, even as we sought shelter in the shadow of our regard for him.

Our highest tribute to him is that we shall stand ready to live now helping to fulfill his hopes and bring to reality his longings. This is the honor we would do him; this is the memorial we would build to him.

—From a selection by
FRED CAIRNS

GREAT OCCASIONS

These hearts were woven of human joys and cares,
  Washed marvelously with sorrow, swift to mirth.
The years had given them kindness. Dawn was theirs,
  And sunset, and the colours of the earth.
These had seen movement, and heard music; known
  Slumber and waking; loved; gone proudly friended;
Felt the quick stir of wonder; sat alone;
  Touched flowers and furs and cheeks. All this is ended.

There are waters blown by changing winds to laughter
And lit by the rich skies, all day. And after,
  Frost, with a gesture, stays the waves that dance
And wandering loveliness. He leaves a white
  Unbroken glory, a gathered radiance,
A width, a shining peace, under the night.

—The Dead, IV
RUPERT BROOKE

We belong to the eternal here and now. We did not begin when
we were born; our origin goes back to the beginningless beginning
of all things. Our biography is the story of earth and sun and
humankind. Do we end when we die?

Something eternal is revealed in everything. Our brains and
bodies are mosaics of the same unknown that underlies the light,
the star, the sea. We do not know what it is but we live in it, and
we call it Life. We belong to the Oneness from which we have
emerged.

—RAYMOND J. BAUGHAN

DEATH

Had I a claim to fame?
   Little to honor;
Save when I spoke her name,
   Gazing upon her.
Then was I crowned of men,
   More than my seeming,
Youth's glorious hope again
   Bannered my dreaming.

So, when our day is past;
   When we lie stilly
Under the earth at last,
   Clod by white lily.
Give me neither tear nor sigh;
Breath but this in passing by,
Where empearled with morning dew
   The high grass above her
Waves, and above me too,—
   "He was her lover!"

—Had I a Claim to Fame?
WILLIAM ROSE BENÉT

The stars shall fade away, the sun himself
Grow dim with age, and nature sink in years,
But thou shalt flourish in immortal youth,
Unhurt amidst the war of elements,
The wreck of matter, and the crush of worlds.

—From Cato
JOSEPH ADDISON

GREAT OCCASIONS

That cause can neither be lost nor stayed
Which takes the course of what God hath made
And is not trusting in walls and towers
But slowly growing from seed to flowers.

Each noble service that men have wrought
Was first conceived as a fruitful thought,
Each worthy cause with a future glorious
By quietly growing becomes victorious.

Thereby itself like a tree it shows;
That high it reaches as deep it grows;
And when the storms are its branches shaking,
It deeper root in the soil is taking.

Be then no more by a storm dismayed
For by it the full grown seeds are laid,
And though the tree by its might it shatters,
What then if thousands of seeds it scatters?

—AUTHOR UNKNOWN

To see things under the form of eternity is to see them in their
historic and moral truth, not as they seemed when they passed,
but as they remain when they are over. When a man's life is
over, it remains true that he has lived; it remains true that he has
been one sort of man, and not another. In the infinite mosaic of
history that bit has its unfading colour and its perpetual function
and effect.

A man who understands himself under the form of eternity
knows the quality that eternally belongs to him, and knows that

DEATH

he cannot wholly die, even if he would; for when the movement of his life is over, the truth of his life remains. The fact of him is a part forever of the infinite context of facts.

—From a selection by
GEORGE SANTAYANA

APPENDIX A

A Ceremony of Adoption

The following is suggested as one possible form for such a ceremony where one might be desired.

(The parents and child having come forward, the minister reads:)

Friends, you come to us today with your newly adopted child. Eagerly you awaited his coming. The days have passed, the obligations of the regulations been completed, and now this child's life has been placed in your care and keeping. Not as a gift of the state, but as a gift from life itself he comes to you. A very special gift because you have chosen and been chosen to receive him.

After considerable thought and planning, you have decided to enlarge your mutual living together. Into your home society has duly placed this child. All of us have a special interest in his well-being and in your successful nurture of him. In due seriousness, but with joy and keen anticipation, we mark the moment when your marriage becomes a family. A child comes into your life, and you come into the life of a child. May the meeting bring happiness to all, growth to all, lasting good to all.

(To the parents:)

As one sign of this adoption you embrace this child with your family name. Will you introduce him to your friends here?

411

(*The parents say:*)

We present to you our son/daughter ——————— ——————.

(*The minister now says:*)

————————— ———————————, we welcome you into your new family and pledge you our love and care.

NOTE: See section I for further readings and prayers to amplify this service.

APPENDIX B

A Rite of Divorce

BY RUDOLPH W. NEMSER

(*Minister:*)

We are here gathered in a place made holy by the aspirations and dreams of many men and women. A place where humanity has encountered what is most sacred. Here people have known themselves before their highest ideals. Here today we bring ourselves and our hopes.

We have come to witness and participate in a solemn and awesome act: a rite of divorce. Divorce is a rite of meaning and import. It must be entered into only with deepest consideration and strongest conviction.

We assemble with many feelings: sadness and disappointment and apprehension. But also, perhaps, for some there is relief and hope and even approval. We have come with many feelings: with mixed feelings.

This ceremony marks the end of a long and intense relationship: perhaps neither as long nor as intense as some might wish, but truly long and intense in the lives of this couple. This ceremony marks the end of a love.

People marry in hope. People marry experiencing many of the strongest feelings they have known: feelings of wanting to share, of faith in themselves, of belief in another, of trust in the morrow, of choosing two before one. People marry in idealism holding not only to the beauty of what is but to the grandeur of what shall

413

be. For marriage is not a moment but a lifetime. Marriage is growth. The wedding ceremony is a declaration of faith in that growth.

But not all marriages are a coming together. Not all marriages are growth. For many reasons a marriage falls short—painfully short—of expectation. And even, in instances, short of necessity.

The days are cold. The nights are long. Again and again. They try to recapture the dream they had; to live the vision they both once believed.

Yet the marriage is a straining. It is a struggle of impossibility. A time when what cannot be becomes too important to be ignored. A time when survival as an individual is at stake.

And all too often, confronted by society's uncomprehending disapproval, the other's disappointment and resentment, one's own specters of failure and inadequacy, the choice must be made to walk alone. Paths must part. And the journey necessity requires ends in this solemn, courageous—and hopeful—time of divorce.

IS IT WITH SUCH SPIRIT OF SOBER AND EARNEST THOUGHT AND DEDICATION THAT YOU HAVE COME TO BE PARTED AND TO SUNDER THOSE NOBLE AND SACRED BONDS AND DREAMS ONCE OF BOTH YOUR LIVES?

(*Couple:*)

It is.

(*Minister:*)

In a wedding celebration are three. So now three mark the start of your lives apart.

For society must be present when such life-changing steps are undertaken. People are social beings. Their deeds affect lives and times they never know. For these, however, they are accountable. With them they must live.

I am here, then, to say to you that, although this is the day of your divorce, your relationship does not conclude. There can never completely be a separation between you. Always there is a past that is shared. Always there are concerns of the present.

414

Ties there are between you. For the meaning and use of these ties, each must be responsible. If you see each other never again their nature will be less demanding. If because of common interests or pursuits, you see each other frequently, or if because of common friends and other enterprise you touch each other frequently, these will call forth your wisest and your best.

These bonds are not to manipulate the other, Not to twist, These are not to control nor to punish.

Let them, rather, be bonds to strengthen. To support. To help each other gain the force and stability you both shall need.

Powerful and courageous, you are yet weak. Days and years of strain and decision-needing-decision are weakening times. That desert of isolation whose only other occupant—the one member of society truly able to hear and understand your cries—is the other: is also weakening loneliness. The callous judgmentalism of a posturing society is also weakening. And too weakening is that destruction of confidence which comes from the shattering of a vision and the inaccessibility of an ideal.

Finally, whether hating or pitying or fearing each other: the truth is that even now—perhaps especially now—in these last times you depend upon one another. Now this too must pass.

Be gentle, then, with the dependence and the fear, the successes and, perhaps, the bitterness of the other.

(Then shall the couple say as they will of the meaning of their divorce and their feelings toward one another—or the following:)

——————————, I do hereby affirm my place in this ending of our marriage, From this day our ways separate and our loves part.

Now I enter into a new relationship with you. I shall treasure always the things we shared that were beautiful. At the same time, I shall hold as valuable and worthy the new and happy in your life ahead.

Above all, I promise to respect you as an individual. We have hurt each other and been hurt. Knowing your strengths and weaknesses, I shall see and honor and treat you as a person. This is my pledge.

415

(Then the bride shall give the minister her wedding ring. And the groom if he has one too. The minister shall say:)

Let the return of this ring(s) be the freeing from a pledge once undertaken and now outlived. As what you exchanged is now returned, so shall you be free to enter into a new life, a new marriage, a new love again. Go forth, not in the hurt of ties wrenched and faith unachieved, but with hope and belief in love yet possible and ties still to be found and held.

(Minister returns ring to groom. And other to bride)

(Minister:)

And so, as you, ——————— and ———————, have stated to one another your intention to live apart and to create lives independent; as you have further declared your common commitment to the health and well-being of one another and to the good of all your lives will touch; and as you, finally, have declared your pledge to trustworthiness—to respect yourself and each other: I now pronounce your marriage to be dissolved.

I summon you in the days that lie ahead—dark days and bright days—to recall the vision and the hopes of this moment. I summon society—family, friends, strangers: well-meaning and ill— to treat now and forever as sacred the decision you have made and the courses ahead which you have chosen.

May all that is noble, lovely and true; all that is enriching and creative; all that is beautiful be and abide in your lives and your homes time without end.

(The couple shakes hands)

APPENDIX C

A MEMORIAL SERVICE

BY GEORGE C. WHITNEY

A memorial service delivered by the Rev. George C. Whitney of the Unitarian Church of Tucson, on May 2, 1962, at the Adair Funeral Home for Adrian Van De Verde, Jr. (August 7, 1930–April 29, 1962).

Pluck softly on the strings of time and know no grief
For green and supple was and is the fallen leaf
And fragrant still within the soft caress
Of happiness.

No sorrow in the triumph of the brave
Or mourning in the night of tears;
Be strong with him, remember that he gave
To us the sunlight of his years.

Treasure the golden hours, make
The light he bravely lit a joyous shrine;
Drink deeply from the cup, for sake
Of him, from life's still sparkling wine.

This time belongs to Adrian, as indeed, all time belonged to him. This then, an interval of remembrance, must share the honesty that was his honesty, the pungent wit that was his, the irredeemable candor and the lovely friendship which we all knew as part of him. We could no more, this afternoon, be grave or be sententious or even formal, in the way in which the world chooses to be so on occasions like this, than he could be grave, sententious and formal.

417

If I should die (and die I must) please let it be in spring
When I, and life up-budding shall be one
And green and lovely things shall blend with all I was
And all I hope to be.
The chemistry
Of miracle within the heart of love and life abundant
Shall be mine, and I shall pluck the star-dust and shall know
The mystery within the blade
And sing the wind's song in the softness of the flowered glade.
April is the time for parting, not because all nature's tears
Presage the blooming time of May
But joyous should be death and its adventure
As the night gives way to day.

Those who knew best the penetration of his mind, sometimes plucked out the quills he had slyly thrust into their pomposity, for Adrian had an unerring instinct in such matters. They knew also the real secret of his life. I think it can be revealed now, for I know that he would not much mind having us remember him in his own truth. There are those who have liked to picture him as a saint, the impeccable symbol of an almost unhuman fortitude. He did share some of these qualities, but they were only a part of his complexity.

Adrian, as he confessed to me and to others who shared his secrets, was really a buccaneer at heart—a benevolent freebooter who sailed the oceans of the mind. It always plagued him that fate required him to wear a certain respectability that he yearned passionately to cast off, and if he had not been bound somewhat to a rather deep ethical awareness, I am sure that he would have liked to have tried his hand at being a scamp and a rogue and a vagabond.

This, of course, he could not and would not do in any dishonest sense, but he delighted in being a pickpocket of ideas, a miser of little treasures picked up in odd moments, and I am sure that nobody ever left his presence without having been relieved of some thought of great value. But he was not content with this, and he took the raw ore of intellect, borrowed and mined from countless sources, and refined it in the crucible of his own sharp thought and brought out a better thing than had gone in.

There was another little secret that he shared with a few and that was the fact that he, Adrian, from his room, was really the ruler of the world. From him, he liked to say, there went, invisibly, tentacles of influence into an empire that stretched to the far corners of the earth. But again, and I do not know the extent to which he fully realized it, while the power and the influence were real enough, they were compounded of love and affection and the desire for goodness and he was the most benevolent of despots as he was the kindest of friends.

We talked about the weather and the shape of women's hats,
We argued over music, soared in space and patched
The troubles of the world.
The universe was in that room and brave the voyage
And splendid were the taut-white sails
To distant winds unfurled.
O, sharing of the heart
That makes the light of intellect a gift
And fastens on the far-flung truths
Of friendship as a fierce possession,
And dares to stand apart
From desperation, in a strength that lies
In mind and will, serenity of purpose
And the courage of the truly wise.

There may be some who would say that there should be no eulogy for him, but I know better. He was understanding enough to know that from our affection there would come words of praise, even as he himself, at the passing of a great friend and valiant companion, had written these words which he insisted that I use as he had written them. I am sure you will agree as I read them that they speak as well of him:

This man was neither an unknown or an equal to those fortunate few of us who knew him and loved him in all the many senses of this overworked word. He was with you

419

when you needed him—and above you by your own estimate, but never his. His very nature would forbid a friend, such as myself, from eulogizing him with conventional trite phrases. He was, instead, a personification of all the things the world chooses to ignore in its mad scramble for sensation. He appreciated the material, but he valued the non-material. He smiled at the ironies in the lives of others but he laughed at those in his own. For years he looked out through the same four walls, but always—the scope of his mind encompassed the whole of our universe. Truly, in quietness and in confidence was his strength. . . .

So, you see, that one who had written so lovingly of Bob Wiessenborn could not, even in the scorn he himself professed to show for humbug, deny to us the same privilege.

Adrian left to us other words he had written. He was, as many of us know, writing a book and had virtually completed it when his tired heart gave up its burden. Here are some of the things that Adrian thought about life, in the raw, unedited version that we now have and which, I am sure, his friends will take as a loving task and polish to the perfection that he would have wished for:

If a man has a soul, he has it before his birth. If I have a spirit, will it expire before my blood clots in my brain? Fear, love, pain and joy—are these things illusions of the spongy mass between my ears or are these emotions at least as real as the physicist's neutrino? In the beginning did God create the heaven and the earth and all creatures thereon? Or in the end did the creature man create God to relieve the lonely ache that is his existence and the throbbing of his questioning mind? Now, ethics. From whence cometh I to go where when I die? . . . The honest man seeks fervently for the answer. The compromising man rationalizes them into nothingness and returns to the loneliness of his sensual existence. . . .

420

(Adrian had developed a philosophy he called "skematicism" which he goes on to describe:)

> Skematicism comes to question the pious, help the honest and crush the compromising. Skematicism incorporates ethical principles of several religions, Christianity, Judaism and Buddhism. The ethic is a human creation and varies with environmental conditions. An important difference between skematicism and Christianity is the abolishment of the Golden Rule—do unto your neighbor as you would have him do unto you. It is felt that this concept permits an individual to force his aesthetic response upon another and in the case of an extremely dominant person gives him the right to create a society in his own image. This has historically been done through coercion and violence. If a substitute ethic is needed, perhaps it should be this: Let your wisdom and justice so impress your fellow men that their actions and your actions will be harmonious with God's universe. . . .

Thus, you see, Adrian, in his search for truth was not above the reverential impertinence of revising even the center of the Christian moral life and it was in token of this that the Unitarian church, with its heresies, was endeared to him.

How strange that one turns outside in
With shriveled bitterness and doubt
And that, another, with an equal fate
Turns heart and friendship inside out.

    How fair the gardens of the mind
    Where seeds of glory flower
    And there, in utter fragrance find
    The sweetness of the fleeting hour.

        How wise the patient heart of one
        Who can the world requite;
        Love knoweth not oblivion
        Nor hope the night.

GREAT OCCASIONS

One could go on and on, even as Adrian himself could go on and on thinking and talking, his mind buzzing as busily as the electrical gadgets with which he delighted to surround himself. One might think of him in terms of the clean precision of a philosophy, such as Whitehead's, or the cogent and warm prose of Einstein on whom his life was in large part moulded, or of Kahlil Gibran—not so much the polished Gibran of "The Prophet" as the somewhat wilder and less restrained Gibran of "The Madman."

Or one might think of Adrian as the ardent hipster, disciple of progressive jazz with which he surrounded himself to the despair of his more proper friends, or in terms of aid to the handicapped to which he gave himself unstintingly, or in terms of the scientific world of which he was an eager lover. But most of all, we remember him as a spark in the twilight of our despair, a counsellor and teacher, confidante, and, at times, a court jester whose attempt at playing the fool betrayed him as being wiser than the king himself. He was the uncommon man, in an uncommon age, and wherever his spirit dwells, I am sure that his sly humor plays counterpoint to whatever solemnity there may be about him.

Let us now praise famous men,
By whom the Lord hath brought great glory.

Such as did bear rule in their kingdoms,
And were men renowned for their power,
Giving counsel by their understanding,
Men richly furnished with ability,
Living peaceably in their habitations;
All these were honoured in their generations,
And were the glory of their times.

Their bodies are buried in peace,
But their names liveth forevermore.
For the memorial of virtue is immortal;
Because it is known with God and with men.
When it is present, men take example of it;

And when it is gone, they desire it:
And throughout all time it marcheth crowned in triumph,
Victorious in the strife for the prizes that are undefiled.
Therefore will the people tell of their wisdom,
And the congregation will shew forth their praise.

—Arranged from Ecclesiasticus 44 and Wisdom 4

And now—let peace, mercy and love, be and abide with you forever. AMEN

ACKNOWLEDGMENTS

EVERY EFFORT has been made to trace the ownership of copyright material. If any infringement has been made, apologies are hereby offered, and the editor will be happy, upon receiving notification, to make proper acknowledgments in future editions of this collection. The editor takes this opportunity to express the deepest gratitude to all authors and owners of copyrighted material for permissions generously extended, and especially to those who have allowed alterations and adaptations.

In some cases it was not possible to use copyrighted material, so the editor would like to suggest that users of this book will find helpful material in *The Four Quartets* of T. S. Eliot and in the *Poems* of Kathleen Raine.

Sincere thanks are due to the following individuals for permission to use their selections:

Waldemar Argow
Raymond J. Baughan
Robert D. Botley
William Brower
Fred I. Cairns
Lon Ray Call
Fred Cappuccino
Paul N. Carnes
Alfred S. Cole
Muriel A. Davies
Sophia Lyon Fahs
William R. Fortner
Charles A. Gaines
Dana McLean Greeley
Robert Edward Green
Ralph N. Helverson
Duncan Howlett
Karl Hultberg
James D. Hunt
J. Donald Johnston
Walter Royal Jones Jr.
Paul E. Killinger
James G. Lawson
Brandoch Lovely

Charles W. McGehee
Angus H. MacLean
David Hicks MacPherson
Robert Marshall
Rudolph W. Nemser
Kenneth L. Patton
Ernest D. Pipes Jr.
Peter S. Raible
William B. Rice
Donald F. Robinson
Elmo A. Robinson
Carl Seaburg
Robert E. Senghas
Ernest H. Sommerfeld
Chadbourne A. Spring
Theodore A. Webb
Robert T. Weston
Walter Muir Whitehill
George C. Whitney
Henry Nelson Wieman
Ruth A. Woodman
Michael G. Young
Robert Zoerheide

Thanks are expressed to the following:

Wilder Foote and Arthur Foote for material by Henry Wilder Foote.
Cynthia Griffin for material by Frederick R. Griffin.
Frances D. Killam for material by Robert D. Killam.
Muriel Davies for material by A. Powell Davies.

And thanks to the following publishers, agents, or individuals holding copyright on the selections specified, for permission to reprint:

Harry N. Abrams for the two selections from Paul Klee's *The Inward Vision.*

George Allen & Unwin, Ltd., for the extract from Bertrand Russell's *New Hopes for a Changing World.*

The American Ethical Union for the selection from Alfred W. Martin's article "Consolations of Ethical Religion" in the March 1931 issue of *The Standard.*

The American Foundation for the Blind, Inc., and Miss Helen A. Keller for the excerpt from Miss Keller's *We Bereaved.*

The American Tract Society, Oradell, New Jersey, for the selection from John Oxenham's "E.A., Nov. 6, 1900" in *Bees in Amber.*

Appleton-Century-Crofts for the selection from Frances G. Wickes' *The Inner World of Childhood* and the extracts from John MacMurray's *Reason and Emotion* published in 1938 by D. Appleton-Century Company, Inc.

Edward Arnold, Ltd., for the excerpt from *Two Cheers for Democracy* by E. M. Forster.

The Association for Childhood Educational International, 3615 Wisconsin Avenue, N.W., Washington, D.C., and Muriel A. Davies for the shortened form of "A Minister Says" from *Childhood Education,* Vol. 31, No. 1, September 1954, by A. Powell Davies.

Louis Auslander, Anna Mary Auslander, and Mrs. Arthur L. Morris for "Holy Ground" by Joseph Auslander.

Avalon Press for the selection from *Patterns in Jade* by Wu Ming Fu.

Beacon Press for the excerpt from *Eros and Civilization* by Herbert Marcuse 1955, © 1966, by the Beacon Press; for the excerpt from "The Immortality of Man" by Jacques Maritain in *Man's Destiny in Eternity* copyright 1949 by F. Lyman Windolph and Farmers Bank & Trust Co. of Lancaster, trustees under the will of M. T. Garvin, deceased; for the poem "Consolation in Time of War" by Lewis Mumford in *The Human Prospect* copyright 1955 by Lewis Mumford; for the abridged excerpt from *The Democratic Man* by Eduard C. Lindeman copyright 1956 by Hazel Taft Lindeman and Robert Gessner; and for the excerpts from *Litany for all Souls* by Lucien Price copyright 1945 by the Beacon Press.

Bishop Museum Press for the selections from *Voices on the Wind* by K. Luomala.

ACKNOWLEDGMENTS

The Bishops' Committee on the Liturgy for the excerpt from the *Collectio Rituum.*

Boys Town Jerusalem, Publishers for the selection from *Duties of the Heart* by Bahya Ibn Pakuda.

Joseph Payne Brennan for "Epitaph for an Earth Lover," copyright 1961 by Joseph Payne Brennan from *The Wind of Time.*

Cambridge University Press for the selection from *Man on His Nature* by Charles Sherrington and the lines from *Poems* translated by F. L. Lucas.

Simon Campbell, executor for the late Joseph Campbell, for the poem "The Old Woman" by Joseph Campbell.

Jônathan Cape, Ltd., for the selection from Vol. 20 of *The Complete Works of Samuel Butler,* Shrewsbury Edition, edited by Henry Festing Jones and A. T. Bartholomew; and for the selections from *The Gate* by Cecil Day Lewis. Jonathan Cape, Ltd., and the Hogarth Press for the selection from "A Time to Dance" by Cecil Day Lewis from *Collected Poems* 1954.

Chatto and Windus, Ltd., and Mrs. Laura Huxley for the quotation from *Orion* by Aldous Huxley. Chatto and Windus, Ltd., and Mr. Harold Owen for "Futility" and "Anthem for Doomed Youth" from *The Collected Poems of Wilfred Owen,* edited by C. Day Lewis.

The Citadel Press for the selection from *Thoughts and Meditations* by Kahlil Gibran. Translated and edited by Anthony R. Ferris. The Citadel Press, 1960.

Collins-Knowlton-Wing, Inc., for part of "To Lucia at Birth" from *Collected Poems,* copyright 1955 by Robert Graves.

Columbia University Press for the excerpt from *Prescription for Survival* by Brock Chisholm.

Rosica Colin Limited for the selections from *The Collected Poems of Richard Aldington* © Madame Catherine Guillaume.

Constable Publishers, London, for the poems "To W.P. I" and "To W.P. II" in *Poems* by George Santayana and for the selection from Prudentius translated by Helen Waddell in *Mediaeval Latin Lyrics.*

Daniel Cory for the selections from the works of George Santayana.

Coward-McCann, Inc., for the anonymous poem "We Must Not Part as Others Do" from *The Book of Restoration Verse* edited by William S. Braithwaite and copyrighted by Brentano's in 1909.

Suhrkamp Verlag for the poem by Herman Hesse from *Gedichte,* copyright 1953 by Suhrkamp Verlag, Berlin.

The John Day Company, Inc., publisher, for the poem from *The Way of Life According to Lao-Tzu* by Witter Bynner, copyright 1944 by Witter Bynner.

J. M. Dent & Sons, Ltd., for the extract from *Greek Poetry for Everyman* by F. L. Lucas; for the selection from the preface by George Santayana to Spinoza's *Ethics* in the Everyman's Library text; and for the selections from the *Collected Poems* of Dylan Thomas, and the Trustees for the Copyrights of the late Dylan Thoms.

Andre Deutsch, Limited, for the

ACKNOWLEDGMENTS

from the poem "The Death of Europe" from *The Distances Poems* by Charles Olson. Copyrighted © 1950, 1951, 1953, 1960 by Charles Olson.

Harcourt, Brace & World, Inc., for "Lo, to the battleground of Life," "What are we bound for?" and "I wonder how you take your rest?" from *Selected Poems and Parodies of Louis Untermeyer,* copyright, 1935, by Harcourt, Brace & World, Inc., and "Irony" from *Long Feud* by Louis Untermeyer, copyright, 1914, by Harcourt, Brace & World, Inc.; copyright, 1942, by Louis Untermeyer; for the excerpt by Geddes Mumford from *Green Memories* by Lewis Mumford; for "love is a place," "love's function is to fabricate unknownness," and "be of love (a little)" reprinted from *Poems 1923–1954* by e. e. cummings, copyright, 1935, by e. e. cummings; renewed, 1963, by Marion Morehouse Cummings; for "nothing false and possible is love," "true lovers in each happening of their heart," and "life is more true than reason will deceive" reprinted from *Poems 1923–1954* by e. e. cummings and copyright, 1944, by e. e. cummings; and for "from spiralling ecstatically this" reprinted from *95 Poems* by e. e. cummings, © 1956 by e. e. cummings; for "Come to Birth" by Abbie Houston Evans from her volume *Fact of Crystal,* copyright, 1953, by Abbie Houston Evans; for the excerpt from *In Tune with the World* by Joseph Peiper; for "As much as you can" from *The Complete Poems of Cavafy* translated by Rae Dalven, © 1961 by Rae Dalven; for "Stars, Songs, Faces" from *Smoke and Steel* by Carl Sandburg copyright, 1920, by Harcourt, Brace & World, Inc.; copyright, 1948, by Carl Sandburg; for the excerpt from *Two Cheers for Democracy* by E. M. Forster; for the excerpts from *Wind, Sand, and Stars* and *Flight to Arras,* both by Antoine de Saint-Exupéry; for the excerpt from *The Journey's Echo* by Freya Stark; and for "Give Way to Grief" from *So That It Flowers* by Melville Cane, copyright © 1956 by Melville Cane.

Harper & Row, Publishers, Inc., for the selection from *Eternal Spirit in the Daily Round* by Frank Carleton Doan, copyright 1928 by Harper & Brothers, Publishers, Inc.; for the reading from *Meditations of the Heart* by Howard Thurman, copyright 1953 by Harper & Brothers; for the lines from *I Speak for Myself* by John Haynes Holmes published by Harper & Brothers, Inc., copyright © 1959 John Haynes Holmes; for "F.O.M." from *Body of Waking* by Muriel Rukeyser, copyright 1954 by Muriel Rukeyser; for the excerpt from "Grass" from *The Fortune Teller* by John Holmes, copyright © 1956 by John Holmes; for "Toward Which" by Thomas Wolfe, in *A Stone, a Leaf, a Door,* selected and arranged in verse by John S. Barnes, copyright 1940 by Maxwell Perkins as Executor; for "Benedictus" and first 2 stanzas of "Agnus Dei" from *Requiem for the Living* by C. Day Lewis, copyright © 1961 by C. Day Lewis, and the first, third, and fifth (with cuts) stanzas of "The Newborn" from *Pegasus and Other Poems* by C. Day Lewis, copyright © 1957 by

ACKNOWLEDGMENTS

Edition) from *The Collected Poems of A. E. Housman,* copyright 1939, 1940, © 1959 by Holt, Rinehart and Winston, Inc., and copyright © 1967 by Robert E. Symons; for the selection from "They Who Choose To Die" from *Selected Poems* by Raymond Holden, copyright 1946 by Holt, Rinehart and Winston, Inc.; for the quotation from *A Passionate Prodigality* by Guy Chapman, copyright 1933, © 1965, 1966 by Guy Chapman; for the poems from *Complete Poems of Robert Frost,* copyright 1923, 1928 by Holt, Rinehart and Winston, Inc. Copyright 1936, 1951, © 1956 by Robert Frost, copyright © 1964 by Lesley Frost Ballantine.

Horizon Press, United States publisher of *Collected Poems* by Herbert Read, for the selection from "The Sorrows of Unicume," copyright 1966.

Houghton Mifflin Company for the selection from *The Wilderness World of John Muir* edited by Edwin Way Teale; for the selections from *The Heart of Emerson's Journals* edited by Bliss Perry; for the selection from *Accepting the Universe* by John Burroughs; for poem #1564 by Emily Dickinson; for "Quaker Funeral" from *Water Ouzel* by William Matchett; for "Words To Be Spoken" from *The Collected Poems of Archibald MacLeish;* for the selection from "Little Girl, My String Bean" in *Live or Die* by Anne Sexton; for the "Song of the Newborn" translated by Mary Austin in *American Rhythm.*

Unity magazine for the poem "Robert M. La Follette" by Lucia Trent in the issue of July 13, 1925.

Corliss Lamont for the poem "To Elisabeth Morrow Morgan" by Margaret I. Lamont and for an excerpt by Corliss Lamont, both from *Man Answers Death: An Anthology of Poetry,* Corliss Lamont, editor, Philosophical Library, New York, 1952; copyright, Corliss Lamont, 1952; and Corliss Lamont and the American Humanist Association for selections from "A Humanist Funeral Service."

Liberation magazine for the poem "Play the Last March Slowly" by Richard Davidson in the issue of December 1959.

Little, Brown and Company for the selections from *The Complete Poems of Emily Dickinson,* edited by Thomas H. Johnson: "Two lengths has every Day" copyright 1914, 1942 by Martha Dickinson Bianchi; "As if the Sea should part" copyright 1929, © 1957 by Mary L. Hampson; "We grow accustomed to the Dark—" copyright 1935 by Martha Dickinson Bianchi, © R 1963 by Mary L. Hampson; and the last stanza of "I see thee better —in the Dark—" copyright 1914, 1942 by Martha Dickinson Bianchi.

Liveright Publishing Corporation for "Old Song" by Hart Crane from *Complete Poems & Selected Letters & Prose of Hart Crane,* copyright 1933, 1958, 1966 by Liveright Publishing Corp.

Walter Lowenfels for the selections from *Some Deaths.*

Luzac & Company, Ltd., for the selection from *Laotze's Tao and Wu Wei* translated by Dwight Goddard and Bhikshu Wai-Tao.

The Macmillan Company for "Two Songs from a Play" from

433

142, © 1965, Pendle Hill, Wallingford, Pa., and to Marion Collins Smith, executrix of the estate of Bradford Smith.

Penguin Books, Ltd., for the selection from *The Poems of Catullus* translated by Peter Whigham; and for the poem by Christopher Okigbo from *Modern Poetry from Africa* edited by Gerald Moore and Ulli Beier.

The Philosophical Library for an excerpt from *De Profundis* by Oscar Wilde and a poem from *A Tagore Testament* by Rabindranath Tagore.

The Pilgrim Press for the adaptation from *Prayers of the Social Awakening* by Walter Rauschenbusch.

R. Piper & Co. Verlag for the excerpt from a poem by Hans Egon Holthusen translated by Marianne Leibholz, and published in *Modern German Poetry*, Grove Press, 1962.

Harriet Plimpton for her poem "Country Burial" from *Out of the North* by Harriet Plimpton, Oxford University Press.

Laurence Pollinger, Ltd., and the Estate of the late Mrs. Frieda Lawrence for "When the Ripe Fruit Falls" and "Our Day Is Over" from *The Complete Poems of D. H. Lawrence,* William Heinemann, Ltd.

Caldwell Titcomb and Alvah W. Sulloway executors of the Lucien Price estate, for the selections from *Mater Gloriosa* and *Hellas Regained* by Lucien Price.

G. P. Putnam's Sons for the selection from *An Almanac for Moderns* by Donald Culross Peattie, copyright 1935 by Donald Culross Peattie, renewed 1963 by Donald Culross Peattie.

Random House, Inc., for a selection from "That Noble Flower" from *Be Angry at the Sun and Other Poems,* by Robinson Jeffers, copyright 1941 by Robinson Jeffers; "The Young Dead Soldiers" from *Actfive and Other Poems,* by Archibald MacLeish, copyright 1948 by Archibald MacLeish; for selections from *Humanist Meditations and Paraphrases,* by Emil Weitzner, © copyright 1965 by Random House, Inc.; for the poem "Advice to Pilgrims" from *Double Axe and Other Poems,* reprinted from *Selected Poems* by Robinson Jeffers, copyright 1948 by Robinson Jeffers; for Section II from "De Rerum Virtute" (*Hungerfield and Other Poems*), reprinted from *Selected Poems* by Robinson Jeffers, copyright 1954 by Robinson Jeffers; for "Inscription for a Gravestone" (*Descent to the Dead*), reprinted from *Selected Poetry of Robinson Jeffers,* copyright 1931 by Random House, Inc., and renewed 1959 by Robinson Jeffers; a selection from "Innocence & Experience" from *Basic Verities,* by Charles Peguy, trans. by Ann and Julien Green, copyright 1943 by Pantheon Books, Inc.; a selection from "I Think Continually of Those" (*Poems*) from *Selected Poems,* by Stephen Spender, copyright 1934 and renewed 1962 by Stephen Spender; a selection from "Wedding" from *Doctor Zhivago* by Boris Pasternak, © copyright 1958 by Pantheon Books, Inc; "Clocks cannot tell our time of day" (also titled "No Time" in *Collected Shorter Poems 1927–1957*) (*Double Man*), reprinted from *Collected Shorter Poems 1927–1957,* by W.

435

ACKNOWLEDGMENTS

John Ciardi for the excerpt from the title poem in *I Marry You* by John Ciardi, copyright 1958 by Rutgers, The State University.

Archibald Rutledge for his poem "Limitless."

Mrs. Duncan Campbell Scott for the stanza from "Afterwards" by the late Duncan Campbell Scott.

Charles Scribner's Sons for "Love Is" (Copyright 1949 May Swenson) from *To Mix with Time* by May Swenson; "The Hatch" (Copyright 1953 Norma Farber) from *The Hatch: Poems* by Norma Farber and "To the Family of a Friend on his Death" from *The Irony: Poems* by Robert Pack (Copyright 1955 Robert Pack), *Poets of Today II;* "Old Woman in the Sun" from *In Rainwater Evening: Poems* by Sheila Pritchard (Copyright © 1958 Sheila Pritchard), *Poets of Today V;* "In Silence" (Copyright 1934 Charles Scribner's Sons; renewal copyright © 1962) from *A Stone, a Leaf, a Door* by Thomas Wolfe; the following poems by George Santayana: "To W.P. I" and "To W.P. II" from *Poems* and "The Poet's Testament" (Copyright 1952 Charles Scribner's Sons) from *The Poet's Testament;* "Exit" from *The Town Down the River* by Edwin Arlington Robinson (copyright 1910 Charles Scribner's Sons; renewal copyright 1938 Ruth Nivison); "Time" from *Moods, Songs and Doggerels* by John Galsworthy (Copyright 1912 Charles Scribner's Sons; renewal copyright 1940 Ada Galsworthy); the following poems by John Hall Wheelock: extracts from "The Part Called Age" (Copyright © 1963 The University of the South), "So Dark, So True" and "In This Green Nook" which first appeared in *The New Yorker* as two of "Seven Sonnets" (Copyright © 1964 John Hall Wheelock), five lines from "Dear Men and Women" first published in *The New Yorker* (Copyright © 1963 John Hall Wheelock) and entire poem "Telos" all from *Dear Men and Women* (Copyright © 1966 John Hall Wheelock); 15 lines from "Night Thoughts in Age" (Copyright 1955 John Hall Wheelock), extract from "Return Into the Night" (Copyright © 1956 *The Georgia Review*), and the following entire poems, "Holy Light" (Copyright 1919 Charles Scribner's Sons; renewal copyright 1947 John Hall Wheelock) and "Epitaph" and Songs II, V, VII, and XIV from *Poems Old and New* (Copyright © 1956 John Hall Wheelock).

Rabbi Abraham B. Shoulson for excerpts from articles by Martin M. Weitz and Joshua Loth Liebman in *Marriage and Family Life—A Jewish View,* edited by Abraham B. Shoulson.

Sidgwick & Jackson, Ltd., for permission to reprint the extract from *Letters to a Young Poet* by R. M. Rilke.

Simon and Schuster, Inc., for the excerpt from *New Hopes for a Changing World* by Bertrand Russell, copyright 1951 (publisher, George Allen & Unwin, Ltd.) and for the poem from *Winter Orchard* by Josephine Johnson, copyright 1935 by Josephine Johnson.

Edwin Seaver for the poem "To Whom It May Concern: Greeting" by Francis C. Cook from *Cross Section,* 1947, edited by Edwin

438

ACKNOWLEDGMENTS

the selection by Al-Hallaj from *Muhammed's People* edited by Eric Schroeder.

John Wiley & Sons, Inc., for the extract from *Death and Identity* edited by Robert Fulton.

Yale University Press for the excerpt from *A Common Faith* by John Dewey and for the poems from *Perpetual Light* by William Rose Benét, copyright © 1919 by Yale University Press.

INDEX OF AUTHORS

THIS INDEX gives the authors and the source of the selections taken from their work. Where no titles are available, the first line of the piece is used.

442

INDEX OF AUTHORS

INDEX OF FIRST LINES

THIS INDEX includes the first lines of the poems in all four sections of the book. The prose selections are not included. The page reference is given.

451

INDEX OF FIRST LINES

I died a mineral, and became a plant, 254
I do not know, 182
If all came but to ashes of dung, 300
If I could find one word, 178
I found myself one day, 401
If we had known all that we know, 184
I give back to the earth what the earth gave, 383
I had not taken the first step in knowledge, 267
I have always loved this solitary hill, 307
I have finished my combat with the sun, 220
I kept my answers small and kept them near, 167
I learned not to fear infinity, 286
I might see more if I were blind, 401
In all he does, whether good or bad, 59
In a man who goes to the beyond for strength, 288
In the singing sun where I am heading, 402
I see what was, and is, and will abide, 242
I shall die, but that is all that I shall do for Death, 289
I shall lose my earthly dwelling-place, 170
I share with you the agony of your grief, 248
Is it right to take your life, 185
I think continually of those who were truly great, 361
I thought of love as a crooked knife, 118
It is a God-damned lie to say that these, 167
It is for the union of you and me, 95
It is innocence that is full and experience that is empty, 6
It is not death that is bitter—*that* for all men stands fated, 184
It is not to diffuse you that you were born, 40
It is our minds that bring, 207
It is the same at the end as it was in the beginning, 259
I told a lie once in verse. I said, 187
I too pass from the night, 377
It was much stronger than they said. Noisier, 252
I wonder how you take your rest, 217
I wonder in what fields today, 198
I would not have this perfect love of ours, 103

Journeying over many seas & through many countries, 194
Joy, how far can you go? 329

Leave me, O Love, which reachest but to dust, 285
Let a joy keep you, 100
Let me die, working, 240
Let me not to the marriage of true minds, 128
Let not young souls be smothered out before, 59

454

INDEX OF SUBJECTS

THIS INDEX refers only to the last section of the book, the readings on death. It will give a quick reference to pieces felt to be appropriate to the indicated topic. This selection cannot be comprehensive. It is merely suggestive, and the thoughtful reader will not let his imagination be limited by this single grouping. References are given by author and page.

461